Intimate Inequalities

Intimate Inequalities

•••••••••••••••••••••••••••••••••••••••

Millennials' Romantic Relationships in Contemporary Times

CRISTEN DALESSANDRO

Rutgers University Press

New Brunswick, Camden, and Newark, New Jersey, and London

Library of Congress Cataloging-in-Publication Data

Names: Dalessandro, Cristen, author.
Title: Intimate inequalities : millennials' romantic relationships in
   contemporary times / Cristen Dalessandro.
Description: 1 Edition. | New Brunswick : Rutgers University Press, 2021. |
   Includes bibliographical references and index.
Identifiers: LCCN 2020043041 | ISBN 9781978823891 (paperback) |
   ISBN 9781978823907 (cloth) | ISBN 9781978823914 (epub) |
   ISBN 9781978823921 (mobi) | ISBN 9781978823938 (pdf)
Subjects: LCSH: Generation Y—United States—Social life and customs. |
   Interpersonal relations—United States. | Intimacy (Psychology)
Classification: LCC HQ799.7 .D3495 2021 | DDC 158.2—dc23
LC record available at https://lccn.loc.gov/2020043041

A British Cataloging-in-Publication record for this book is available from the British Library.

♾ The paper used in this publication meets the requirements of the American National
Standard for Information Sciences—Permanence of Paper for Printed Library Materials,
ANSI Z39.48-1992.

www.rutgersuniversitypress.org

Manufactured in the United States of America

Contents

Preface

You Are Who You Date?

As we move through the world, our interactions with different individuals and groups help each of us learn who we are, what our identities mean to us personally, and how we are perceived by others. While this is true more broadly, I think this process can be magnified when it comes to romantic and sexual relationships. For instance, in my experience conducting interviews for this book, it was not uncommon to hear millennials frequently stress that their most noteworthy intimacy experiences have been transformative—have taught them valuable lessons about the world or about themselves. Though individual biographies around sexual and romantic intimacy are unique to each person, what we all share is the ability to use our experiences to gather information about who we are and what we want out of our lives and relationships. As I argue in the coming pages, experiences are important to millennials—or those who have birth years from the early 1980s to the mid-1990s—since rather than rely solely on tradition, the current cultural conditions surrounding us in the West compel us to figure out for ourselves who we are and what we want out of life.

Though I am—like my participants—a millennial, this book is not about me. However, I wanted to use this preface as an exercise in reflexivity by showing how our individual lives connect to those of others, and how personal experiences connect to larger patterns beyond just ourselves. For instance, take Whitney's story. Whitney (a pseudonym) and I are both White, middle-class women who have had romantic and sexual experiences with men. Despite some evidence that millennials and other younger adults value gender equality, Whitney shares that she still grapples with negotiating gendered expectations that men her age may not face. As a twenty-eight-year-old woman who is not in a serious relationship, Whitney is starting to feel pressured by those around her to find a committed partnership and possibly get married: "[My sisters] have ideal relationships, really good guys. So of course, I'm getting the pressure of 'You're next! You're the last one!' . . . It puts pressure on me. . . . I've just been hopping around so much, [maybe] it's just time to settle down somewhere." Even though she is feeling good about where she's at right now—in a new, long-distance relationship that allows her to have a boyfriend and still have her day-to-day freedom—the idea that it's time to "settle down" is starting to weigh on Whitney. As a woman in my thirties, I understand how Whitney feels about the anxieties related to aging and finding a partner. I also worry about getting older and balancing intimate life expectations while pursuing my own personal (nonromantic) interests. Although it seems there are more conversations happening now that disavow the idea that women must be married to get the most out of their lives, gendered expectations around the importance of pursuing committed intimate partnerships persist.

Though Whitney deals with stressful gender expectations, she also admits that she is relatively privileged when it comes to social class. Her good fortune became especially apparent in one of her previous relationships with a working-class boyfriend. At the same time, Whitney shared that her experience caused her to wonder more about the significance of their class differences. In an example of what she meant by this, she shared, "Yeah, there were differences. . . . [For example,] I questioned why he'd be using food stamps when he was a student. Was it abusing the system, basically? I questioned that. And I never actually said this out loud, but the fact that he was doing student loans and whatnot, yet his father had an RV [recreational vehicle] and four snowmobiles in the garage—it was like, hmmm, something wasn't right!" In this quote, Whitney's experience with her ex-boyfriend reinforces a message about class differences. Her account marks her ex-boyfriend and his father as potentially dishonest people—an assessment that Whitney relates to their class position. The implication of Whitney's account is that it assigns value judgments to social class status and conveys the idea that compared to middle- and upper-middle-class people, working-class or poor people may be shady, suspicious, or not have their priorities straight.

Though I was initially taken aback a bit by Whitney's story, upon reflection I had to admit that I've participated in similar judgments myself. For instance, in my early twenties I shied away from the prospect of becoming romantically involved with men who had not gone to college or were not university students due to the misguided assumption that we would probably not have the same values and goals around pursuing higher education. Also during that time, I received advice from a friend that pursuing a romantic interest who was wealthy might be a bad idea, lest I be rejected for not coming from the right class background.

Though Whitney and I have different biographies, both of our stories reflect the shared idea that maybe it's best to stick to romantic partners with a class position similar to your own. This message is not neutral—it reinforces the understanding that the "type" of person you are is supposedly related to your social class and can also predict compatibility.

Though Whitney's story is different from mine, there are similar ideas about identity, power, and status in society influencing both of our stories. While we may indeed be distinctive in the intricacies of our stories, it is nevertheless apparent that there are things we share. The messages about class and gender that we have garnered through our experiences are seemingly much the same: class operates in a clearly hierarchical manner, and normative expectations for women still very much involve intimate partnership with men by a certain age.

Yet, while it is interesting and perhaps comforting to explore our similarities, it is equally as important, if not more so, to consider differences. Race and sexual identity do not figure prominently in Whitney's story, which is likely due to her identity as a straight White woman. However, as I discuss in the coming pages, the option of not having to think too much about sexual identity or race is usually not available to those who do not identify as White and/or as straight. Since the millennials interviewed for this book use their stories to make sense of their individual selves, their places in society, and even their partners, what is said and mulled over is as significant as what goes unsaid or unnoticed. Further, while Whitney and I have vivid understandings of where we have struggled, it may be less obvious to us how our actions may affect others. Unbeknownst to her, Whitney's ex-boyfriend may have perceived her disdain toward his use of food stamps, and it may have had some impact on his understanding of himself or his understandings of what it is like to date women like Whitney. It is easy to recognize one's own struggles and dilemmas, but it is sometimes more difficult to see when we might devalue, misinterpret, or even exacerbate the struggles of someone else.

The stories I share throughout this book are from millennials who are like me and are from millennials who are not like me. Their stories reveal shared experiences, and different experiences, among a group of young adults concentrated in the western United States. Throughout the rest of the book, my own narrative is absent in order to center the stories of the millennials I interviewed. It is my hope that through examining their stories we can begin to see how identity- and status-based inequalities are often perpetuated, and sometimes challenged, through routine intimate relationship experiences. It is also my hope that in examining these millennials' stories we may better understand how to address lingering identity- and status-based inequalities in our private, and also our public, lives. This book is about millennials and how they use their relationship stories to make sense of themselves, their partners, and how they subsequently navigate social and identity differences—based on race, social class, gender, sexuality, and age—in their intimate lives. However, I argue that what millennials do in intimacy is bigger than them. The traditions of the past, as much as the expectations of the present, help inform how millennials make sense of and navigate their intimate lives. Millennials' stories reveal how the landscape of intimacy is changing . . . or in some cases, how it is not.

Intimate Inequalities

1

Introduction

• •

Millennials, Intimacy, and
Negotiating Inequalities Today

On a hot summer day, I meet twenty-four-year-old Delilah at a coffee shop near the university where she is pursuing a master's degree.[1] A self-professed coffee lover, Delilah plans to go into education after she is done with school. At twenty-four years old, Delilah and her peers have been labeled "millennials"—a term associated with a generational cohort thought to be socially and politically distinct from those who are older and younger. Generally speaking, millennials are those with birth years from the early 1980s to the mid-1990s who are now in their twenties and thirties. Having moved less than a year prior to the interview, Delilah is new to the Mountain West region of the United States. Although she is new, with her outgoing personality she has already started making friends. It is one of those friends who told Delilah about my study. Like most of the millennials I interviewed, Delilah's stories about her intimacy experiences touch on a range of emotions—happiness, sadness, disappointment, irritation, excitement, confusion, and other feelings in between. Also like the other millennials in the study, Delilah's unique combination of identities seems to heavily influence her intimacy experiences.

Delilah is young, straight, middle-class, and Black. In one instance, she shared that since she is Black and on the dating scene in a majority White city, race sometimes brings up uncomfortable feelings and situations. For example, she spoke about feeling uneasy around some potential intimate partners out of a fear that they might see her as a dating "experiment" due to her race: "I have had White males try to talk to me and things like that. I think that, I think I'm not comfortable with it. . . . [This] recent [White] guy . . . I'm like, maybe he's not [racist], but then, I don't know. It's hard to explain, but sometimes I just feel it! And I just feel like, sometimes, that I'm this experiment for him and he's trying to see where it's gonna go. . . . And I think a part of me thinking that he might be exoticizing me made me apprehensive about the whole thing." Delilah's story raises important questions. If media reports are correct, millennials are supposed to be adept when it comes to navigating social differences in their lives.[2] They're a generation who grew up being fed popular messages asserting that girls can do anything boys can do, where you come from has no effect on where you are going, and that race doesn't (or shouldn't) matter. Yet despite the *idea* that millennials may have mastered navigating race, class, and gender when compared to older adults, Delilah's story indicates that negotiating differences is a routine—and often uncomfortable—part of her romantic and sexual intimacy experiences. Her experiences—and the messages they send about race, class, gender and other categories of difference—undoubtedly also help shape how she thinks about herself as a middle-class Black woman. It seems that millennials' romantic and sexual intimacy stories can tell us much about how they are negotiating social differences and issues of equity in their lives. Yet these stories receive less attention than they perhaps should.

Unlike Delilah, twenty-five-year-old Oscar has lived in the Mountain West his entire life. Oscar is athletic and determined when it comes to both sports and his career goals. He is also Latino and gay/queer with a bachelor's degree and a middle-class lifestyle.[3] However, he comes from a poor background. Oscar shared that his single mom supported his siblings and him on poverty-level wages while he was growing up. Yet today, Oscar is confident that, thanks to his education, he will not face the same financial constraints as his mother going forward: "I'm not afraid of anything financially, whether I'm gonna be freelancing [or working for a company]. . . . I'm never gonna go poor again in my life! I've worked too hard for it, and I know . . . how to provide for myself." Despite his background and his respect for how hard his mother worked to support him, Oscar believes that being working-class is incompatible with the values he has now. He said about his hometown, "Mediocrity is encouraged and celebrated there. There's a billboard [for a junior college] that I want to burn every time I go into town . . . and the slogan on it is, 'Who says you have to leave home to get an education?' And I just think that's so horrible, to celebrate living in your parents' basement well into adulthood, and just getting an, honestly, mediocre education. I just don't understand where that [desire] comes from."

Perhaps unsurprisingly, Oscar also expects his romantic partners to share his views, and explicitly states that he doesn't think a relationship would pan out with a partner who is working-class. However, in Oscar's experience dating a man from an affluent background, differences in upbringing caused issues in the relationship: "He was super rich. I was putting myself through school. . . . Still to this day, actually, he's graduated and still living off his parents' money. So that caused a lot of problems [in our relationship]." One of the big issues in Oscar's previous relationship was tension stemming from the fact that his boyfriend didn't have to work very hard to access class privilege. Although this still bothers him in the present, Oscar also believes he will eventually marry someone who is similar to his ex, citing affluence as one of the characteristics comprising his romantic "type."

Though I will return to both Oscar and Delilah in later chapters, their statements raise important questions about the extent to which social and identity differences have ceased to matter much in millennials' intimate lives. Oscar's class expectations clash with his class experiences, while his romantic partners often come from more privileged backgrounds than his own. How does he deal with issues that come up due to these differences? Are common goals enough to overcome the past? At the same time, Oscar's and Delilah's experiences have probably helped them learn new knowledge about themselves, about their partners, and about what they can and cannot tolerate in the context of intimacy. How have their experiences dating partners who are different from themselves helped them gain insight into not only who they are as people, but who their partners are as people? I argue in this book that Oscar, Delilah, and other millennials routinely negotiate the meanings attached to gender, class, race, age, and sexual identity in their experiences with intimate partners. Yet remarkably, despite widespread curiosity in the media and in our society when it comes to millennials' lives, we really have little knowledge about how millennials navigate differences and inequalities—while they work through their own complicated identities—in the context of romantic and sexual intimacy.

Compared to their grandparents and even their parents, life for younger cohorts in the United States today seems vastly different in almost every way imaginable. Millennials in the United States are more diverse in terms of race, sexual identity, gender identity, and have more freedom and choice in their intimate lives than generations that have come before them (Coontz 2006; Rosenfeld 2009).[4] For instance, thanks to changes such as the abolishment of antimiscegenation laws that criminalized interracial marriage and the expansion of same-sex marriage rights at the national level,[5] millennials are seemingly free to form romantic and sexual relationships with whomever they choose regardless of race, class, religion, gender, or sexual identity. When compared to the past, we have legally and technically made progress in terms of possible intimacy choices, and millennials themselves attest to valuing socially progressive views on issues related to race, gender, and sexual identity (Pew Research Center

2018).[6] This tendency toward more progressive values compared to older groups is even found among millennials who might be stereotyped as socially conservative, such as those belonging to the Church of Jesus Christ of Latter-day Saints, for example (Riess 2019). It thus seems easy to assume that millennials should be past some of the communication issues and struggles that older generations had to face. Yet, at the end of the day, is this really the case?

Despite broadening freedom and choice in intimacy, when it comes to how millennials actually approach navigating social and identity differences in their intimate relationships, research often generates as many questions as answers. On the one hand, some research suggests that millennials are more likely to take an approach to intimacy and sex that is open-minded and less traditional. Compared to older generations of adults, millennials and other younger cohorts are more likely to cohabit before marriage (Manning, Brown, and Payne 2014; Sassler and Miller 2011), more likely to embrace casual sex (Bogle 2008; Wade 2017), more likely to identify as LGBTQ+ (GLAAD 2017; Williams Institute 2020), more likely to form intimate relationships with someone of a different race (Joyner and Kao 2005), and frequently profess a desire for gender egalitarianism in their relationships (Gerson 2010; Lamont 2020). However, puzzles remain. For example, research also finds that young adults struggle to achieve gender equality in romantic relationships (Dalessandro and Wilkins 2017; Gerson 2010; Lamont 2014). When it comes to marriage, younger people still generally tend to pursue partners from race and class groups similar to their own (Cherlin 2013; McClintock 2010). Further, in contrast to the gains of the last decade, millennial acceptance of LGBTQ+ identities has dipped slightly in the last few years and is still low among some groups of young people (GLAAD 2019; Worthen 2020). Given all of these seeming contradictions, how can we even begin to make sense of what's going on in millennials' intimate lives or to decipher how millennials actually approach differences and potential inequalities in intimacy?

In an attempt to answer this question, *Intimate Inequalities* examines U.S.-based millennials' own stories about their intimacy experiences.[7] Over the course of three years, I interviewed sixty millennials about their past and present experiences with dating, romance, sex, and their intimacy goals for the future. The stories millennials shared with me illustrate how they make sense of their intimacy experiences, dilemmas, tensions, successes, and goals as they are coming into their own as full adults. Unlike other research studies, which sometimes center primarily one category such as gender, social class, sexual identity, age, *or* race, I use interviews with a diverse group of millennials in order to investigate how *all* of these factors intersect in their lives and experiences. As the population of the United States continues to become increasingly diverse, an approach that considers how different identities and social factors shape the experiences and self-understandings of younger adults is crucial. The approach I take in the coming pages allows me to capture a snapshot of some of the nuances of millennials' approaches in their own private lives.

Though romantic and sexual intimacy is just one part of millennials' lives, it is an important arena for working out social and identity differences. While some contexts—such as the workplace—may require social niceties that hide racist, sexist, or classist sentiments, millennials' private lives can reveal how they actually navigate social and identity differences with some of the people with whom they are closest: intimate partners. Although individually unique, I take the view that personal stories are also always connected to larger social institutions and forces, and are informed by broader understandings of social identities and statuses such as race, gender, class, sexual identity, and age (Giddens 1991; Plummer 2005; Riessman 1990; Wood 2001). Thus, while personal stories reveal how millennials approach difference in their experiences with individual partners, they also reveal clues regarding how millennials are thinking about entire *categories* of difference—such as race, class, or gender—as well.

On a broader level, it is worth asking if millennials' stories about navigating intimate inequalities—or their stories about navigating social and identity differences between themselves and their partners, and the potential tensions and issues that arise in the process—suggest a lessening of broader inequalities as we move into the future, or the social reproduction of inequalities. This book asks, first, what millennials' own accounts can tell us about how they are making sense of themselves, partners, and broader categories of difference in the context of intimacy. Following the first question, this book also asks how millennials negotiate and solve dilemmas related to social and identity differences in intimacy. Third, I speculate on what the answers to the first and second questions reveal about millennials' more wide-ranging approaches to navigating inequalities in their relationships, and how their approaches might provide insight into millennials' ability to navigate social and identity differences in their interactions more generally. Relatedly, what might we expect from millennials as we go into the future? In order to speak to these questions, it is important to first parse out the conditions under which millennials in the United States are currently living and navigating intimacy. In the next few pages, I contextualize millennials' lives and explain further how we can examine millennials' intimacy stories for insight into answering the main questions of this book.

The Changing Landscape of Young Adult Intimacy: Are Millennials Unique?

When it comes to romantic and sexual intimacy in millennials' lives, the extent to which millennials are unique compared to older and younger generations in the United States is unclear. However, broad social and technological changes suggest that millennials' lives are different from those of older cohorts who came of age in the recent past. For instance, compared to older adults, millennials and other young people in the United States are spending more time dating and hooking up before getting married; that is, indeed, if they decide to get married at all.[8] A peek at the statistics on marriage—a classic demographic measure of intimacy patterns—demonstrates this change over time. For example, the percentage of millennials who are married is currently around 44 percent. While marriage is not going extinct, this figure is a steep drop from the 81 percent of similarly aged young adults who were married fifty years ago (Barroso, Parker, and Bennett 2020). Further, the age at first marriage continues to inch upward. According to recent calculations from the United States Census Bureau (2018), the average age of first marriage is now at around twenty-eight for women and thirty for men. This is a marked increase from even a decade ago, when the average ages hovered around twenty-six for women and twenty-eight for men.

Yet looking at statistics on intimacy changes around marriage only reveal part of the story when it comes to shifts millennials have faced compared to previous generations. While critics may contend that millennials are "ruining" marriage (as they have "ruined" or "killed" other popular activities, such as giving diamonds and golfing), we have seen a similar pattern before.[9] For instance, historically, marriage rates decline during times of economic insecurity (Hill 2015). As social researchers know well, changes in the public and private spheres connect (Dernberger and Pepin 2020), and, for many millennials, economic prospects look increasingly bleak. Thanks to high levels of debt and stymied work opportunities stemming largely from the Great Recession (and more recently, the COVID-19 pandemic), many millennials are poised to be financially worse off than their parents (Harris 2017; Kalish 2016; Jones 2020; Rinz 2019). When it comes to economic gains, one media outlet recently went so far as to call millennials the "unluckiest generation in U.S. history" (Van Dam 2020). Based on historic trends that show strong links between economic conditions and intimacy choices (such as timing of marriages), we can say with some certainty that millennials' economic misfortunes probably relate to their approaches to marriage and other intimacy choices as well (Coontz 2006; Edin and Kefalas 2005; G. Lee 2015). At the same time, it's difficult to tell whether these changing intimacy patterns make millennials unique or whether they are simply responding to the current world in ways comparable to those in the past who were faced with similar economic precarity.

However, one social and cultural change characterizing millennials' lives does involve something previously unseen: the rise of information and communications technology. The rapid ascendance of phone and computer technology is a historically new change that is influencing how millennials live, work, and date in ways we have not seen before—and millennials themselves also aren't sure how they feel about it (Dalessandro 2018a). Millennials are arguably the first generation to collectively realize that technology—from a human communication standpoint—can be both a blessing and a potential curse.[10] As it relates to relationships, technology can provide millennials with more options, since they can meet many more and different kinds of people—across greater physical distances—than past generations could at the same age. However, meeting people online and using technology to traverse intimate relationships also comes with uncertainty—especially around communication (Dalessandro 2018a). Perhaps more than anything, technology is one factor implicated in a more *general sense of the unknown* that millennials are experiencing in their lives in this historic moment. Though I don't provide an in-depth discussion of millennials' views on how technology is impacting their relationships in this book, I do discuss their views elsewhere (see Dalessandro 2018a) and find that many of these millennials see technology as just another factor contributing to the generalized uncertainty that characterizes their lives.

Depressing economic circumstances and the rapid ascendance of digital technology are two factors characterizing millennials' lives that matter for how they approach and cultivate intimacy. Yet both of these conditions also represent a broader reality for millennials: rapid change. Indeed, the general ethos of rapid social and cultural change—and the accompanying uncertainty—is perhaps the dominant factor overshadowing millennials' lives and relationships. However, while media or popular press conversations sometimes bemoan these changes, they may not be all bad. Millennials are seemingly asked on a continual basis to adjust to a world that seems to change drastically year by year (and sometimes month by month), and their beliefs about intimacy could arguably benefit if they relate to the breaking down of some of society's more nefarious inventions such as racism, sexism, or other forms of discrimination and inequality. Millennials may use digital tools to find a variety of romantic partners and explore their sexual selves in ways unavailable to past cohorts. Their experiences with rapid change might also mean they are flexible in their beliefs about intimacy—that there is no one *right* way to structure intimate life. Millennials may have the confidence to make their own choices rather than feel pressured to live their lives in a way that society tells them they *should*. The rapid social changes millennials have faced could also be leaving them better equipped to understand and navigate social and identity differences. As they harness new technological tools and embrace social and cultural change, millennials may be doing a better job at navigating race, class, and gender-related tensions and inequalities than generations past. However, on these points we simply do not know if this is true or just truthfully too optimistic.

Almost Adult: Cultural Change and Emerging Adulthood in the West

Although some of millennials' experiences, such as economic insecurity, may not be unknown in history, other social conditions surrounding millennials in the United States are arguably new. In addition to technology, the rise in "emerging adulthood" as a contemporary phenomenon is one that undoubtedly impacts millennials' approaches to their romantic and sexual relationships. Further, both the cultural conditions giving rise to emerging adulthood and the new expectations attached to emerging adulthood seemingly make the examination of millennials' intimacy stories all the more important for understanding them.

For scholars, emerging adulthood is a period that falls between adolescence and full adulthood and is characterized as a time of transition in which young people leave behind adolescence and prepare for their adult lives (Arnett 2000). Though often discussed in a Western context, there is some evidence that emerging adulthood is increasingly useful for understanding the lives of twentysomethings across the globe (Gala and Kapadia 2014; Obidoa et al. 2019). Emerging adulthood research argues that this time period (or life stage) affects young adults through their twenties and possibly into their early thirties in some cases (see J. Silva 2013), although factors such as social class, race, geography, and gender all matter for how young people themselves experience emerging adulthood. Emerging adulthood is not exclusive to millennials, although much of the emerging adulthood literature published in the last two decades *has* profiled millennials since their birth years (the early 1980s through the mid-1990s) correspond to the age range studied by emerging adult scholars. Until very recently—since "Generation Z" has begun entering their emerging adulthood years—most research and discussions around "emerging adults" were generally synonymous with describing the millennial experience.[11]

A number of social and economic factors experienced by millennials—including the restructuring of the labor market, increasing student loan burdens, the advancement of contraceptive and reproductive technologies, and more—have transformed reaching adulthood into an extended, multiyear project (see Arnett 2004; Risman 2018; Settersten and Ray 2010; J. Silva 2013). Yet in addition to the importance of concrete changes, explorations of identity—in which young adults investigate who they are and what feels true to them—have emerged as something that many young people expect to pursue during their emerging adulthood years (Arnett 2004, 2016; Dalessandro 2019b; Nelson and Luster 2015; J. Silva 2013; Waters, Carr, and Kefalas 2011). Perhaps unsurprisingly, these explorations take time. Similar to Oscar and Delilah from the beginning of this chapter, millennials use emerging adulthood to figure out their identities, explore what they want out of life, and discover what it is they want out of their intimate relationships during the time they spend transitioning to full maturity. Although structural changes in the United States have helped shape the rise of emerging adulthood, emerging adults themselves often experience this transitional time period in individualized, and even emotional, terms (Dalessandro 2019b). Many millennials use emerging adulthood as a time to explore before (ostensibly) solidifying their fully developed adult identities.

More generally, a number of scholars contend that there has been an increase in the cultural importance assigned to individuality and personal choice in the global West (Freeman 2014; Rosenfeld 2009). The newfound emphasis on choice seemingly gives millennials more freedom and flexibility, and considers their feelings and emotions, in decisions about life and identity. Young people are no longer required to make decisions out of necessity but may do so out of personal desire or if something feels right and true to them. For example, while marriage was at one time a near-universal expected component of adulthood in the United States, at present marriage seems just one option among many (Coontz 2006; Sassler and Miller 2011). Further, that one's emotions even have an expected place *at all* in intimate institutions such as family and marriage is a historically recent phenomenon (Coontz 2006). Considering the rise of emerging adulthood and the cultural emphasis on emotions, individuality, and choice, many millennials have long, drawn-out intimacy histories during their emerging adult years, and these histories also serve as a resource in which millennials can work through their feelings, identities, and make sense of themselves. Given this cultural context, we can observe in millennials' stories how they have been dealing with making sense of themselves in their own intimacy experiences as they transition to full adulthood.

In the West, both the rise of emerging adulthood and cultural changes that center individual emotions and choice mean that millennials are at a time in their lives when they are actively negotiating their identities as mature people with particular gender, race, class, age, and sexual identities. They are deciding what they want, and expect, out of their adult lives and intimacy futures. They look to their experiences for clues about what feels true to them and how they should live their lives. Researchers such as Furedi (2004), Illouz (2008), and Irvine (1999) have written previously about how shifting cultural conceptions of emotionality impact individuals' approaches to making sense of themselves. However, despite emerging adulthood scholars' documentation of the importance of identity exploration, we know less than we might expect regarding how these changes apply to millennials and other young adults in the emotional, personal context of romantic and sexual intimacy.[12]

Crafting Identity and Intersectionality in Intimacy Stories

Researchers of emerging adulthood have pointed out that narratives and stories can reveal information about individuals' lives that is challenging to gather using other methods (Dalessandro and Wilkins 2017; J. Silva and Corse 2018). How people negotiate meanings and identities is difficult to gauge quantitatively, for example. This book thus centers millennials' stories—gathered in an interview setting—in order to address the aforementioned research questions. Methodologically, individuals' stories gathered through interviews provide insight into the nuances of their lives (see R. Weiss 1994), and stories about intimacy in particular can be especially useful for helping us examine how broader social inequalities manifest in people's routine experiences (Plummer 2005). Yet despite a long history of thinkers who argue that the examination of stories in particular is integral to understanding how individuals craft, make sense of, and negotiate their identities in relation to others both inside and outside of intimate contexts (Irvine 2013; Labov and Waletzky 1997; McAdams 1993; Plummer 1995; Rose 2003), with few exceptions this body of literature has not described the lives of millennials or other young adults.

The process of storytelling—or relaying a narrative to a listener—helps the individuals sharing their stories to give meaning to their own identities and membership in different groups as they explain themselves to someone else (Mason-Schrock 1996; Plummer 1995; Somers 2004; Wilkins 2012). In this book, I treat personal storytelling as a constructionist project and active site of meaning-making in which individuals assign significance to the events and experiences in their lives (Hiles and Cermak 2008; Irvine 1999; Polletta et al. 2011; Wilkins 2012). The stories that people tell about themselves serve an important purpose. Stories help individuals work out who they are at the same time that they present themselves to others. As storytellers, our own beliefs about ourselves can be reaffirmed, or sometimes challenged, by others' reactions to us. In this way, storytelling is a profoundly social process that has implications at the individual level (Plummer 1995).[13] For millennials, storytelling serves as an important resource that helps them negotiate their identities and construct their understandings of who they are as raced, aged, classed, gendered, sexual people. This is especially important as millennials try to situate themselves in an ever-changing and confusing world.

While the storytelling I investigate here centers individuals' negotiations of their own identities, these negotiations are rooted in ideas that go beyond the level of the individual. It is in the intricacies of millennials' identity constructions—and connections to broader ideas about inequality—that intersectionality becomes an integral component. To consider identities intersectionally is to also note how individuals' complicated lives and selves are rooted in larger social systems of inequality. Though intersectionality is not in and of itself a theory of identity, it can be used to make sense of intricate identity negotiations that are rooted in structural, systemic webs of privilege and oppression (P. Collins 1990, 2019; Crenshaw 1991; Madfis 2014).

In this book, I consider intersectionality first as a methodological tool, since I specifically seek to investigate evidence of enduring social inequalities in intimacy and sites of resistance among a diverse group of people. At the same time, I consider intersectionality as a framework because it is a useful instrument that we can use to understand and make sense of the nuances of millennials' intimate lives and how their complicated social statuses and identities play into their intimate experiences and decisions.[14] Intersectionality itself is currently "under construction" as a theoretical and methodological tool (see P. Collins 2019), and my perspective is that it can be useful when applied to both research design and analysis. However, one seemingly consistent point of agreement among prominent intersectionality scholars is that intersectionality is ultimately concerned with identifying (often obscured) structural webs of privilege and oppression and with exploring how to address unfair and detrimental social inequities (P. Collins 2019). This is one of the goals of my project as well, since I seek not merely to describe millennials' intimate lives and approaches to intimate inequalities, but to think about why enduring inequalities persist and what knowledge and actions might be needed to address them. Intersectionality itself has sometimes proven difficult to apply in research, and debates over how to use intersectionality can make appropriate application less clear. However, in this book, I try to provide some examples of how intersectionality might be used to understand people's lives and experiences, and to explore how, when, and why social inequalities manifest in intimacy according to millennials' stories about their relationships.

In sum, millennials' intimacy stories serve as an important source of information for how they are thinking about their intimate lives, and how they negotiate with partners who may hold different identities and perspectives than themselves. Millennials' stories of navigating intimacy can reveal how they situate themselves as classed, gendered, raced, sexual, and aged people in their experiences with partners. Simultaneously, how millennials situate themselves does not occur in a vacuum. They draw from, and affirm through storytelling, broader ideas about raced, classed, gendered, sexual, and aged groups. Millennials work through their own understandings of themselves and come to conclusions about potential intimate partners—and the identity categories to which partners belong—in the process. Further, by taking an intersectional approach, we can better capture the nuances in millennials' stories.

While I used the last few pages to explain the reasoning behind my focus on millennials' intimate stories and lives, before going further I should discuss in greater detail the particular millennials interviewed for this project and how I found them. While I do spend—what may seem to be—extra time describing the millennial interview participants here, I do so for a reason. Because investigating how millennials navigate difference is one of the core topics of this book, I need to explicate the demographic differences of the millennials in the interview group as well as my own positionality as the (millennial) researcher.

Methods, Participants, and Researcher Positionality

Motivated by a lack of research on "older" (past age twenty-two) emerging adults, between 2012 and 2015 I interviewed sixty millennials between the ages of twenty-two and thirty-two. While the study targeted millennials in two cities in the U.S. Mountain West, I interviewed participants in rural and suburban areas as well.[15] All names I use throughout are pseudonyms. Since this study focuses on millennials in a particular area of the country, it offers a snapshot of how millennials in a particular context navigate intimate inequalities in their lives.[16] The group of millennials recruited for the project is purposefully diverse. Of the sixty participants, half identify as men and half identify as women. Most participants identify as cisgender (i.e., their gender corresponds to the gender they were assigned at birth), although two participants (Marcus and Taylor) identify as trans men and three more participants (Spencer, Aaron, and Jeremy) acknowledge that they also have criticisms of the expectations attached to rigid gender binaries or take a genderqueer approach to gender in their lives (see appendix A). The average age of participants is twenty-six and a half for men and twenty-seven for women. Forty-one participants identify as heterosexual or straight. The nineteen remaining participants identify as lesbian, gay, bisexual, and/or queer in terms of sexual identity.

Racially, forty-four participants are White, while the remainder are either Latino or Latina (7), Black (5), "Brown," meaning Middle Eastern in one case and South Asian (Indian) in another (2), or identify with being mixed-race (2). For social class, I do not rely primarily on self-descriptions due to the tendency of people in the United States to consider themselves generically "middle-class" (Gilbert 1998; Sherman 2017). Rather, I discern class using a combination of participants' descriptions of their backgrounds, their educational attainment, their current careers, and future plans. Though I discuss class more below ("A Note on Language"), I generally group participants into three classed groups: class-advantaged, class-disadvantaged, and upwardly mobile. In terms of class background, thirty-five participants come from middle- or upper-middle-class backgrounds and twenty-five come from working-class or poor backgrounds. I group working-class and poor backgrounds together because, in most cases, working-class and poor millennials seemed to experience similar levels of economic instability growing up. However, seventeen of those from working-class and poor backgrounds aspire to middle- or upper-middle-class futures. These seventeen—whom I call "upwardly mobile"—expect to occupy middle-class status in full adulthood. Oscar, who was profiled in the opening of this chapter, is one example of an individual who belongs to this classed group. Upwardly mobile millennials expect to occupy middle- to upper-middle-class status by gaining access to middle-class career paths, usually with the help of a university education. This upwardly mobile group is growing in the United States (Cataldi, Bennett, and Chen 2018), although existing literature often conflates class background with current class status. Drawing from the work of Bettie (2003), who also highlights the importance of identity and status expectations in determining how young people navigate their lives, this book considers throughout how expectations work alongside backgrounds in determining millennials' strategies for making sense of themselves and negotiating difference.

At this juncture, it is important to note as well how my own identity as a millennial could have influenced the interviews. I discuss my own positionality in further depth in appendix B, although it is also worth mentioning here. I do believe my own identity as a millennial helped participants feel more comfortable in opening up about age-related anxieties and tensions since it's possible that participants assumed, as their similarly aged peer, that I would have at least some understanding of their experiences. Of course, this was likely not the case for every participant. However, it is my impression that I achieved enough rapport with participants that they revealed to me information they would feel comfortable revealing about themselves in any other context where they could expect confidentiality. While I asked these millennials questions about things I was curious about, I also left them space to discuss certain topics or relationships for as long, or as little, as they liked. In doing so, I attempted to gather information on the experiences and issues at the forefront of millennials' minds—those experiences, issues, intimate relationships, and intimacy goals that they themselves found most significant to their own biographies.

In analyzing the over 1,200 pages of transcripts from my interviews, I focused on the messages that millennials' stories communicate through the interview process itself as an active site of meaning-making and identity negotiation. The interview process helps millennials understand themselves, potential partners, and broader identity categories as they work through what everything means (see Holstein and Gubrium 1995). It must be said, though, that taking an approach that focuses on the meanings millennials construct in their stories does not discount the sincerity of participants' stories. Rather, I believe most (if not all) of the millennials interviewed are honest in their stories about their lives. Nevertheless, I focus on how millennials' stories are illustrative of how they give *meaning* to identities and how the meanings communicated in stories inform how millennials navigate difference. These meanings are important because while they inform how millennials make sense of themselves as gendered, classed, raced, aged, sexual people, they also help millennials work through what it means to be a certain gendered, classed, raced, aged, or sexual person more broadly. These meanings not only help millennials understand their experiences with individual partners, but they can additionally inform how they approach other areas of their lives as well. The meanings millennials negotiate also relate to their actions, and provide insight into where they are at—and where they are going—when it comes to their ability to navigate social and identity differences (and potential issues that arise due to those differences) in their lives.

Chapter Overview

The chapters that follow examine different aspects of millennials' intimacy stories. In each chapter, I explore how in telling stories about their intimate lives and experiences, millennials actively make sense of themselves, and their partners, as gendered, classed, raced, aged, and sexual people. In the process, I examine how millennials reconcile, explain, and deal with issues related to navigating difference and inequalities in intimacy. Lastly, I incorporate into each chapter a discussion of whether my findings suggest that millennials are challenging, or rather upholding, intimate inequalities rooted in categories of difference. Most chapters center a category of difference that these millennials most typically discuss negotiating in their intimate lives. I start with gender and follow with chapters that respectively center how millennials navigate age, race, and social class identity. I then move to explore millennials' views on their intimacy futures (which for many, includes marriage) and how they reconcile their identities with their future goals and plans. I show throughout how complicated power differences—which are rooted in millennials' social and identity statuses—shape their experiences, how they talk about themselves and partners, and how they work through dilemmas in their relationships.

While chapter 2 centers gender differences in women's and men's accounts, it also examines how gender intersects with social class, age, and sexual identity in stories about negotiating gender and gender-related issues in intimacy. This chapter begins with a discussion of two major differences between women's and men's accounts: the distinctive ways that women and men discuss their gendered personal agency in relationships, and the distinctive ways that women and men talk about learning from their gendered experiences in relationships. I also discuss how social class, sexual identity, and age identity relate to how millennials make sense of gender. While millennials' accounts indicate that gender-based tensions and inequalities prevail in their relationships, I also find evidence of resistance to gendered interpretations of intimacy expectations in a few cases.

Chapter 3 centers age. To explore how millennials navigate age concerns, I use their stories about dating older partners. I first examine relationships between women and men, and show how gender, age, and class inform these stories. A number of women and men both have experience navigating age concerns in romantic and sexual encounters with older partners, although how millennials make sense of themselves and their partners differs by gender. I find that while straight men dating older women cast women as primarily desirable as sex partners (but not partners with whom to make a commitment), straight women are more ambivalent about dating older men. I argue that the stories of both groups uphold gendered, aged power dynamics. I subsequently move on to examine the stories of LGBTQ+ individuals with experience navigating age discrepancies in intimacy and find that the experiences of some LGBTQ+ millennials challenge gender expectations. However, LGBTQ+ millennials often struggle with age-related concerns despite seemingly being more transgressive when it comes to gender.

In chapter 4, I center racial differences and examine how race intersects with gender, social class, and sexual identity in millennials' intimacy stories. This chapter investigates how millennials are discussing and making sense of race and racial differences in intimacy in light of the idea that race should no longer matter. While I find that millennials generally express that they do not want to use race as a factor in making intimacy decisions, three patterns in their accounts—exoticizing and othering, the influence of family and friends, and a prioritization of Whiteness—serve as barriers to progress. Since millennials use their stories to make sense of their own racial identities, the identities of partners, and racial differences more generally, these stories should give us pause. Unfortunately, those millennials who seem the most knowledgeable about how race matters also tend to be those who bear the brunt of racial inequalities in intimacy.

Chapter 5 focuses on millennials' stories about their experiences (and expectations) with negotiating social class differences in intimacy. In addition to considering intersections of class with other categories of difference, this chapter also illustrates the importance of *both* class origins *and* class expectations in structuring millennials' accounts. Those with class-advantaged goals expect partners to also embody similar goals and values. These same millennials also try to distance themselves from a class-disadvantaged lifestyle and, consequently, class-disadvantaged partners. Simultaneously, the importance of social class background is also apparent since millennials from working-class and poor backgrounds often have awkward interactions with those from more affluent backgrounds. The tension between class background and class expectations causes a disconnect, especially for upwardly mobile millennials whose backgrounds seemingly contradict their class goals. This chapter explores how class-coded language contributes to the construction of "desirable" versus "undesirable" partners, and also considers how class intersects with gender and sexual identity in millennials' negotiations of social class.

While previous chapters generally focus on discussions of the past and present, chapter 6 explores millennials' plans for their intimacy futures and how gender, race, class, age, and sexual identities and concerns figure into those plans. Since most expect marriage, this chapter profiles millennials' views on marriage. While straight women and men take marriage for granted, gender and class still matter in how they approach marriage. Compared to straight participants across gender and class categories, LGBTQ+ millennials have a more nuanced understanding of marriage and are often more critical of marriage as an institution. This chapter demonstrates that rather than a decline in the importance of marriage, millennials see marriage as important and practical, although gender, age, class, race, and sexual identity concerns shift the meanings attached to marriage among millennials. Marriage is still the expected last stop on millennials' route to maturity via intimacy, but it is far from one-size-fits-all.

Finally, in chapter 7, I conclude by integrating the arguments contained within the previous chapters and—in keeping with my goal of not just identifying, but trying to address, inequalities—discuss in depth how to think about the findings and move forward. I explore what millennials' stories tell us about how they make sense of themselves, how they negotiate differences and inequalities in intimacy, and how the ways in which millennials make sense of their private lives suggest they will challenge, or resist, inequalities going into the future. I believe that while there seems to be more work to do, the same channel that suggests millennials are sometimes struggling—their stories—might also offer potential transformative power.

A Note on Language

It is important to touch on a few language choices I have made throughout this book and to clarify why I have made these choices. The first, and perhaps messiest, category that requires clarification is social class. Social class is arguably the least straightforward of all the demographic factors and identities I discuss throughout this book, which is also a reflection of the messiness of social class in U.S. society more generally. I primarily categorize millennials into three groups based on both their class backgrounds and their class trajectories, which I believe is the most accurate method of class categorization for these millennials. I classify one group of millennials as class-advantaged, which means they came from a middle- to upper-middle-class background and are expecting to occupy at least middle-class status in full adulthood. Class-advantaged millennials are those whose parents often have college degrees and/or professional jobs and who are themselves pursuing similar educational and career trajectories. These participants also discussed growing up in middle-class neighborhoods. I did not interview any millennials who would classify as downwardly mobile—or those who likely would not reach at least middle-class status despite a comfortable class upbringing.

The second group are those I classify as upwardly mobile. These are millennials who come from poor or working-class backgrounds yet are on track to occupy at least middle-class status in full adulthood most often through pursuing and obtaining a bachelor's degree or, in a few exceptions, by securing middle-class jobs without a degree. For example, these millennials had parents with little to no higher education and working-class jobs or a precarious work history, and grew up in poor or working-class neighborhoods. These millennials also often started out with limited access to cultural capital, or the cultural knowledge and understanding needed to access class privilege (Bourdieu 1993). However, through luck, mentorship, or other fortuitous events, these millennials found themselves with personal or institutional support that enabled them to pursue higher education or middle-class career trajectories, and so their aspirations for middle- to upper-middle-class adult life seem within reach. Numbering seventeen participants, this group is actually larger than I anticipated. I attribute the relatively high number (almost 30 percent of those interviewed) to the research site: the areas surrounding two cities in the U.S. Mountain West that are going through an economic boom, boast a number of public universities, and are attractive to upwardly mobile young people from both inside, and outside, the state.

The final group is comprised of millennials from working-class and poor backgrounds who will likely occupy that class milieu going into the future.[17] I term these millennials class-disadvantaged because, relative to the other two groups, they have not had the same opportunities in terms of social class and are comparatively disadvantaged in this way. Though they grew up poor and working-class like the upwardly mobile group, these millennials seem likely to stay working-class or poor. I myself do not think the language of "disadvantage" is necessarily perfect, and the use of this language does not imply that these millennials have bad lives. Rather, it communicates that these millennials have had—and will probably continue to have—struggles based solely on their lack of access to classed power and resources in a neoliberal, capitalist society that devalues working-class and poor people. In chapter 5, it becomes clear that many millennials themselves buy into the idea that being class-disadvantaged is not only undesirable, but indicative of some moral or personal failing. Thus, I term this group class-disadvantaged since they face both economic and social insults as a side effect of their class position in U.S. society.

In addition to class, there are other language choices I would like to mention as well for the sake of clarity. Some readers may have already noticed that while I list millennials' sexual identities as "heterosexual" on demographic charts (appendix A) and occasionally refer to heterosexuality, I prefer to use the term "straight" to refer to these participants instead. My reasoning for this is that those millennials who identify this way usually consider themselves "straight." Thus, especially given the essentializing nature of terms like "heterosexual" and "homosexual" (Blank 2012), I prefer to use "straight" due to history, participants' own use of the term, and also to signify that "straight" sexual identities are still normative in the United States relative to other sexual identity options. With one exception, references to "straight" sexual identity throughout this work are applied to cisgender participants interested in heterosexual relationships with other cisgender people.[18]

Lastly, I have decided to refer to Latinx participants throughout the book as either "Latino" or "Latina" (corresponding to gender). There are compelling arguments for and against using the term "Latinx" (see Guidotti-Hernández 2017; Trujillo-Pagán 2018; Vidal-Ortiz and Martínez 2018).[19] However, the primary reason I choose the more gendered option is that no participants actually used the term "Latinx" in reference to themselves or any relatives. Instead, participants alternated between "Hispanic" and "Latino" or "Latina," or, as in one case, "Latin." While this trend might be changing since I completed these interviews, I try to honor participants' descriptions of themselves here as they appeared at the time of the interviews.

2

He Said, She Said

• • • • • • • • • • • • • • • • • • • •

Making Sense of Gender
through Stories

Compared to some of the other discussions covered in this book, arguably no topic has received more attention from social scientists—and the popular media—than gender issues in millennials' relationships. To put it succinctly, researchers often find evidence that gender inequality continues in young people's relationships, and that women usually lose out in this regard (see Armstrong, England, and Fogarty 2012; Bogle 2008; Dalessandro, James-Hawkins, and Sennott 2019). The doggedness of this trend is striking when we consider that calls for more egalitarianism have been in place for over fifty years in the United States, and that younger people themselves tend to support calls for equity (GenForward 2018). Despite their ideals, millennials can't quite escape persistent unequal gender expectations.

A comparison of the stories of Zoey and Connor provides some insight into how millennials are negotiating gender-related issues and struggles in their relationships. Upon meeting Zoey (twenty-five years old, White, straight, class-advantaged), I am immediately struck by how cool she seems—like a successful Instagram influencer. Yet despite my impression of Zoey as a confident, self-assured twenty-something, her story reveals that she often struggles with gender power inequalities in her relationships. Zoey believes one of her ongoing problems is that she has a pattern of catering a little too much to the needs of her boyfriends. Further, she says she is often overly tolerant of their bad behavior. For example, Zoey has experienced a pattern of emotional abuse in her intimate partnerships. She shared about one ex, "I really wanted him to be close with me. [But] every time I tried to get close with him, he would get defensive. And he would say mean things, or, he was pretty emotionally abusive. But then we would have really wonderful, great moments. And that would counteract the bad ones. So, it was able to sustain for such a long time because I was always hopeful that we would be able to break past this barrier." Though it seems that Zoey encountered some emotional struggles in that relationship, she justifies putting up with the behavior of her ex by highlighting that there were good times, too. Further, Zoey also believes that she has even achieved some empowerment through being able to overcome the less desirable experiences: "I've definitely grown. I'm fortunate that happened, in a way, because it's made me into a stronger person. I'm not willing to be so passive anymore. But I'm also upset that it happened because I'm not as sweet as I used to be. I can definitely be a jerk sometimes!" Even though Zoey has had some troubles in intimacy, she emphasizes her ability to learn and grow, framing her experience as a way to ascertain valuable lessons despite being on the receiving end of boyfriends' bad behaviors in the past. While useful for Zoey, her ability to explain the bad as a growth opportunity also downplays how unfair it is that she has experienced hurtful treatment.

In a rare occurrence for this study, I spoke separately with Zoey's current boyfriend Connor (twenty-six, White, straight, class-advantaged).[1] Connor also has a self-assured and approachable energy about him. He is tall, dark-haired, polite, and met Zoey on an online dating site. While Zoey voices some frustration over having to take on much of the responsibility for trying to make emotional headway with her partners—including in her current relationship—Connor admits that he often relies on his partners for their support. He confesses that this is the case in his relationship with Zoey:

> I think she's probably more there for me than I am for her. . . . I don't know if I am doing my best. Maybe I should try harder! But yeah, I definitely want to be there for her more. And I think grad school, [*laughs*] honestly I think grad school's to blame at least for a big chunk of that. You know, it's just hard and demanding and that's something she doesn't have to deal with, but I do, and it kind of just takes a toll sometimes. . . . She does a good job of [being supportive], she's amazing. But I definitely think I could improve in that area.

Though Connor believes he should give Zoey a level of support that is closer to the amount she offers him, he hasn't quite taken the steps to provide that support yet. His explanation for why he has not done so largely centers on his efforts to build his career. He claims he *will* contribute more emotionally, once he has more time. He reasons that he doesn't quite have the tools—or the time—to reach his goals just yet when it comes to offering emotional support in his relationship.

While Zoey, like many women in the study, discusses some of the bad experiences she's had (and continues to have) in relationships, she believes that ultimately these experiences can be used to inform her own self-awareness and self-improvement. Connor, like many men in this study, acknowledges that although he has sometimes been aloof in his past relationships—and to a certain extent, is also somewhat aloof in his current one—he hopes to change that at some point in the future. However, he believes he will only be able to change once he is ready and able to change. The differences between the stories of Zoey and Connor are important and have implications for how these two millennials make sense of themselves as gendered people, how they make sense of gender as a broader category of difference, and how they use their knowledge of gender to address gender issues and inequalities in their own lives. For example, Zoey's story is influenced by broader gendered expectations, yet her story also reinforces the idea that women are emotional caretakers in relationships and must navigate around men's needs. Connor's story, in contrast, communicates that women do more support work in relationships while men are occupied with other concerns—in Connor's case, economic and career goals. Further, the gendered approaches of Zoey and Connor are conditioned by their understandings of age, their social class positions, and their straight sexual identities as well. For instance, Connor's idea that he must wait until he establishes himself economically before he can contribute more emotional effort in his relationships is something that, we will see, is gendered as well as classed.

Focusing primarily on gender and the intersections of gender with several other categories (age, sexual identity, and social class), this chapter serves to explore how ideas about gender inform millennials' stories, how they negotiate gender and gendered dilemmas in intimacy, and how their stories challenge—or conversely, shore up—intimate inequalities rooted in gender and gendered expectations. Ultimately, while I do indeed find that millennials continue to struggle with some issues and tensions around gender in intimacy, their stories also reveal insight into why these struggles persist.

Gender Inequality in Intimacy

A bit of background with regard to the state of millennials' dealings with gender is useful to explore here. Similar to the dynamics we can observe in Connor's and Zoey's differing accounts of their relationships, research on young adults consistently finds that women and men have different gendered experiences in their relationships (Bell 2013; Bogle 2009; Dalessandro and Wilkins

2017). For example, compared to young men, young adult women have fewer orgasms during sexual activity, must contend with "slut-shaming," have more reputational concerns and conflicts over the practice of hooking up, and are often held responsible for preventing pregnancy and sexually transmitted infections (STIs) (Armstrong, England, and Fogarty 2012; Bogle 2009; Dalessandro 2019a; Dalessandro, James-Hawkins, and Sennott 2019; Hamilton and Armstrong 2009). In more committed or long-term relationships, women are typically saddled with the responsibility of keeping relationships afloat, taking care of men's emotional needs, childcare, and other emotional and care work tasks (Edin and Kefalas 2005; Wilkins and Dalessandro 2013; Wilkins 2004). Despite slow change toward more equity (Graf and Schwartz 2011) *and* many U.S. young adults' professed desire that gender roles and expectations be less rigid or more equal, gender inequalities prevail (Ciabattari 2001; Dernberger and Pepin 2020; Eaton and Rose 2011; England 2010; Gerson 2010; Hochschild 1989; Lamont 2014). As we have seen with the examples of Zoey and Connor, and as we will further see later, many of the millennials I interviewed share stories that are consistent with these previously documented trends. While the millennials here rarely admit to preferring inegalitarian relationships—which suggests that they value gender equity in principle—their stories reveal tensions and struggles when it comes to navigating awkward gender power inequalities in their intimate lives. Adhering to traditional gender expectations may be fine for some millennials, but since research has shown that many millennials profess to wanting to move past traditional gender norms, we must explore where, why, and how stagnation exists.

Yet in addition to gender, other factors—such as class, age, and race—always matter in individuals' negotiations of gender inequality. For instance, past research has found that class is important in structuring gendered approaches to intimacy (Edin and Kefalas 2005; Edin and Nelson 2013) and that claiming an LGBTQ+ identity may relate to a concerted effort to challenge gender conventions in particular (Lamont 2017). As the stories in this chapter reveal, there is much more for us to learn about how identity and status intersections are important in millennials' negotiations of gender in intimacy, and how these negotiations reflect patterns of gendered power more broadly. I investigate throughout how gender intersects with several other categories in millennials' negotiations of gender and gendered dilemmas. First, I explore the two main differences I found between how millennial women and men understand gendered experiences in their accounts.[2] They differ in strategies for making sense of personal (gendered) agency and in making sense of intimacy experiences as those that contribute (or do not contribute) to gendered personal growth. Both of these patterns reflect millennials' attempts to understand gender and gender differences and inequalities in intimate contexts. However, these differences also reflect unequal approaches to—and experiences of—gendered dilemmas.

Gender and Personal Agency

One key difference I found between millennial women and men is that the women's portrayals of themselves in their relationship stories, like Zoey's, tend to revolve around navigating the needs of partners. In contrast, men's stories stress the need to do what's best for themselves, even if what men want conflicts with the desires of their partners. Among the women, stories about having difficulty ending unwanted relationships provide an example of women's portrayals of themselves as reluctant to dictate the trajectories of their relationships. The women's stories are seemingly rooted in traditional gender expectations of femininity as passive and responsive in romantic contexts.

For instance, take the story of Faith (thirty, White, straight, class-disadvantaged). Faith is blonde and petite with a calm demeanor. She is also one of only four women interviewed who has ever been married. However, Faith and her husband are currently in the midst of a trial separation. While Faith appears eager to end the marriage, she also seems to be leaving the decision to divorce up to her husband. She admits that she does not really want the relationship to work out, as her feelings for him have diminished and she started seeing someone else even before they decided to separate. However, she still feels awkward about making the final decision to end things without his input: "With my husband, I'm hoping that it doesn't [work out]. I'm hoping that he'll really enjoy just being free. . . . So I'm kinda hoping he just wants to move on after. We're taking a year separation and we're just seeing how it goes. But in a way I'm hoping that he doesn't wanna get back together." In terms of whether she would pursue divorce if her husband does want to stay married, Faith said, "I don't know." Going through with a divorce would undoubtedly come with a string of logistical complications (such as arranging housing and childcare, for example).[3] Due to their separation, Faith is already living her life as a single working mom with her sons and without her husband. Yet still, Faith primarily discusses her husband's feelings and opinions about the relationship as integral to the outcome of their marriage. She does this even though she already knows that she wants out. In approaching the situation this way, Faith downplays her own agency and leaves the decision making up to her husband.

Other women's delayed breakup stories illustrate their (apparent) reverence for men's wishes as well as their desire to uphold feminized expectations of being "caring" partners (Dalessandro 2019a). The story of Molly (twenty-six, White, straight, class-advantaged) regarding her high school and college boyfriend provides an example. Molly is a self-assured Midwesterner living in the Mountain West who works in counseling. Molly recounted that her boyfriend's feelings directly impacted her choices about partying and socializing in college even though she was both a year older and left for college while he was still in high school: "I would say Tyler was pretty controlling, but not that I was really aware of. Like, I didn't label it as that until post-breakup. Um, he was definitely, like I would say I probably didn't party or didn't do a lot of stuff because I knew it would cause too much drama with him. . . . I remember having fights, or very intense conversations, about if I stayed out really late or what I was doing." Due to her boyfriend, Molly sometimes avoided socializing entirely.

After she decided to end it, Molly spent six months "officially" breaking up with Tyler, largely because she felt guilty about hurting his feelings: "I initiated a conversation with Tyler that was basically along the lines of 'I don't know where we're at, this is a lot of work, I think we maybe should see other people' . . . um, and that didn't [go] too well. Um, and I didn't have the energy—I don't know, courage?—to just flat out end it. . . . So this was like, April, [but] we weren't fully, clearly, officially, in his mind there's no chance of us getting back together, broken up until the end of October." Though Molly ultimately took steps to end the relationship, she portrays Tyler—who did not want to end the relationship—as being able to keep things going for another six months. Molly said she lingered toward the end out of respect for Tyler's feelings.

Similarly, Renee (twenty-six, Black, bisexual, class-advantaged)—who has a casual yet reserved style, striking gray eyes, and works as a writer—recounted a past relationship in which her boyfriend was not just controlling, but emotionally and verbally abusive as well. Just as she was trying to end the relationship, they were in a car accident. While Renee was driving, she lost control of the car because her boyfriend was drunk and kept putting his hands on her. In the aftermath, his injuries were severe because he wasn't wearing a seat belt: "So, long story short, we flipped over. His body got ejected from the car. . . . And during that time, I had already been thinking, I need to get away from [him]. . . . But then after that happened, I didn't want it to look like, you know, 'I don't want you because you're all [hurt]', and then I was driving, so, 'Oh, I messed you up and I'm gonna leave you now!' So I stayed with him until he could walk and he was himself again." In this case, Renee was both concerned about her boyfriend's recovery and how she might look if she broke up with him too soon after the accident, especially because she sustained only one minor injury ("some stitches") from the accident: "I was like, oh, what am I gonna do? That would be terrible for me to just, like, leave." Renee's concerns about the relationship had to do with a combination of her own guilt, fears about how she might look to others if she left, and also how that might make her boyfriend feel even though she admits that during the relationship, he showed little regard for her feelings.

Zoey, who was introduced in the opening of this chapter, offers another example of the lengths women can go to protect men's feelings. She shared about one of her relationships,

> When we decided to solidify our relationship, even then I knew I didn't want
> to be with him. I didn't want to be his girlfriend. But, a couple weeks prior, he

had asked what the deal was between him and I, and I was like, "Oh we're just hanging out, we're having fun dating. Why do you ask?" . . . And then, like, a couple weeks went by, and we kept hanging out here and there, and he asked again if I wanted to be in a relationship with him. And at that point I would have felt bad saying no twice, so I decided to say yes.

Further, Zoey added that she sometimes avoids ending her relationships, and that when faced with the prospect of breaking up, it can be a "relief" when a boyfriend decides to end things first: "I'd feel a sense of relief that I didn't have to be the one to do it." Like Faith and Molly, Zoey admits to putting off ending relationships. In allowing a partner's feelings and desires to determine whether a relationship will continue, she thereby avoids a possible gender transgression. However, Zoey has to endure an unwanted relationship as a result.

Interestingly, many of the millennial men interviewed emphasize much more often the importance of their own desires—rather than desires of partners—in making decisions in, and about, relationships. Patrick (twenty-four, Black, queer, class-advantaged), an affable graduate student, provides an example with his discussion about his ex-girlfriend. In his discussion about his relationship, he approaches the topic of marriage pragmatically: "I always wanted to be involved in politics. That's another arena where, obviously, a spouse helps. I was always told that I was supposed to be a minister, I was supposed to preach. So obviously a spouse helps in that arena." For Patrick, having a spouse could be a benefit to his career due to his understanding that ministers and politicians are viewed more favorably when married. Hunter (twenty-four, White, straight, upwardly mobile)—who is talkative, likes to philosophize, and was applying to law schools when we met—said something along the same lines as Patrick: "I would like to see myself married. I would like to have a wife with kids, you know? [It helps] if I'm running for office, or climbing up the judicial [ladder]." Though Hunter expresses some cynicism around marriage, he also admits that it's something he wants because he imagines that being married will help him reach his professional goals.

Like Patrick and Hunter, the account of Dawson (twenty-nine, White, gay, class-advantaged) also shows that he thinks about how relationships can be beneficial to his own development even though he discusses a past relationship with a man. Dawson strikes me as easygoing, but serious when talking about important issues. While Patrick points out that relationships can help with career/public image, Dawson frames a past relationship as helping with his own sexual identity exploration: "I don't want to paint it like I was messing with his emotions, but I definitely was experimenting with [my ex], trying to see, what does this look like? Can I get this person to like me, to love me, and how am I gonna respond to that? . . . So I was doing a lot of boundary work, um, to sort of maintain his desire and his attention without having to be anything, necessarily, without any obligation to him." Unlike the women's accounts, Dawson's does not suggest that he structured his behavior around his partner's wishes. Instead, he considers what the relationship could contribute to his own developing sense of self. Dawson's gender identity and understandings of gender matter for how he approached his past relationship.

The story of Joel (twenty-four, White, straight, class-advantaged) also provides an example of how men afford themselves agency in their accounts. Joel is a people-person who, by his own admission, would also probably always rather be skiing or doing something athletic. For Joel, a woman with whom he had a casual intimate relationship—Lydia—suddenly took things to a more serious level when she revealed to him her mental health struggles: "She has a lot of depression issues and stuff like that, and she called me during the summer trying to commit suicide. So, I went down to help her with that stuff, but then she was thinking I was trying to date her, and I was like, 'We live over three hours apart. It's never gonna work. I'm not gonna be the one who *saves* you from this. You're gonna have to start anew and find somebody for yourself and make it work.'" Joel declined to take emotional responsibility for Lydia, instead telling her that she was going to have to sort out her issues on her own. This is interesting because Joel's three-hour trip suggests that he cared about Lydia in some capacity (even though the relationship was casual). However, Joel also said that in light of her mental health struggles he did not want to enter into a more serious relationship. Joel's story reveals that unlike some of the stories told by women, he did not feel obligated to be (or stay) in a romantic relationship in order to help a partner make it through a difficult time in their life.

These millennials' stories demonstrate not only gender differences in how they experience and make sense of their relationships, but also different approaches based on efforts to live up to gendered expectations. Gendered ideas about men as independent, and about women as natural caregivers, seemingly inform women's and men's gendered portrayals of themselves and their own agency in stories. While men portray themselves as in control, women portray themselves as unwilling to challenge men's moods (even if their actions suggest otherwise—such as by initiating a breakup, for example). While women cast themselves as acting in response to partners, men cast themselves as being generally in control. Women's and men's gendered ways of making sense of their experiences help perpetuate ideas about how women and men are different and the dissimilar ways that women and men approach gender and gendered issues in relationships. Women are seemingly self-sacrificing, and men are seemingly self-serving. While the truth of what actually happens in their relationships is undoubtedly more complicated, ideas about gender perpetuated in these millennials' accounts help reinforce generic gendered expectations, which in turn help inform personal gendered identities and, on a larger scale, contribute to the perpetuation of gender inequalities in intimacy. Another area in which women's and men's stories diverge—and help simultaneously hide and perpetuate the importance of gender—is in making sense of intimacy experiences as an opportunity for personal growth.

Gender and Personal Growth

To these millennials, relationship stories offer an opportunity to reflect on—and make sense of—the meaning and purpose of their relationship experiences over time. According to millennial women's stories, partners (and experiences with partners) are central to women's evolving sense of (gendered) self. While relationship stories are also important for demonstrating change over time in men's stories, many men's accounts downplay the extent to which partners might influence their personal growth process. Similar to stories about agency, stories about growth help obscure the extent to which gender matters and simultaneously convey important messages about gender.

The stories of Kara, Paige, and Hallie illustrate how women make sense of their encounters with gender inequality as experiences of learning and personal growth. Kara (twenty-nine, White, straight, class-advantaged) has a funny, sarcastic sense of humor and loves science fiction. She shared with me that she would characterize her prior relationship with her ex-boyfriend Cole as "manipulative." According to Kara, after Cole actively pursued her and they began a relationship, he started trying to convince her that they should have an open relationship in which each of them was free to date, and have sex with, additional partners.[4] Kara was uncomfortable with this and tried to communicate with Cole about it, but she eventually gave up and went along with his wishes. In retrospect, she believes, "he manipulated me. So, I'm a little angry about that. He's one person I do not want to talk to ever again." Though Kara believes the relationship conjures up memories of bad experiences, she also said she believes that all is not lost: "I think in some ways the relationship was good for me, because you know I saw how crazy and ridiculous the situation was and it kind of taught me, oh, you're an idiot, Kara. Maybe I owe Cole a thank you, but I am NOT gonna tell him that!" Similar to the accounts in the last section, and to Zoey's story from the chapter opening, Kara went along with an uncomfortable situation by deferring to her partner Cole. Ultimately, Kara recounts the relationship as a negative experience, but one that she believes did teach her to be more assertive.

The story of Paige (twenty-two, White, straight, class-advantaged) is similar to Kara's in that she also believes she experienced emotional manipulation in past relationships. When we meet, I notice that Paige has expressive eyes that light up when she talks about her new puppy. When asked about her previous experiences, Paige gives the example of her on-again, off-again relationship with an exchange student named Dane. During the entirety of their relationship,

Dane flip-flopped between responding to and ignoring Paige's text messages. After several months of back-and-forth, Paige described the last straw of the relationship:

> But still, 'cause I am stupid and can't get a hint, I'm just like, "I'm gonna make this work, 'cause we would be perfect together!" . . . Then the last time that we hooked up. [*pause*] OK, so the whole time, he had had a problem [keeping his penis] hard. Also, kind of graphic, I'm sorry! And I tried a lot of things to make it not so. And then the last time we hung out, he pretty much blamed it on me and said he didn't have that with anyone else. Like, it was pretty much my fault that his penis wasn't working! . . . I pretty much said, like, "I'm never gonna be good enough for you, am I?" . . . That was like, the end. And I'm actually really glad that's how it ended, with him being a total asshole, 'cause otherwise I would have been like, well, maybe this can work.

Despite being upset, Paige explained that after the incident, she came to the realization that "I was like, I am not myself 'cause I've just been obsessing over these guys. And I'm not valuing myself as much, and I just kind of needed to go through this, all this crap, really, to just be like, I want to work on myself." Like Kara and other women interviewed, Paige makes sense of her experience as an opportunity for growth. Further, Paige's case suggests that without the bad experiences, she may never have realized that taking care of herself, and advocating for herself in relationships, is important.

A third example comes from Hallie (twenty-seven, White, straight, class-advantaged). Hallie has a commanding, yet inviting, presence that serves her well in her job as an event coordinator. Hallie shared that she entered into a "toxic" relationship during her last year of college: "I just met someone 'cause I was lonely, and I looked the other way even though I knew I shouldn't be looking the other way." After they had been dating for a time, Hallie discovered that her boyfriend was cheating on her when she acquired an STI. She was especially upset because she had recently also gotten an intrauterine device (IUD) for birth control and her doctor warned her that STIs can be especially dangerous for women with IUDs. Yet despite being angry, Hallie largely blames herself for the incident and considers it an opportunity in which she learned about the kinds of men to avoid: "I couldn't turn the other cheek anymore [after the diagnosis]. I couldn't pretend. It's like, ugh, this is just so stupid. Yeah he's a jerk, but it's my fault for going along with this for as long as I did. I was settling. I just needed some companionship because my friends were leaving and there was nobody around. I was lonely. I just let someone violate me, basically. And that was the last time. That *was* the last time, 'cause I'm getting married and my fiancé would never do that!" In Hallie's view, her ex-boyfriend is "a bad person," but she also believes it is her fault for putting up with him for as long as she did.

Hallie goes even further in contrasting all her ex-boyfriends with her current fiancé. She sees her current relationship as the happy ending she deserves after many years of dating men who caused trouble and hurt her: "[My fiancé's] not a liar, [he's] not cocky, [he's] not this, that; like, things I'd already decided, I'm not dealing with that again. . . . [But] I don't really regret anybody I dated, 'cause they all gave me a tidbit of something where I'm like, oh, I'm not putting up with *that*, I'm not dealing with *this* kinda person. They all taught me something along the way, so I don't regret anybody." Hallie's stories about her experiences are important because they demonstrate that she will not let men "violate" her ever again. Instead, she can take comfort in knowing that she has overcome her experiences and ended up with a good guy not in spite of her experiences but *because* of them. Hallie believes her experiences taught her to differentiate the good men from the bad.

While the stories of the women convey the idea that personal growth comes out of negative experiences with partners, men's stories suggest that personal growth has different origins. Rather than discuss how partners have changed them, the men's stories tend to focus on how they have changed themselves. The story of Rob (twenty-six, White, straight, class-advantaged) provides an instructive example. Rob is a tall, bespectacled, and bookish man originally from the West Coast. Like other men, Rob's approach to pursuing partners has changed as he has gotten older. Rather than seek out partners for superficial attributes such as how they look, he now appreciates other qualities: "Attractiveness is not the only component [to a potential partner]. I would say I was probably more fixated on how the girl looked before [in the past]." Tommy (twenty-eight, White, straight, upwardly mobile), a no-nonsense small business owner, has a similar view: "I feel like as I've gotten older, it's not all physical. It's really what's going on the inside too. . . . Now I realize . . . maybe [I] should [start] judging people on things other than superficial qualities." However, unlike the women quoted previously, Rob and Tommy generally credit their own self-reflection, rather than experiences with actual partners, for bringing about this change.

Luke, (thirty-two, White, straight, upwardly mobile), a tireless optimist who seems to be always smiling, illustrates the extent to which men's understandings of change are self-directed. Unlike Rob and Tommy, Luke isn't sure his criteria for partner selection has changed much over time. However, he believes that it will change once discovers what he wants out of life:

I think that's [when] I will change, is once I move. Or, once I figure out where I wanna go, I will begin to figure out what I wanna do with my life, who I wanna become, and what great things I want to accomplish. Until I know what those goals are, I won't have a place of certainty with women and where I wanna go with them because I still haven't discovered myself yet. So, it would be premature to go into something if it would be anything different from [the relationships] I've been in, 'cause what I've been in is something that has no future—but it does sustain itself!

Luke's account is interesting because, especially when compared to those of the women above, it demonstrates the conviction that change starts with him rather than with his experiences with partners. Whereas women understand themselves as changed through their relationships, men's stories suggest that change is a self-paced, personal choice. Eddie (twenty-six, Latino, gay, upwardly mobile), a wiry personal trainer, shared that a few relationships ended in the past due to his lack of readiness to commit: "I'm not saying it was my fault or anything [that the relationships didn't work out], 'cause I didn't do anything wrong, but definitely it was because of the fact that I wasn't really ready to, you know, ground myself at that point." Unlike the women discussed earlier in the chapter, Eddie does not blame himself for past relationships that failed, saying he "didn't do anything wrong." The relationships simply did not work out because Eddie did not commit to them working out, which he considers a personal preference rather than a problem.

In reality, men can and likely do have bad experiences with partners, and women frequently initiate the dissolution of unwanted relationships. However, while women construct their experiences with men as important to their own development, most men here don't discuss their experiences in relationships as having a noteworthy impact on their propensity to learn, grow, and change. This is important, because in making sense of how they navigate gender differences millennial men construct themselves as able to grow outside of the context of intimate relationships, whereas millennial women paint relationships as important to the project of who they are as women. This is also interesting considering that, according to research, it is *men* who seemingly benefit the most from being in committed relationships (see Riessman 1990; Siegler et al. 2013). Further, solutions to some of the gendered issues millennials discuss are also typically individualized. This individualization puts the focus on personal failings or successes rather than social systems. Whereas women's solution is to learn from individual mistakes and move on to better partners, men's catalyst for change is their own individual will to change.

Given increased awareness of gender issues and inequality in the United States over the last half century, it might be surprising that these women and men have different interpretations of their experiences. One reason for the seeming gap is that these stories are personalized, which can get in the way of recognizing larger patterns (see Riessman 1990). However, another factor contributes to this seeming awareness gap as well. In order to understand how these millennials might be able to explain away the importance of gender, we must consider how specific age understandings are important in millennials' stories.[5]

Gender and Aged Expectations

With few exceptions, the millennial women and men interviewed do not usually understand their gendered experiences in relationships as gendered. The exceptions to this are most often those who have been exposed to feminism and gender studies through education.[6] This is the case with Colleen (twenty-five, White, queer, class-advantaged). Colleen is in school while also working in victim advocacy, and she has a strong sense of commitment to helping those in need. She recalled that her ex-boyfriend forced her into sex when he was drunk. However, instead of brushing it off, she confronted him about it: "He raped me, and we talked about it, like, six to seven times. . . . We talked about it a lot, which is a lot more than most women get. . . . I think he was just real drunk, and yeah I was studying gender and sexual assault then. But that's what made me really interested in masculinity, because I think he just really wanted to have sex, and [I asked], why?" However, the awareness exhibited by Colleen—that sexual assault and rape prevalence relates to destructive masculinity expectations, and that rape can still happen even in committed relationships—is not common. Instead, young women and men draw on understandings of their age status as adults-in-progress to make sense of gendered experiences.

Some of the stories already introduced hint at how age matters for interpreting gender. For instance, we saw women discuss how negative experiences in relationships are the result of not knowing any better, and men discuss how they have changed (or will change) over time. However, women and men also use age explicitly to either explain, or explain away, certain behaviors. The story of Morgan (thirty-one, White, bisexual, class-advantaged) provides an example of the use of age expectations to explain gendered inequality in her relationships. My first impression of Morgan is that she is sensitive and thoughtful. Morgan describes her first serious boyfriend as "a horrible guy" who was emotionally abusive, controlling, and aggressive in his efforts to separate her from her family and friends. However, Morgan explains her ex-boyfriend's actions—and her tolerance of his actions—as a symptom of immaturity: "You know, unfortunately [with] the first boyfriend, you learn all the bad lessons. . . . Of course being a first love I was completely blinded." She also added, "Yeah, that was my first, my first horrible two-year relationship. [*laughs*] But yeah, I'm glad that I did learn [and] that I at least took away from it [that] I didn't fall into a pattern." Morgan talked about her boyfriend as "psychotically jealous" and misogynistic. However, she explains her decision to stay in the relationship as a sign of immaturity. Further, even though she was mistreated, she believes that at least she has learned from the experience and has since moved forward.

Similarly, Paige (introduced earlier) discusses being hurt by a few romantic interests during her college days. However, she blames these bad experiences mostly on herself by saying that it was actually her fault for tolerating being treated badly and for being "desperate" for a relationship in the past: "I was not comfortable [being assertive] or saying anything that could be seen as an ulti-matum to a guy before, 'cause I was much more desperate at that time." How-ever, again, through her negative experiences, Paige believes she has learned how to value herself as she has grown up.

Women also frame youthful vulnerability as a state that is replaced with more control and agency in adulthood. This is the case with Leah (twenty-six, Brown [Middle Eastern], queer, upwardly mobile)—an artistic, statuesque, and sociable graduate student—who connects her own experiences to those of the undergraduates in the university classes that she teaches:

> Mostly I see young women—the problem is, I get so fucking frustrated and so angry when I see and hear things, when I see women who are seemingly disempowered. It just blows my mind. And it doesn't blow my mind that they are that way, because I fucking understand. I was there. I've seen so many people in relationships, and you just have to let them experience that. Like, in my experience, there's no other way to learn than to suffer. You know? And that's pretty intense. But I see young women all the time . . . using fucked up, crazy excuses. Like, "Oh my boyfriend got too drunk, I couldn't turn in my homework." You know, shit like that. And you know, that's probably the truth, that your boyfriend fucking distracted you, because you devote yourself entirely to him, and it just makes me fucking *burn* inside!

As a graduate student, Leah's exposure to feminist literature and ideologies led her to be one of the women with a better understanding of the importance of gender. Nevertheless, Leah still uses age to explain gendered experiences and what is needed to overcome them. She points out that there's "no other way to learn than to suffer" when it comes to gaining a higher level of understanding about relationships. However, she has confidence that women's empowerment comes with age (and with more experience in relationships).

Men also use age to explain past behaviors and experiences. A quote from Reid (twenty-eight, White, straight, class-advantaged), a quiet man who works in finance, illustrates how many of the millennial men interviewed generally make sense of gendered behaviors as aged: "When I was younger I was imma-ture, probably made immature decisions, said immature things. And now I have the conscience to know [that] what I'm saying affects other people's feelings. You know, [I ask myself] 'Is it gonna affect the relationship I have with this person, maybe other relationships that I have?' So I think that my identity has changed in that sense. [I'm] more mature [and] act like an adult." Reid admits here that in the past he may not have been as mindful of his partners' feelings. At the same time, his realization is consistent with patterns discussed previously in that this change comes from his own awareness rather than specific experiences.

Dylan (twenty-four, White, straight, class-advantaged), who is fun loving and likes the outdoor recreation that the Mountain West has to offer, also said that he did not always consider the feelings of his partners in previous relationships and struggled with putting himself in their shoes: "Full-disclosure, openness, and communication were things I struggled with. I'm a lot better with them today. I make it a point to be as open and honest, and communicate, as much as possible, because I believe that's essential to have any sort of valuable relationship. . . . I guess back in the day, I was more of a taker. [*laughs*] So yeah . . . I wouldn't always say what was on my mind, and if questioned about it, a lot of times I wouldn't, like, give the honest answer 'cause I knew it wasn't the answer that would always benefit me." In retrospect, Dylan said, "I can see where I probably wasn't being the best person I could have been." Although today he considers himself more "mature" and less of a "taker" than he was in the past, this is a change that he developed with time. For Dylan, maturity brought with it more considerate behavior.

Similarly, Eddie (introduced earlier) reflected that in his younger years he probably hurt some of his previous partners with his attitude and actions: "When I was younger, I knew going in that I didn't want a relationship with anyone. So, even when I was dating someone, I knew it would be nothing long term. I'm a jerk like that! Yeah, unfortunately with me, I don't wanna sound like a bitch or anything but, it was just one of those things where, back when I was younger, I was a huge asshole." Eddie's story, like those of many men, links immaturity with being selfish and aloof when it comes to dealing with intimate partners. Conversely, maturity means realizing that the feelings of partners are important.

While the women and men here both attribute changes in their approaches to relationships to changes in maturity, gender has an impact on how women and men apply aged understandings in their stories. While men's understanding of coming to maturity focuses internally, women's understanding focuses on the development of maturity through their experiences with others. Millennial women reason that their efforts working through bad relationships help them understand themselves as strong, resilient women. Millennial men's efforts are instead constructed as mostly self-directed. While women use relationship stories as a way to seemingly gain more control over their lives as they come into their own as adult women, men's bad behaviors could be explained away as simply immature.

The stories of the millennial men here seem to take an almost laissez-faire approach to gender issues in intimacy. That is, men's stories don't indicate that gender causes many problems for them, and men also don't typically locate the development of a confident, masculine self in their intimate relationship experiences. In contrast, millennial women cast intimacy stories as an important part of developing into adult women. Despite wanting to move beyond gender, millennials' stories indicate the persistence of gendered ideas that help shore up inequalities. Though these patterns come across very strikingly in most participants' accounts, social class differences add an additional layer of nuance when we consider how millennials make sense of gender in their relationship stories.

Gender and Social Class

In light of the differences between millennial women and men outlined here, it is also important to consider how social class might be important to how these women and men portray themselves in their stories. Indeed, I find that class-disadvantaged women and men divert somewhat from other classed groups of women and men in the study when it comes to making sense of gendered approaches to relationships and potential relationship issues. For example, while the class-advantaged and upwardly mobile men interviewed downplay emotions and the extent to which the influence of partners matters for their sense of personal identity, class-disadvantaged men are more inclined to acknowledge their emotions in their stories. Conversely, compared to upwardly mobile and class-advantaged women, class-disadvantaged women generally portray themselves as more independent and less emotional. Thus, for these millennials, making sense of gender and navigating gender-related issues is a project that is also conditioned by class.

For example, quick-witted maintenance worker Noah (thirty-two, mixed-race, straight, class-disadvantaged) discusses throughout his interview (in detail) his own emotional state and feelings with regard to his relationships. Noah told an emotional story about his breakup with one of his first serious girlfriends:

On Valentine's Day I went downtown and spent two or three checks on balloons, cards that played music, stuffed animals, candy, anything I could think of. . . . [I had to] get on the bus from [downtown] to [the neighborhood], then walk about six miles with all that stuff back to the house. So I walked in, like, "Happy Valentine's Day, baby!" And gave her all the stuff. She threw it on the ground, looked at me and said, "Where have you been all day?" You know, like it wasn't obvious that I was shopping for her all day long! She didn't give me a chance to explain why I was a little bit late. So, I couldn't handle it no more. After lying to me about being pregnant, and her being ungrateful about everything I was trying to do for her, I packed one bag—one bag of clothes.... [I got] a ride to my friend's house.

Compared to the men quoted previously, Noah's story is notable for its specificity. Though class-advantaged and upwardly mobile men acknowledge feeling positive or negative emotions as a result of their experiences, most do not go into this much detail. For comparison, here is the complete account of class-advantaged Reid's experience with his high school girlfriend: "Yeah, pretty much all of high school I dated the same girl. So, I think, sophomore year we started dating, and we dated 'til we graduated, so it was a long time. So we grew up [together], we went to the same middle school, kindergarten, and I don't really know how [but] it blossomed in high school. She had an older brother who I played sports with, and I knew her whole family. And, yeah, I don't know that's about all I got! I don't know, what else you looking for? [*laughs*]" Contrast Reid's complete account with only an excerpt from Noah's account, and there is a striking difference in both the level of detail and the amount of emotionality shared during the interview.

Similarly, Troy (twenty-six, White, straight, class-disadvantaged), a gig worker with a serene personality, includes many details in his account. His breakup story is even more emotional and detailed than Noah's:

With her, it was complete honesty, even if it hurt.... But regardless, that diminished after a while, and a lot of our dreams that were dreams, were just dreams still.... You know, we were broke. You know, we couldn't afford much. There was a point where we were grocery shopping at the dollar store for a little while until I got that good job where I was the [manager] of my own department, kinda deal. And, by that time there were already so many years, and so many things talked about that never happened. I feel like that's what gave her cold feet, you know what I mean? And, uh, that really crushed me, 'cause it was tough and I was working my ass off, and I was really trying. There's no doubt about that. You know what I mean? I gave all of myself to this girl. There was even a day, like I said, we were so broke, and she had an infected tooth.... I actually went out, and luckily it was wintertime, 'cause I went house to house shoveling snow with boots that had holes in 'em, and let my feet freeze and everything and made just enough money to get her tooth pulled for her. It was like, things like I would do, you know what I mean? That didn't matter because I loved her. It just didn't matter at all. It didn't cause me any pain or suffering because I'm helping somebody that I love, and that was amazing. But yeah, of course, like I said, things talked about that never happened. I think gave her the cold feet, and she just tried to disappear and make her own dreams come true, which is totally understandable. I mean, we were young—twenty-two to twenty-four—you know, in that age range, and we were serious talking about getting married, and being a fiancée, and husband, and all that wack[7] stuff. But um, you know, yeah it was wild. It's making my heart beat thinking about it! [*laughs*] But, um, no she left me and it was probably the best thing—even though it makes my heart flutter like that, and gives me all those crazy emotions from the past, it was actually probably the best thing that could have happened to me at that age because I had not known myself, and neither did she. . . . It took a couple years after, you know. It was wild, like if she wouldn't have ran away from me, I wouldn't be the person who I am today, of course. So, I can only thank her, instead of regret it.

While the accounts of Noah and Troy apparently contradict the more controlled stories of the men already profiled, considering social class sheds light on these seeming outliers.

As hinted at in the preceding pages (and addressed more in the coming chapters), economic and career power is both important to, and expected by, class-advantaged and upwardly mobile men. These concerns help structure men's gendered approaches to their relationships—men are in control in terms of both class/economic power and gender power (which can go hand in hand in U.S. society). In contrast, class-disadvantaged men have more challenging experiences with paid work. For these men, emotional stories that demonstrate how much they care about their partners can actually be a way to live up to masculine expectations when economic strategies either fall short or don't exist as a possible pathway (see Edin and Nelson 2013). Class-disadvantaged men's emotional approach helps address the gendered dilemma of lacking access to the economic and class resources that seemingly continue to be important to normative masculinity in a U.S. context.

Viewing men's stories, across class lines, through the lens of masculinities theories can also add more insight. While class-advantaged men can assert gendered control through downplaying their emotions and asserting the importance of their economic pursuits, class-disadvantaged men might assert a more "hybrid" masculinity form that still asserts power, albeit in a slightly different way than that exerted by more privileged men (Bridges and Pascoe 2014; Connell and Messerschmidt 2005). For instance, Noah and Troy use emotions to paint themselves as good, chivalrous, responsible partners in much the same way more privileged men might do so by focusing on their ability to be financial providers. Both class-advantaged and class-disadvantaged men can exert power over women, although social class helps structure how men make sense of, and wield, gendered power (see also Pyke 1996).

On the other hand, class-disadvantaged women actually come across more matter-of-fact in their stories compared to other classed groups of millennial women. Katelyn (twenty-two, White, straight, class-disadvantaged), an athletic brunette with pin-straight hair, provides an example. Rather than paint her current relationship in romanticized terms, Katelyn emphasizes the logistics of how she and her boyfriend became a couple: "On Craigslist I just found a house to live in. . . . And he had done sort of the same thing around the same time . . . like, moved to [town] from a random Craigslist thing. So, yeah, his roommate became one of my good friends and I started going over to the house a lot, and met him, and we were kinda friends for a little bit and then after that we started dating." Katelyn's story is also interesting because she thinks she might get engaged in the near future. However, she doesn't romanticize her relationship. In contrast, class-advantaged Molly (introduced above) gushes about her fiancé: "Yeah, with [my fiancé] Andrew it was—[I'm] cheesy and cliché pulling on these horrible narratives—but I knew. I did. I knew [he was the one]!" In this study, the class-disadvantaged women, compared to more class-privileged and upwardly mobile women, tell less ornate stories about their relationships.

The account of Jasmine (twenty-seven, Black, straight, class-disadvantaged) adds some insight as to why some class-disadvantaged millennial women might be less emotional and more matter-of-fact. Jasmine, who appears to have a fun side as the pink streak in her hair suggests, is rare among the participants because she has two children. While she would like to find a man who can be a father figure to her kids, she said that she has a hard time with men sometimes because they expect her to take care of them as if they were an additional child: "I have three kids? No, I only have *two* kids, for real, for real. I'm not gonna take care of you, I'm not gonna pay your bills. I don't know what to tell you, but you better do something! . . . I'll get bored. Or, it's just taking too long to get progress. And then I'll be done with the relationship." As a parent, Jasmine's children come first. Due to being busy as a single mom working multiple jobs, she simply does not have the availability to attend to the needs of a partner who would be greedy with her time and money. For Jasmine, practicality is a concern since she communicates that first and foremost she needs to make sure she and her kids have what they need.

Chelsea (twenty-six, White, queer, class-disadvantaged), a barista who also has a funky sense of style demonstrated by the dinosaur T-shirt that she wore to our interview, pushed back on her fiancé when she interpreted his actions as conforming too closely to traditional gender roles: "He's like, 'I'm not trying to be condescending, I'm trying to protect you,' and I'm like, 'Look, when you're looking at me as a woman and saying "I need to protect you" . . . you're basically telling me I'm not capable of taking care of myself without your help.'" Chelsea has proven to herself throughout her life that she can take care of herself, and so her fiancé suggesting otherwise is offensive to her. Contrast Chelsea with Ruby (twenty-eight, White, straight, upwardly mobile), who said about her fiancé, "If I lost him now, I don't know what I would do. I love him so much. . . . We feel like we're the only couple since Romeo and Juliet to feel this way, and I think that's hilarious!" While Ruby's story is more theatrical, the accounts of the class-disadvantaged women here are not as romantic and instead seem to relay the message that romanticizing men and traditional romantic tropes is unhelpful or impractical.

What remains less clear is how to comprehensively explain these gender differences, which are seemingly conditioned by class. However, we can speculate that while class-disadvantaged men might be *more* emotional as a way to demonstrate masculinity in the absence of economic prowess, class-disadvantaged women might be *less* emotional in their stories to communicate feminized class identities that convey resilience and strength. Compared to more privileged women, working-class and poor women have not had the same opportunities historically to live out culturally idealized images of femininity. Although some of these older gender expectations have ostensibly fallen out of favor (or at least have somewhat shifted) in many communities throughout the United States, class-advantaged millennial women still exhibit some romanticization around their relationships with men. Further, while more privileged women can rely on spousal income and outsource domestic labor if everyday life becomes too difficult to manage alone, poor and working-class women have always had to balance domestic duties with working outside the home (Coontz 1992). These practical concerns might influence ideas about a (classed) feminine identity in the context of intimacy.

What is also interesting is that women's trajectories—rather than their background alone—seem to determine approaches to gender. For example, though they share a background, the accounts of upwardly mobile women (as we saw earlier) more closely match those of class-advantaged women. This suggests that not just background but *expectations* of identity are important in helping determine millennials' approaches to negotiating differences and issues in their relationships. As we will also see later (such as in chapter 5), backgrounds are significant, but are not necessarily deterministic when it comes to how individuals will make sense of their lives. Expectations should not be discounted in discussions of millennials' approaches to negotiating difference.

Ultimately, class-disadvantaged women and men—and indeed all the millennials in this chapter—work through concerns about gendered power in light of their classed positions. For class-disadvantaged men, the absence of the promise of economic prowess makes communicating emotional commitment important to a masculine sense of self. Due to the precarity of working-class labor, class-disadvantaged women cannot assume that they will find spouses in their social networks from a similar class position who will be able to support a family the same way that class-disadvantaged men cannot assume that they will be able to support a family on the low-wage work typically available to men in this group (Edin and Kefalas 2005; Edin and Nelson 2013; Johnson and Mollborn 2009). Thus, while men on a class-disadvantaged trajectory can make use of emotions to make sense of themselves as caring partners in the absence of economic prowess, women on a class-disadvantaged trajectory might be more emotionally cautious than other women because they expect that while romance is nice, practical concerns must be prioritized.

These classed approaches to gender that I have just described do arguably upset men's central place in gendered stories. Decoupling masculinity from economic prowess—a trait often central in U.S. constructions of hegemonic masculinity—changes how gender emerges in discussions about intimate relationships. It could be argued that the accounts of class-disadvantaged millennials thus offer a challenge to class-advantaged versions of gender expectations that perpetuate inequalities. However, class-disadvantaged women and men still must navigate broader gender expectations. For example, in Troy's story, part of the reason his fiancée left was that he could not financially support them both (thus not living up to hegemonic masculine expectations to provide). Jasmine also balked at the idea of having to financially support a spouse or boyfriend. Despite current normative expectations of gender not being a good fit for their lives, class-disadvantaged millennials must still seemingly contend with gender expectations in relationships that appear most achievable to those in more privileged groups.

Simultaneously, that class-disadvantaged millennials diverge from class-advantaged millennials shows that making sense of gender is not a fixed process. This raises more questions about how millennials' approaches to gender could challenge deeply rooted inequalities sourced from ideas about essentialized gender differences. In fact, I find that the stories of some millennials who have understandings or approaches to gender that explicitly challenge the idea that gender is essential, natural, and unchangeable might add further insight into how stories around gender—and as a result, gender inequalities—might change.

Complicating Gender, Complicating Inequality?

The stories of several millennials stand out because they further highlight the importance of complicating gender assumptions and expectations when it comes to millennials' understandings of gender and their own gendered experiences. The accounts of Aaron, Spencer, Jeremy, Marcus, and Taylor are useful to examine because each of these men either has a gender identity different from the one they were assigned at birth or an explicitly fluid understanding of gender. Aaron, Spencer, and Jeremy are cisgender or genderqueer men who try to incorporate a fluid approach to gender into their lives, and Marcus and Taylor are trans men. Their accounts show that uprooting gender essentialism—or the idea that gender is binary, fixed at birth, and unchangeable or strict—may provide insight into how to better challenge the inequalities that seem to accompany most cisgender millennials' typical approaches.

Marcus and Taylor demonstrate the potential in challenging gender as fixed. Taylor (thirty-one, White, queer, upwardly mobile) is a tech industry worker who also strikes me as slightly shy, and his account aligns largely with those of cisgender men. Even though he was assigned "female" at birth and did not begin his gender transition until after high school, Taylor gave an account of a past relationship (and breakup) that looked most like those put forth by cisgender men from the same class position:

> In hindsight I was eighteen, young and impressionable and just kind of still figuring out what I wanted for myself and for my partner and for my future life. And I think—she didn't act like thirty-five in the beginning. She was very young and high-spirited. But then I think you kind of know who you are when you're thirty-five. I mean, you know better who you are. And we just kind of grew apart. I mean I was a much different person at twenty-five than I was at eighteen whereas she was pretty similar at forty-one to who she was at thirty-five. And I just didn't romantically feel attracted to her anymore. And when I started talking about transgender feelings she was not supportive at all. So I just knew that that was not something that would get me to where I wanted to be in life.

Like other men, the patterns in Taylor's account include a demonstration of agency in making relationship decisions and sticking mostly to the facts in the story. Thus, Taylor's account offers evidence for the importance of personal, classed gender identity in structuring a gendered approach to intimacy. Gendered approaches to intimacy are largely a factor of millennials' own gender identities, and, as we'll see directly below, understanding gender as fluid, changeable, or not a natural extension of sex assigned at birth might open up opportunities for challenging gender inequalities.

Unlike Taylor, who seemed quiet, Marcus (thirty-one, Black, queer, upwardly mobile) is an open book when it comes to sharing stories about his personal life. Marcus works in public health and wore a bowtie to our interview, which he tells me is one of his favorite accessories. Marcus is also trans, although compared to Taylor his account generally took a more macro approach to problematizing gender as a category of difference. In particular, he tried to steer clear of what he considers to be the "negative" aspects of masculinity:

> I feel like when I look at people in the queer community—whether it's trans guys, or butches, or studs or what have you—it's unfortunate that a lot of us didn't have appropriate male role models. And so, we kind of like, make up and piece together what we think masculinity is and, a lot of the times, unfortunately it comes from these negative things we see—either the media, the community, or whatever. . . . And I was definitely there at one point, and

looking back on it, I'm like geez that was wack! [*laughs*] You know? And I would say that since transitioning, I'm able to just—I dunno, able to just be more comfortable with myself. And I take on, and enjoy, being the young Black guy who will say things that maybe people have never heard a young Black guy say. Or, be that person who challenges masculinity for themselves, and for the people they come in contact with on a regular basis. And I think that, you know, kinda going through the overcompensating masculinity phase, and the second puberty phase, [*laughs*] you know, this is what I've come to. And I go out of my way to not be that guy. In everything that I do, I go out of my way to not be *that guy*.

As Marcus mentions, his particular experience as a queer Black man (who works in public health) seems to also have influenced his concerns about gender and how he is perceived.[8] Though I save discussions about the intersections of gender and race primarily for chapter 4, it is noteworthy to mention here since it is important to Marcus's story and his approach to gender. Marcus's understanding of gender as both a larger social force and as more fluid than fixed has caused him to think about gender in more structural terms, which seems related to his ability to challenge restrictive gender expectations as well.

Spencer, Aaron, and Jeremy were all assigned "male" at birth and also have queer understandings of gender. These men's stories are thought-provoking because they combine elements of previously discussed masculine and feminine patterns found in other accounts (all three men were on class-advantaged life trajectories). Spencer (twenty-five, White, gay/queer, class-advantaged)[9] proved an interesting participant because by the time he was interviewed, I had already started noticing the gendered patterns discussed earlier in this chapter. Spencer is full of life and loves to always be learning new things. He kept mentioning that his (sometimes negative) experiences in relationships have taught him a lot: "I think that the biggest thing I learned about that relationship, *through* that relationship, was to stand up for what I need and to be really mindful about that when things aren't working out." When describing his gender identification, Spencer said, "I'm perfectly happy being a guy. I don't want to be a girl," but "emotionally and mentally" he feels connected to femininity. Spencer also switches between feminine and masculine self-descriptors when talking about his present and future self, such as through expressing interest in being a "trophy wife." He said, "I think everything's a gradient, there's no black and white, especially with sexuality and gender. There's just so much fluidity!" Though Spencer is "perfectly happy being a guy," his understanding that gender is fluid seems to open up more possibilities for communicating how he talks about himself and his experiences in relationships.

Compared to Spencer, Aaron and Jeremy have a similar approach to gender. Aaron (twenty-six, White, queer, upwardly mobile), who has a classic fashion sense and works as an artist and art director, said, "I don't think sex and gender are as simple as we want to categorize them, and a lot of my friends don't fully understand that, you know?" Aaron, like many women I interviewed but unlike the men, also admitted to experiencing emotional abuse in relationships and that he believes the experience taught him some valuable lessons: "I fell in love with a friend of mine once who was a total dick, and that was really bad, because I was kind of constantly pining and trying harder and harder to win his affection, and I was kind of being toyed with for a long time in this really emotionally abusive way. That was bad. . . . I've learned to kind of, like, not get too attached so quickly—and not let other people get attached so quickly. Let things move slowly. I think I've learned that I like that, and that it feels healthy for me." Unlike many of the other men on class-advantaged trajectories discussed in the previous section, Aaron admits that he has spent time reflecting on his relationships and that they have left important emotional impressions on him.

Jeremy (twenty-six, White, straight, class-advantaged) has a similar story. He has tousled light brown hair and wears a band T-shirt to our interview. Jeremy identifies as straight and as a genderqueer man, and this identification seems to have important implications for how he talks about himself in the context of his relationships. In a departure from some of the other men previously discussed, he acknowledged that he felt taken advantage of, and hurt, by multiple *women* he's dated in the past. Jeremy even described one instance of being coerced into sex by a woman he was dating:

> So emotionally, Willow took advantage of me. [Then] I dated a girl Alisha who, we were drunk, I told her no, and she definitely forced herself on me. . . . Afterwards I felt taken advantage of, because I told her no and she pushed past that. And I think my testosterone kicked in, like, there is a woman who wants to have sex with me! So, let's fornicate! But yeah afterwards I felt [bad], 'cause I said I didn't want to. My brain had already stopped having sex, and then she was drunk, I was drunk, and I didn't stop her. But I regretted it afterwards. I regretted having sex with her. Initially I said no, and she kept going. So I felt taken advantage of, yeah.

Rejecting the idea that gender and gendered traits are uncomplicated and predetermined seems to open up possibilities for Aaron and Jeremy to admit to being hurt and taken advantage of in their past relationships, regardless of the genders of their partners. Jeremy's case is particularly notable, because he openly grapples with trying to make sense of his experience with unwanted sex. Other straight-identified men I talked to may have had similar experiences with unwanted sex or assault, but if so, they did not discuss those experiences in their interviews.

Besides Aaron and Jeremy, I speculate that some of the other men *have* had experiences in relationships that could be categorized as coercive or problematic. However, a convergence of gender, age, and class expectations structure what men share in their stories. Jeremy's account suggests that other men on class-advantaged trajectories may have had bad experiences with partners that they chose not to highlight due to their own understandings about how men are supposed to enact masculinity. Though Jeremy still grapples with what happened to him, admitting that experiences like his can happen to people like him is a departure from the idea and stereotype that men are always tough, desiring of sex, and can't be assaulted. Jeremy's and Aaron's openness about their experiences challenge harmful stereotypes about men and masculinity, and brings forth a conversation about the possibility that men can (and do) experience sexual assault. Understanding gender norms and expectations as complicated can challenge the idea that women and men always experience fundamentally different realities in their relationships and lives.

While the accounts of these millennial men don't suggest a definitive answer for how to "solve" intimate inequalities and issues around gender, what some of them do indicate is the extent to which having a queer approach to gender might open up the possibility of at least challenging gendered expectations in intimacy by understanding that gender and the meanings attached to it are not fixed. Also tellingly, most of the men I just discussed had heavy contact with queer friend groups, and all identified as queer themselves in terms of sexual identity or gender identity. Other research, such as that from Lamont (2017), has indeed found that contact with queer communities and peers seems to impact how individuals approach gender expectations in their own intimate lives. Striving to complicate gender in one's own life may relate to challenging gender and gender inequality on a larger scale. At the same time, however, most millennials interviewed did not seem to have a solid grasp on the idea that gender—both their own genders and gender more broadly—can be fluid and change. Further, research has shown that these queer approaches to challenging gender do not obliterate all inequalities (Lamont 2017), and unresolved is the issue of how to better address gender inequality in the lives of cisgender millennials who do not come across queer approaches to gender in their lives or communities. Challenging gender inequality by challenging gender itself may be a step in the right direction and open up possibilities for expression that are not limited by the constraints of gender binaries, but it remains to be seen how (and if) this solution could be applied on a larger scale.

Conclusions

I would like to impart some concluding thoughts by checking back in with Zoey and Connor, the couple with whom I opened this chapter. In addition to discussing her past and current relationship, Zoey and I spent some time in the interview talking about her future. If her relationship with Connor ends, where would she go from there? Zoey has hope that things will be different for her going into the future, but she isn't so sure that she can achieve her goals:

> It's just, when you're not emotionally committed to a relationship or you don't have expectations for anything, it's a lot easier to be in a relationship. But once you're, like, expecting more or you want more from somebody, and they're not fulfilling that, then it's really incredibly frustrating. And it's really frustrating when you know that you can't ask it from them. You can say something, but you can't change people. You just have to accept that it's not going to work, [*nervous laugh*] which is the most frustrating part of it. But yeah, going back into dating, I would definitely not commit to anybody unless I knew that they were going to be there for me and be the person that I'm looking for.

Like some of the other women, Zoey lamented that while she thinks she deserves better emotional support than she is currently getting, she has realized that she "can't change" how her partners act. She feels she has grown and she has a deeper understanding of what she wants out of partners and relationships due to her experiences. Even though she insists that she won't commit to future partners unless they are emotionally supportive, she believes that she also has only so much control in the situation since she can't change how others act.

Compared to Zoey, Connor is more optimistic about his relationship future. However, he also admits that committing to Zoey—or any partner—through something like marriage is probably at least ten years out for him (which would make him at least thirty-six years old at the time of marriage). This timeline is connected to the amount of time Connor needs to set up his career, which he is prioritizing before marriage. As a young man on a class-advantaged trajectory, his timeline is linked to the idea that he is supposed to be a breadwinner:

> I think [Zoey's] a really interesting, smart, and progressive person—yet when it comes down to it, when you've been in a relationship for several months—to a year, even, really—girls just wanna be treated! [*laughs*] I feel like that's how it is in the experience I have dating or being in relationships. I think girls expect that to varying degrees. Which, I don't really like that. It's this thing where guys have to treat girls. It's weird. It's a weird balance. [Zoey's] very career driven I feel like, and she's always gonna wanna have a career. But whenever that [idea] originated . . . men were the breadwinners and women were treated because men had money. I dunno . . . unfortunately, I think some of that has carried over to now. Yeah, and that still exists in my relationship, even, where it's expected that she should be treated, or whatever. . . . It's not awful, it's just

something you have to deal with. [*laughs*] It's just something I have to deal with that I don't think she has to deal with.

Connor reveals that he expects himself to live up to the masculine expectation to be a breadwinner, and even though he doesn't necessarily like it, he doesn't challenge it either.[10] Connor's nonchalance almost hides his discomfort. However, ultimately he just accepts that this is the way things are when it comes to gender relations in intimacy. Unfortunately, as Connor and Zoey approach their relationship in different, gendered ways—and make sense of their shared relationship in different gendered ways—they seem to struggle with finding what they want and need as individuals as much as they sometimes struggle with delivering what the other needs and wants out of the relationship.

In thinking about Zoey, Connor, and the other millennials profiled here, it does not seem that they have entirely figured out how to negotiate gender expectations—and the related inequalities—in their relationships. In many ways, millennials struggle with gender as older generations have also struggled. While women take care of the emotional side of things—especially when it comes to helping men—men worry about tending to their own self-development. Women paint themselves as relational, while men paint themselves as independent, even though the "truth" of the matter is likely somewhere in between for most. These ideas manifest in individuals' stories because broader ideas about gender have persisted even though there have been many changes in both private and public, such as the movement of women into the labor force (Wong 2017). Women's and men's struggles persist because despite change, some underlying assumptions about gender differences circulating on a larger scale in U.S. society seem to have remained the same. Even class-disadvantaged millennials—whose stories differ in important ways from their peers—tell stories along gendered lines and suggest that women and men take unique approaches to gendered dilemmas.

It appears here that only those millennials who purposefully try to challenge hegemonic or conventional ideas about gender itself—both in their own lives and more generally—show much variation in their stories when it comes to potentially challenging inequalities. This suggests that background or gender assignments are not deterministic when it comes to how millennials may approach gender (or other issues, for that matter), and exposure to new understandings of issues and personal goals can shift individuals' approaches. As more young people are exposed to queer critics of gender and sexuality (Robertson 2018), we may see more transformative change in approaches to gender among millennials and other young adults going forward. However, because many millennials tend to individualize their intimacy stories, the extent to which their own stories are informed by systemic ideas, and the inequalities that relate to those ideas, is sometimes obscured. While stories have transformative power, they also have to power to reaffirm the inequalities and injustices that were also experienced by older generations of Americans. When social systems are not part of the story, individualized approaches that reaffirm ideas about inherent gender inequalities and differences can get in the way when it comes to addressing intimate inequalities around gender.

This chapter has also shown that the delicate intersections of social categories must be considered when thinking about potential solutions to millennials' relationship issues. In the examples discussed here, having life experiences or understandings that challenge the gender binary offer some hope that gender inequality might not always prevail. However, as this chapter has also shown, gender inequality is complex and intersects with many other categories of difference. When we consider these other categories, the landscape of negotiating not just gender—but other differences as well—is complicated even further.

3

Age Is Nothing but a Number?

● ●

The Importance of Age in Intimacy

Romantic and sexual intimacy stories can tell us much about how millennials see themselves as gendered, classed, raced, and aged people. However, how millennials discuss their intimate partners is important and revealing as well. For instance, take the account of Lee (thirty-two, White, straight, class-advantaged). My first impression of Lee is that he fits what the media might portray to be a stereotypical image of a millennial: he chooses a brewpub for the interview and dresses in the tech industry uniform of a plain T-shirt, hoodie, and jeans. Though Lee seems self-assured, his discussions about what he wants out of his intimate life reveal some uncertainty. He wants "something more serious" out of his intimate relationships with women—by which he means a committed, monogamous relationship. At thirty-two, Lee is getting older and believes it might be time to think about getting more serious about his love life. However, he also finds himself attracted to partners who aren't interested in commitment: "The wild, outgoing ones—those are the ones I've always been attracted to. . . . No one's ever looking for anything that serious. Um, and so it's kinda gone like that, like one dating thing per year has been kinda the average. But, and then I keep telling myself, ahh that sucks. Like, that was fun, but I want something more serious next time. . . . I want someone I can really get into, confide in, and trust, spend time with, share worldly experiences with—I want all that, you know?" In this excerpt, Lee portrays himself as ready to make a change compared to how he has previously approached intimacy.

Yet despite his yearning for a different approach to his relationships, he also admits that something gives him pause when it comes to pursuing the kind of intimate experiences he says he wants: his anxieties around finances. As we saw in chapter 2, financial prowess continues to be an important signifier of successful masculinity for class-advantaged and upwardly mobile men especially. Lee also discusses how his fears relate to his decisions about romantic relationships: "I feel like I'm not making as much money as I should be making to be able to do the things I want to do, and you know, even [with] dating." In other words, Lee expresses that he wants committed monogamy, but isn't sure if he is worthy of it yet.

However, Lee does have a partner who—he admits—is interested in making a commitment. Unfortunately, he does not consider his current partner to be commitment material. According to him, this is largely because she is thirteen years his senior:

> I already knew from the beginning, I don't want anything more than the physical side. . . . I do want to start a family. So it was that, the age difference, and so I knew from the beginning that I didn't want to do anything, didn't want to get serious with her. But um, so then we were going on and off. She would get too clingy, then I was like, "I can't do this, you're getting too clingy." Then we would get back together, and uh, and then she's like, "OK fine. It's totally fine—I can do this without the emotions," and we'd do that for a while. Then she would get clingy again. It would just, it would go like this, on and off. Now we're kinda at the point where, we're totally just—it sounds so bad— but we're totally just using each other [for sex] until we find something more serious. She's on internet dating sites, I'm on internet dating sites, and we agree that until one of us finds someone we're more interested in and want to formally date, then our casual arrangement will end.

Even though his current partner expresses interest in commitment—which is what Lee says he wants—he rebuffs this suggestion due to her age. Incidentally, her age is also convenient for Lee, since the idea that she is too old to be considered a serious partner alleviates the financial pressure to provide—something Lee expects he would encounter in a relationship with a younger partner.

Lee's account of dating an older woman looks similar to those of the other straight millennial men in this study with sexual and intimate experiences with women around ten (or more) years older. For Lee, the age difference can be both convenient and strategic. Lee and other men portray older women as suitable sexual partners, but not "serious" (meaning committed, monogamous) girlfriends. Men's accounts suggest that older women are more laid-back and that, compared to younger women, they won't put the same pressure on them to make monogamous commitments. When women, such as Lee's partner, do hint that they are interested in commitment, men fall back on gendered, aged understandings to justify why it just wouldn't work. Lee's account of this relationship with an older woman accomplishes two tasks. First, it helps him work through his understandings of himself as a millennial man on a specific class trajectory. Lee is relatively young, and his relationship with this older woman gives him the opportunity to have a sexual relationship whilst building his wealth and keeping his options open for a younger partner. Simultaneously, Lee's story reveals his ideas about the intersection of femininity and age. Lee is unwilling to pursue a serious commitment with his current partner because, to him, she is too old. While Lee's account is personal, it conveys messages about men, women, age, social class, and sexuality more broadly.

About half the millennials interviewed (fourteen women and fourteen men) discuss dating partners around a decade older. While some of these individuals discuss dating partners a few years younger, they talk much more, and more significantly, about dating older partners during their young or emerging adulthood years. Millennials' stories about dating older partners have implications not only for their understandings of their own aged, classed, gendered sexual identities, but for their understandings of their partners as well. Further, as Lee's account illustrates, these stories convey broader messages about categories of difference. This chapter engages how millennials navigate age differences in intimacy, but also continues to explore how understandings of age intersect with other categories of difference (gender, social class, and sexual identity) in the process. In the coming pages, I first explore how straight women and men discuss navigating age differences in their relationships, noting the significance of social class throughout. Next, I explore how sexual identity slightly shifts the content of millennials' stories about navigating age. Most notably, I find that millennials' approaches to age differences reveal much about their understandings of the intersection of gender and age meanings, and that when it comes to age in intimacy, gender and sexual identity matter for how millennials perceive age differences. Those "outdated" ideas about men aging gracefully at the same time that advancing age chips away at women's social value? These millennials' accounts suggest that these ideas still linger.

Making Sense of Age Differences between Partners

The importance of age in the context of millennials' relationships has received much less attention overall when compared to other factors, such as gender. While sociologists are increasingly interested in intimate relationships across the life course (see Carpenter and DeLamater 2012; Montemurro 2014), research less frequently explores the significance of age, and age gaps, in intimate partnerships (for exceptions, see Alarie 2019; Mojola 2014; T. Silva 2019; Warren 1996). More generally in the United States, intimate relationships between older men and younger women are much more normalized than any other age-gap relationships, and the numbers reflect this trend. For example, among straight married couples, over 25 percent of marriages include a husband who is at least five years older compared to 6 percent of marriages in which wives are at least five years older than their spouses (Kershaw 2009; Wade 2009). Among couples who have divorced and remarried, 20 percent of men have a spouse at least ten years younger compared to only 5 percent of women (Livingston 2014). Lee's reluctance to embrace his relationship as "serious" hints at tenuous social acceptance when it comes to relationships between younger men and older women in particular. Yet outside of the context of marriage, information about age differences among daters, unmarried partners, and casual sex partners is largely missing. Information about *millennials'* specific experiences with romantic partners from different age brackets is also lacking.

While there is much more to learn about heterosexual or straight-identified individuals' experiences with age discrepancies in relationships, we also know little about LGBTQ+ millennials' experiences with intimacy across age categories. Some research argues that "gay culture" glorifies youth and that young people are prized and sought-after as intimate partners (Bartholome, Tewksbury, and Bruzzone 2000; Kaufman and Phua 2003; Schope 2005). However, research has less often compared LGBTQ+ individuals' approaches to age differences in intimacy to the approaches of straight cisgender individuals. Especially considering the importance of gender in age discrepancies *and* the seeming propensity of some LGBTQ+ people to challenge gender conventions (as seen in chapter 2), it is important to explore more fully how LGBTQ+ millennials approach age in their romantic and sexual relationships. Among my participants, I find LGBTQ+ identity might relate to finding different meanings in age-discrepant relationships. Though not as popular among scholars, the stories millennials share about traversing age in intimacy are as important as stories about gender, race, and class in millennials' explorations of themselves, their partners, and in deciphering what these identity categories mean and how to traverse them. These stories are also important because age is a potential site of inequality, and one that can relate to other kinds of inequalities (such as gender) as well.

Age Differences in Relationships: Straight Men's Stories

Besides Lee, some other straight men who discuss having romantic and/or sexual relationships with older women are Christian, Brian, Adrian, and Luke. In terms of social class and race, these four men are diverse. Christian and Adrian are both Latino, although Christian is upwardly mobile and Adrian is class-advantaged. Brian and Luke are both White, although Luke is upwardly mobile and Brian is class-disadvantaged. However, despite these differences, all four men frame their stories about intimate relationships with older women as inherently temporary. Twenty-eight-year-old, mild-mannered Adrian reveals during our park bench interview that he is college-educated and has a professional job. However, while in college, Adrian was in a band and always on the go. During those years, he carried on relationships with several older women simultaneously: "During that time, I actually had relations with a few ladies that were a little bit older than me . . . like ten years, twenty years [older] . . . and I kinda, you know, actually really liked it. They were kinda more relaxed, just chill—nicer to hang out with. . . . [With younger women] you kinda always feel like you have to always do something fun, do stuff. I guess I've always been a little more laid-back and low-key, you know? . . . I thought it was pretty cool, you know, as a younger guy, having an attractive older lady." As a college student, Adrian appreciated that older women seemed more "laid-back" than younger women. Similar to Lee's current relationship with his older partner (discussed in the chapter opener), at the time he was dating older women Adrian did not feel confident pursuing a more "serious," emotionally monogamous relationship with a woman his age because he thought a relationship with a younger woman would require more work and resources.

Also according to Adrian, his relationships with older partners were sexual and not committed, "Mmm, no, not really [serious], 'cause that's not really what they were looking for either. So for me at the time, it was kind of a good situation for both of us." Adrian's account of his past experiences with older women paint the experience as a win-win for both parties. Dating older women allowed Adrian to access sexual relationships without having to worry about providing economically or making a more serious commitment—which highlights his class anxiety as a musician and college student without a high-paying job. At the same time, his story cast this setup as unproblematic for older women as well, whom he characterizes as mostly interested in sex and not in committed relationships.

Twenty-six-year-old Christian comes across as gregarious and likes to insert jokes into his conversations when possible. Like Adrian, Christian's accounts of his experiences with older women also show the relationships as short-term and based on sex rather than on romantic commitment. For example, he smiled as he recounted a story about being "kidnapped by a cougar"[1] at a music festival a few years ago:

> I was like, well, it's about like nine or ten o'clock right now, and I'm not going to sleep for a little bit. Well, I'm going up to go up to the bar over here and go check that place out. And she's like, "Well, I'm actually heading that way too because some of my friends are over there." So we just kind of went, and we

were talking, and she was pretty open about things. She was very clear about her intentions, at first, which was like, for me it was kind of different because, you know, for a lot of the [young] women that I've had experience with, sometimes their intentions aren't very clear. I think that comes with age, too. . . . And then it kind of got to the point where we were just like about to part ways for the night, and she was just like, "Hey, you know this might sound a little forward or something, if you want to maybe come back to my tent and stuff, whatever." I had to think about that one because my friends are probably going to be looking for me. . . . But then, yeah, I was like, "OK, let's go." We drank a little bit, smoked a little bit, talked, and then we just kind of started fooling around and [the sex] happened.

Like Adrian, Christian treats his sexual encounter with a "cougar" as a fun, sexual learning experience rather than as an example of a serious sexual and emotional commitment. The stories of Lee, Adrian, and Christian cut across racial lines and say something important about the intersection of masculinity and social class. These stories reinforce the idea that men on class-advantaged trajectories (whether upwardly mobile or from an advantaged background already) should take their time and explore themselves sexually before committing to the intimate partners with whom they will make serious monogamous commitments. The women they believe they will commit to are either similarly aged or younger. Despite praising older women for their laid-back attitudes, the straight millennial men in this study never discuss older women as ideal or preferable as long-term partners even though they also said they believe younger women would be more demanding of their money and time. Older women are constructed in men's stories not as committed partners, but as casual sex partners. Young men also communicate that older women can help with men's sexual, but not emotional, needs—reinforcing the idea that young men have predominantly sexual, but not necessarily emotional, needs.

The story of Luke (thirty-two, White, straight, upwardly mobile) also demonstrates that many younger men consider older women to be primarily short-term partners. Luke—the eternal optimist introduced in chapter 2—is in a relationship with an older woman. However, despite actually living in her home, Luke insists that the relationship is temporary: "She's a lot older than me, and we're just in different places in our lives. . . . Because, I don't know, it's like, getting to a point where I'm thinking five years down the road. You know, I'll be thirty-six, thirty-seven, and if I'm gonna have a family, the woman—if she's going to deliver [a baby]—is going to have to be of a certain age, within a certain parameter. You know, there's no parameter with guys like there is with women. . . . I guess age does come into play. I guess I think about that a little bit." Like Lee, Luke sees his relationship with an older woman as temporary while he waits for a more appropriate (younger) partner to come along.

Also similar to Lee, Luke draws on the idea that younger men cannot, and should not, plan to start families with older women. Luke said, "I've been with the same person—living together just as I have in other relationships—but there's no future in it. [There's no] long-term future because of the goals that I'm gonna be having." Luke does not believe he has reached his economic potential yet. Once he does this, he believes a marriageable partner will come along. In general, Lee, Adrian, Christian, and Luke treat relationships with older women as uncomplicated sexual experiences. Men's acceptance of women as partners is influenced by their beliefs about the importance of women's reproductive capabilities, although as Luke points out, men believe this "parameter" to be largely applicable only to women. Ultimately, since men don't construct older women as long-term partners, older women are cast in a role that supports millennial men's young adult freedom and does not distract them from reaching their economic goals.

While men's classed anxieties about the demands of younger women make older women a tempting choice, ideas about gender and age can transcend class as well. Brian (twenty-five, White, straight, class-disadvantaged) has piercing blue eyes and is soft-spoken, but he has much to say. He recently worked as a chef but is now between jobs. Although his class orientation makes him unique compared to the men already discussed, Brian also confirms that his past experiences with older women were short-term. His experiences with older women were primarily rebound relationships—casual relationships that he pursued after breaking up with a long-term girlfriend his own age. He still sees benefits to dating older women, albeit with the caveat that men might have to be careful as older women could get the wrong idea about the seriousness of the relationship:

> Hanging out with them would create the idea of a relationship in their minds, even though that wasn't something they would say with a verbal connection, like "Oh, we're in a relationship?" They just kind of assumed once it got to a certain point. [*laughs*] But it was probably the most interesting experience of my life. . . . They also don't seem to create drama over reasons that don't need to be [dramatic], either, which made for a very interesting experience for me, and I didn't know whether to attest that to maturity, or whether you just get to a certain age and stop giving a fuck about certain things that make you angry because it's not worth your time.

Brian's quote, similar to those from Lee, Adrian, and Luke, indicates that intimate experiences with older women are primarily a novelty and that men don't plan on these unions turning into "serious" relationships. Regardless of what women want out of relationships (casual sex or emotional commitments), men see themselves as being in charge of defining what the relationships mean. Men's stories indicate that older women's desires and expectations from their relationships with younger men are diverse. Some women seem to primarily want sex (the case with Christian), whereas others want more emotional intimacy (the case with Lee). However, regardless of what women want, young men generally see themselves as in control of defining—and getting what they need from—the relationships.

These men's stories are noteworthy, and perhaps surprising, given the testimonies of the women and men in chapter 2. In that chapter, millennial men claimed that they are becoming more selfless and attendant to their partners' needs over time, while millennial women claimed that they are gaining more agency and control as they age. However, young men's stories here suggest that older women may have less negotiating power in their relationships after all. The men's accounts also suggest that men may only be willing to cede some power *for certain partners*, not for women more generally. One more quote about Lee's relationship is illustrative: "When [the relationship] started, she wanted to be serious. She was like, 'You know, I really like you. I don't wanna keep it a secret. I wanna tell everyone,' you know? She was like, 'Yeah, everyone would be really happy for us!' And I'm like, no." Despite Lee's testament that his partner agrees their relationship should be casual, Lee clearly states that she wants a more serious commitment. Lee flatly refuses, instead insisting that his definition of the relationship be honored.

The men's stories institute a clear aged and gendered boundary: according to these millennial men, the most marriageable partners are young adult women (probably in their twenties). However, older women can serve as a convenient placeholder so that men can access sexual relationships while they establish themselves economically, or enjoy other pursuits, during young adulthood. Across class, men agree that older women are probably not suitable as long-term partners due to men's own understandings of gender and age.

Men's stories about dating older women are very revealing in terms of how men make sense of themselves as gendered, aged, and even classed individuals. Men's stories help define young, straight masculinity as sexual, in control, and not preoccupied with fertility concerns and constraints. Conversely, men understand women as subject to the constraints of age. Men's stories indicate that women are most valuable as long-term partners if they are young, and that women's relative power over men diminishes as women age. Research on college men's process of sorting young women finds that those men consider primarily hookup material those women whom men believe are "low-status." The same men see "high-status" women as monogamous relationship material (Sweeney 2014). While status sorting in this previous work is based largely on class and race, the millennial men's accounts here show that age can be an important criterion for sorting as well. On the other hand, straight young women have different things to say about relationships with older men and how age relates to men's power.

Age Differences in Relationships: Straight Women's Stories

Like men's stories, the stories of straight women in relationships with men communicate and reinforce ideas about women's aged, classed, gendered sexuality and the aged, classed, gender sexuality of their partners. Yet the stories of the women differ significantly from those of the men. Millennial women's approach to older men is characterized by a few points. First, women discuss older men as confident, powerful, domineering, . . . and potentially dangerous. Women do not discuss being able to control the outcomes of their relationships with older men or dictate the terms of the relationships. Women do, however, discuss older men as being entitled or expectant. Women sometimes believe that older men assume women will "give" themselves over to men, whether that be in terms of sex or their time and attention. Lastly, a small number of women admitted to pursuing older men specifically because they believe older men to be more mature and better-resourced than younger men. Taken together, women's stories help uphold prevailing ideas about gender, class, age, and power.

Millennial women's stories about their dating experiences with older men are often laden with conflict and tension. One of these conflicts has to do with differences in commitment expectations that women sometimes attribute to age. The story of April (thirty-two, White, straight, upwardly mobile) illustrates some of the tensions present in women's accounts that can be attributed to age differences. April—who has sun-kissed, freckled skin and wears her hair in sandy-colored braids to our interview—had a relationship in the past with an older fireman when she was in her early twenties. However, at the time, he wanted to get married whereas April was still figuring out what she wanted out of life: "We started dating, and we actually lived together, for, I dunno, six months maybe? He was older, and he was really looking to have some babies and [a] wifey, and I wasn't down." Part of April's apprehension was around her own status as an upwardly mobile woman trying to return to school. She feared that getting married would derail her goals. This makes sense given the idealization of young adulthood among women as a time to explore self-development, and to be cautious about making adult commitments prematurely (Hamilton and Armstrong 2009).

Marissa (twenty-two, White, straight, upwardly mobile) has a quirky and inviting personality and works with special needs kids. Marissa is like April in that she had an older ex-boyfriend, Vince, who wanted to get more "serious" than Marissa was comfortable with:

> [Vince] had a kid, and he had had serious relationships. And so he was a lot different than, like, a male my age coming to me and asking me to go out. Like [he said], "Let me treat you to dinner," and then you know, [he was] calling me and not just sending me some stupid, flirtatious text—being mature about it.

And the reason we stopped dating was because it was like, we're not on the same life path right now. I was kinda just wanting to hang out, and he was wanting something more serious. Like, [he'd say] "Let's go out on a date." And I was just like, "Let's hang out whenever I'm available!" And he was like, "Mmm, no. I'm trying to find someone to settle down with." And I wasn't.

Marissa's story helps define her as a young woman on a certain classed path, yet it also says something about older men as partners. Interestingly, while young millennial men who date older women discuss taking steps to define the relationship so that it aligns with their goals, millennial women do not do this. Instead, women like April and Marissa, who are not looking to get married in their early twenties, simply opt out of the relationships. While men's stories strip older women of power, young women's stories paint older men as powerful. If women do not agree to older men's terms, they opt out of the relationships instead of trying to change the terms.

While April and Marissa did not attest to feeling physically or emotionally threatened in their experiences with older men, other women are not so lucky. Kara's and Delilah's stories illustrate the danger behind ongoing gendered power disparities that are seemingly exacerbated by age. While in high school, Kara (twenty-nine, White, straight, class-advantaged) had a boyfriend who was actually a coworker of hers in his twenties. While the age difference made Kara feel "cool" at first, she believes it ultimately gave her boyfriend the confidence to pressure her into unwanted sex: "I think I was just so excited that this hot older guy was paying attention to me, so I felt like, OK, I'm being a grown up. And losing your virginity is a sign that you are a big girl, even if I wasn't. I wasn't very mature at that point, but I thought I was. . . . I didn't call it [this] at the time, but I would say it was date rape. I didn't wanna do this, and I didn't know that I could say no." Kara communicates that she did not have the power to say no due to the aged, gendered power dynamics in the relationship. Kara's experience with an older partner is striking, especially in contrast to those men's stories already discussed.

Similar to Kara, Delilah (twenty-four, Black, straight, class-advantaged) has concerns about the potential for unequal power dynamics when older men date younger women. She believes that older men who pursue younger women can be "super sketch"[2] because, comparable to Kara's point, she believes older men sometimes purposefully look for young, naïve women whom they believe can be manipulated:

I went out with an older man, and to me, he was just super childish. And for me, I guess, if you're significantly older than me, I'm expecting you to have something to offer 'cause you're older, and—not necessarily monetarily—but I'm expecting your mind to have developed a little bit more. And I think he thought I was super naïve, and he treated me as such. . . . I think there's a type of young woman that these guys are looking for, and I just wasn't it. . . . Someone who's naïve, or is turned on by a car—someone who is easily bought, and for me it's just like, yeah, it's a beautiful car. I mean, that's nice and everything, but it's not gonna make me drawn to you more than if you were driving something else! It's just not. It's not my car! [*laughs*] What does it do for me?

Delilah believes some older men are more interested in exchanging money and gifts for sex and companionship than in finding an intellectual equal. Her story constructs older men as powerful even if they act immature or not "developed." Unfortunately, Delilah's story also says something about young women more generally. While she does not see herself in such a way, she does believe there are "naïve" women out there who regularly fall for older men's manipulative tricks. Speculatively, it could be that some older men prefer younger women because they believe they will be more easily swayed than older women. However, based on what we know from the millennial men's accounts above, it may also be likely that some older men pursue younger women because young women are constructed as more desirable partners based on the persistent association between youth and women's social value.

Unlike men's stories about older women, women's stories about older men afford older men power in relationships and social power more generally. Both younger and older women seem to be less powerful, and younger and older men relatively more powerful, in stories about partnerships between women and men. Yet despite some of the issues they face, the straight women are unique from the straight men here in that a few admit to *preferring* committed partnerships with older men. These women frame their preference as an attraction to maturity and, sometimes, access to resources.

Stephanie (twenty-eight, White, straight, class-advantaged), a very tall and curly-haired photographer, said that she prefers older men because they are more mature: "Especially the guys in their early twenties, like, they're a little crazy for my taste . . . the puffing up of the chest and who can drink the most, who can wear the lowest cut tank top, who can, like, be the most 'bro.' Like, all of those things that are really, like, juvenile to me are very off-putting." At the same time, Stephanie is attracted to her boyfriend—who is almost ten years older— because he offers financial security, and she believes this will be beneficial due to her future family plans: "Both of us are very much into like the traditional nuclear family structure, which is so interesting because, like, a lot of women [my] age fought really hard to not have to stay at home. . . . Those people aren't me, so it doesn't matter what they think. But it's definitely interesting. . . . Again, it's nice to have a partner that's on board with that idea. And if we're fortunate enough to have children and financially stable enough to have one parent stay at home, we'd like to do that. . . . Logistically speaking it'll probably be me at home and him earning." Stephanie likes that her boyfriend is older and therefore more established in his career than most men her age. This is especially attractive to Stephanie because she strives for a "traditional" family setup in which her partner acts as the main breadwinner (see Hochschild 1989).

Despite the migration of women into the workforce, Stephanie's plans are not entirely stigmatized among all class-privileged women (Hamilton 2016). Thus, she only grapples slightly with the idea that she's comfortable leaving breadwinning up to her partner. While she believes some millennial women might find her approach off-putting, Stephanie states that "it doesn't matter what they think." However, making a similar admission would likely be much more difficult if Stephanie were a young man due to the continued association of masculinity with the need to financially provide (Edin and Nelson 2013). Indeed, recent research has shown that in heterosexual couples, women's and men's lack of paid employment is often conceptualized differently, with upper-middle-class women seeing their husbands' unemployment as especially problematic, while the same cannot be said of husbands with unemployed wives (Rao 2020). For Stephanie, a preference that men be the breadwinners influences her inclination toward older men who are ostensibly better resourced when compared to younger men.

Another woman with experience dating older men is Faith (thirty, White, straight, class-disadvantaged), whose story adds classed nuance to these women's views. Faith is unique among the women described previously due to her class. Faith also decided to get married at a young age and did not put off having her two sons. However, as she is now going through a marital separation, she questions her past choices. Faith attests that she originally agreed to her marriage for reasons peppered through other women's accounts: her husband expected it, she felt that he was the one with the power to make the decision, and she was hoping her marriage would help her find more economic security. She said, "There was just all this pressure—it was assumed we were gonna get married," but that marriage also felt like "kind of an escape . . . from everything. Like, get married, get out of [my hometown]." As I discussed in chapter 2, even in the context of Faith's marital separation, she is giving her husband a great deal of say in whether the marriage should continue. Faith's story communicates classed differences in understanding the timing of marriage—a theme I explore in greater detail in chapter 6. However, gendered power inequality seems to transcend social class here as well. Only Faith's decision to actually get married while in her early twenties sets her apart from her peers.

Taken together, these millennial men's and women's stories illustrate how gender, class, and age intersect and have implications for the women and men telling the stories, their partners, and inequalities more generally. While men's stories highlight men's agency in their experiences with older women, women's stories afford men more power with age.[3] While men feel comfortable setting the terms of their relationships with older women regardless of their partners' preferences, women usually seem to opt out of their relationships with older men if there is a conflict. While men portray older women as laid-back, attentive to men's needs and willing to bolster men's attempts to explore themselves sexually and establish themselves economically before moving on to (ostensibly) more marriageable partners, women portray older men as steadfast in their authority. The portrayals in the stories of the men and women here help shore up aged, classed, gendered identity claims, which inform how millennial men and women navigate their relationships in real time. Both women and men use these stories to make sense of their own identities, and to think through what it means to be a young man or woman relative to what it means to be an older woman or man in sexual and romantic contexts. These stories thus help define masculinity and femininity more broadly in the process. At the same time, I also find that sexual identity has an impact on how millennials traverse age in their romantic and sexual relationships. While the stories so far have discussed the views of straight cisgender millennials, those millennials with LGBTQ+ identities provide additional insight into the intersection of gender, age, and sexual identity in intimacy.

LGBTQ+ Millennials and Navigating Age

Some of the LGBTQ+-identified millennials interviewed for this project also have experience dating older people.[4] Their experiences sometimes echo, yet also sometimes subvert, the patterns previously outlined. For instance, take Leah's story. Statuesque and artistic Leah (twenty-six, Brown[5] [Middle Eastern], queer, upwardly mobile) details age-related tensions with her ex-girlfriend Casey: "Our [ten-year] age difference was absolutely one of the reasons we're not together— just because we're at different stages in life." In explaining this further, Leah shared,

> My [older] sister and I don't speak because I think she's evil, and controlling, and manipulating, and very mom-ish; like, she wants to be in charge. And I saw those things in Casey. So I was like, maybe it's just when you get to that age, you think you know everything and so you see someone who's ten years younger than you and you wanna, like, counsel them on how to live. And people can't tell me how to do things. I have to try and suffer and fail and learn from that. That's how I learn. I don't like people telling me what to do. . . . So Casey and I, we went on a fucking road trip—this is a really good example. . . . First of all, it's like a fifteen-hour drive from [the city] and she drove both

ways—wouldn't let me drive! . . . And then she packed a whole bunch of snacks—she told me not to bring any food. But when I am on the road, I wanna eat a whole bag of puffy Cheetos and fucking Gatorade and, like, M&M's! That's the kind of shit I eat on the road—you know, I want a fucking cheeseburger! That's the only time I allow myself to indulge in those things, you know? But she packed all these bougie-ass[6] snacks from Whole Foods like kombucha and carrot sticks. I was like, goddamn it. And I woke up from my first nap, which was from, like, five to nine in the morning. I woke up and I was hungry! So I reach back and pull out the beef jerky and, like, half a piece of pita bread. And this is what I wanna have for breakfast, and she just looked and me and said, "Do you know how much fruit is back there?" And for the next three hours, she just badgered me about eating a piece of fruit! Look, I just want beef jerky for breakfast, fucking let me have it! [*laughs*] You know? Just little things like that drove me fucking nuts!

In this excerpt, Leah compares Casey to her domineering older sister in that Casey tries to control Leah's actions by "telling [her] what to do." Similar to her straight peers, Leah is able to define her own youth by contrasting herself with Casey. While Casey acts mature and maternal, Leah still wants to be irresponsible and have fun. However, Leah's story is unique in that it does something that straight men's accounts of dating older women do not: it casts an older woman in a powerful, and even domineering, role.

The idea that older partners can be too powerful, and that the motives of older partners can be suspicious, shows up in both straight and LGBTQ+ individuals' accounts. However, in LGBTQ+ millennials' accounts, these patterns are not gender-specific for either millennials or their older partners. For example, men who date older men do encounter some of the same issues as women who date older men. However, their status as men does not protect them from awkward power dynamics with *older* men. Spencer (White) and Oscar (Latino), who are both twenty-five years old and gay/queer-identified, both had experiences in relationships with older men where they felt their partner was a bit too paternalistic. Spencer, for example, went through a "daddy phase" right after he graduated from college; he meant this not in the sense that he participated in an organized sexual subculture[7] but rather that he was interested in dating older men. In this case, the age differences caused issues:

I was trying it out just out of curiosity, and I think [my boyfriends] were hoping for something more long-term. But what I found out with the first one, there was no way in hell that would ever work. At the time, I was twenty-two/twenty-three, and he was forty-five. Just like, no—that's a big difference in age! I admire couples where there's a big difference in age, but it does matter in a lot of ways, 'cause we're just in very different chapters of our lives. And the second one was completely insane, and I only dated him for about three weeks until I found out how crazy he was! It was very much him wanting to lock me down and make me his wife and stuff, and I was, like, nooooo!

Spencer's approach to his relationships with older partners looks similar to some of the relationships that straight women describe. In his early twenties, Spencer was not ready to have a partner "lock [him] down" yet, and he ended the relationship as a result. Oscar's experience is even more closely linked to the "daddy" idea. He explained:

> So [the relationship] was really nice, actually, until shit got weird. . . . But anyway, he sought me out, was super persistent, and kept trying to buy me drinks, dance with me. So finally after two weeks of him bugging me, I was like, "Fine you can take me on a date!" And it was really nice, 'cause I'm a very independent person, and when I go out on a date I'm usually the person to pay for things, I'm usually the aggressor. And I was the one being pursued, which was weird. . . . I thought it was just gonna be a hookup, and that's when he kept asking me to go out and whatnot. So I let him take me to dinner, and then it just kind of kept happening more consistently, and honestly, it was really nice until he disclosed this one thing to me. . . . I asked him, "Why do you go after young guys?" And he said, I think he even said the word "father." But he said something about how comforting it is to provide for a younger man and be a father figure to them, and it freaked me out! . . . And I'm like, I wanna date someone, not have a dad that I have sex with! That's really weird. . . . I just didn't know how to handle it, and it just ruined the whole relationship.

For both Spencer and Oscar, the power dynamics in their past relationships seem clear. Older men—regardless of the gender identities of younger partners—expect their visions for the relationships to be prioritized. Oscar even relates that the dynamic he describes can be typical among other young gay men he knows. Spencer and Oscar share this unequal power dynamic—which is based most notably on age—with straight women. The class tensions present in some women's accounts show up here as well. As upwardly mobile (Oscar) and class-advantaged (Spencer) young men, neither wanted to settle down and get involved in a serious monogamous commitment while in their early twenties. Though these sets of stories refer to older men, LGBTQ+-identified millennials tell stories of awkward, unequal power dynamics in the context of intimacy with older women as well.

Bowtie-wearing, public health professional Marcus (thirty-one, Black, queer, upwardly mobile) recalls a past relationship with a woman who had a tendency to date younger partners. At the time, Marcus was only a teenager while his girlfriend was twenty-seven years old:

> In hindsight, her being twenty-seven—[it was] not a healthy relationship, I'd say! As far as good things, I'd say [I] definitely learned a lot of, like, sexual things, you know, which is nice. . . . [But] I was a kid. [*laughs*] You know? I was seventeen. Granted, I've always been what's called an "old soul," or whatever—but I was a kid, and she was not. So it leaves the question, what is with this person—this grown person—who for whatever reason identifies with this kid, you know? For whatever reason, you know, it's odd. [*laughs*] That's just how I think about it now. But my brother—this one time he was dating this really older woman, and I was like, dude—and she had a lot of issues. I was like, one, you gotta ask yourself, what does she want with you? Two, you live with your mom, she's got a kid, what is it with her? You know what I'm sayin'? That she's identifying with a guy who's ten years younger, who lives with his mom, and *she's* somebody's mom? You know? There's some kind of disconnect. [*laughs*]

Speaking from both his own experience and using his brother as an example, Marcus casts suspicion on older women who are interested in younger men. Marcus paints this behavior as potentially predatory and infers that older women with interest in younger partners might be manipulative, emotionally or mentally immature, or have an ulterior motive—similar to the ways in which older men are portrayed in stories above. Like Marcus, recall from chapter 2 that Taylor (thirty-one, White, queer, upwardly mobile) also had a relationship with an older woman that started in his late teens. Although he is seemingly less suspicious of older women than Marcus, Taylor also did say he was "young and impressionable" at the time and that "age played a factor" in his decision to end the relationship when he reached his twenties.

Tamara (twenty-nine, mixed-race, queer, class-advantaged), who has a septum piercing and prefers to bike places rather than drive out of concern for the environment, is currently dating an older woman. Tamara's girlfriend also routinely seeks younger partners, about which Tamara said, "I think there are certain things I get angry about, because of her age. She does date a lot of younger people, and I'm like, why? . . . I'm like, well of course you're gonna have issues with someone who's twenty-four years old when you're forty! Like, why are you relating to this person, and why do you think you're gonna spend the rest of your life with this person who's barely even coming into the world, you know?" For both Tamara and Marcus, older women could potentially be just as suspicious as the older men discussed in other millennials' accounts. While not necessarily flattering, the stories of these LGBTQ+ millennials all grant older women more agency than they are granted in the stories of straight young men.

One last case that is less consistent with the patterns—but is still important to mention here—is Gabriel. Gabriel (twenty-five, Latino, bisexual, upwardly mobile) is opinionated and works as an engineer. He sees himself as somewhat of a social outsider who commented that his responses would probably be different compared to those of other men. Gabriel also affords older women agency in his story about his current fiancée, Corinne. In some ways, Gabriel's story shares elements with those of other men who have intimate experience with older women. For example, Gabriel shared that he likes his fiancée Corinne (who is more than ten years his senior) because she is secure in herself, a trait he has not seen as much in younger women. He said he prefers "the security of an older woman, as opposed to younger ones—ones who haven't gotten over their shit." However, unlike other men in relationships with older women, Gabriel explicitly rejects "the assumption that young is good." Further, Gabriel's exploration of his own bisexual identity seems to have opened up his mind to designing his life outside "convention" (his own wording). Thus, his approach to the age difference between Corinne and himself makes some sense considering that Gabriel explicitly tries to reject normative expectations related to gender and age in his own life.

Besides Gabriel's case, LGBTQ+ millennials' stories often reveal similar age boundaries as those in straight millennials' accounts. For example, while some older adults are more likely to want to be "serious," younger adults need time to play around and to explore self-development. However, LGBTQ+ millennials' accounts of dating older partners break down gender differences to an extent. An LGBTQ+ identity upsets ideas about gendered stereotypes of *women*, although they most often uphold unequal power dynamics based on age. While these stories do not necessarily suggest more equality in intimacy, they do at least suggest slightly less constraint in terms of gender if not always in terms of age.

While this section has highlighted the messages that LGBTQ+ millennials' stories convey regarding partners, and gender and age more broadly, these stories say something about the potential of millennials' own LGBTQ+ identities as well. Similar to what I found in chapter 2, an LGBTQ+ identity might be related to being better equipped to challenge gender expectations in certain cases. This is perhaps not surprising, as an LGBTQ+ identity is sometimes associated with deliberately challenging gender normativity, and other recent work has found that some groups of younger LGBTQ+ people try to explicitly challenge gender inequality in their intimate relationships and lives (Lamont 2017; Robertson 2018). Thus, it makes sense that millennials with these identities would challenge gendered expectations in their accounts. However, the LGBTQ+ millennials interviewed here often grapple with ongoing issues related to unequal age-based power dynamics in their romantic and sexual relationships, even if their struggles are sometimes not as gender-specific as those of their straight peers.

Conclusions

In thinking about the patterns I have just discussed, it is useful to check back in with Lee from the beginning of the chapter. As Lee made clear, he doesn't see his current relationship with his older partner as a relationship that he will maintain for much longer, as he is looking for a younger woman with whom he might start a family. However, though Lee seems to know what he wants, there are complications:

> I'm not trying to just throw caution to the wind anymore and just date, or you know, whatever. I am looking for something, I do want something more serious. . . . I wanna feel excited about, you know, about someone, really get into them. . . . I look out there on internet dating sites for girls that are around my same age—twenty-nine/thirty/thirty-one type of thing—I feel like a lot of them are looking for the same thing, but too fast. They want that *now*. [Women say] right now, "[I want to find someone to] spend the rest of my life with, someone I can settle down with, get married." Even though I want that, I don't want that to all happen in a month. I feel like there would be a lot of pressure from them, like, "Let's hurry up!" Because of the biological clock they might feel, like, "I need to start making babies!" I don't want that pressure, but I still want that, you know?

Unfortunately, what Lee likes about his current relationship with his older partner is very similar to what he doesn't like about it. He likes that it is temporary and no strings attached. Yet he wishes he could find another relationship that he is more interested in committing to long term. However, his impression of the kinds of partners he would like to commit to long term is that if he agreed to a relationship, he would immediately feel the pressure from them to start planning for marriage and children—something that makes him nervous, despite admitting it is something he wants.

Among Lee and other straight millennial men, relationships with older women allow them to solve certain issues and to make sense of themselves as (aged, classed, sexual) men in the process. While popular culture may sometimes glamorize relationships between younger men and older women (or "cougars") as a sexy novelty, these relationships can serve specific roles in young men's lives. The accounts of the men here suggest that older women provide them with a way to access sex and casual companionship as they take their time in figuring themselves out, and establishing themselves economically, during their transition to full maturity. Millennial men also indicate that they are the ones who determine the terms of their relationships with older women. Thus, perhaps not unlike previous generations of men, millennial men continue to construct themselves as in the position of power, regardless of whether their partners are the same age or older. While these stories are from men's point of view, they are still significant in thinking about what might happen for women in intimacy as they age. Will women find their agency to the extent that they expect (as discussed in chapter 2)? Though I did not interview any older women, recent work indicates that older women who date younger men do indeed portray themselves as taking on a submissive role in relationship formation with younger partners. For example, Alarie (2019) has found that women over forty in particular sometimes take on a passive role in relationships with younger men. Though some research has found that sexual exploration—similar to that which men's stories have described—can relate to more empowerment for older women (Walker 2018), my findings here call into question the hope that women categorically harness more power in relationships as they age, and that men—young and old—will make space for women's power.

Besides the stories of straight millennial men, the stories of straight millennial women also support men's claims to power and afford older men with gendered power in intimacy. Although this power can sometimes be cast as dangerous, it nonetheless generally goes unchallenged. Women paint older men as deliberate, in control, and, sometimes, manipulative. However, instead of dictating the terms of the relationships like younger men, if women are not on board with older men's terms, they usually decide to just opt out of the relationships rather than challenge men. While young women can demonstrate agency in deciding whether they want to opt into, or out of, these relationships, they do not try to change men's terms. Thus, it seems that at least among straight millennials, age does little to disrupt traditional gendered power dynamics in relationships. In many cases, age differences make gender power inequalities more pronounced.

In our search for some evidence of progress, we might look to LGBTQ+ millennials. LGBTQ+ young people—like their straight peers—also use their stories to draw gendered and aged boundaries and meanings, although their accounts of unequal power dynamics are less gender-specific. However, while older women are notably afforded more power in LGBTQ+ stories, this does not mean that there is necessarily more equality in these relationships, since age-based issues and tensions are clearly visible in most millennials' accounts across sexual identities. LGBTQ+ millennials still struggle with issues related to age-based power dynamics in their relationships.

Though less often a topic of discussion when it comes to millennials' relationships, stories that illustrate millennials' age understandings (in the context of other categories of difference) are revealing when it comes to how they navigate inequalities and power issues. As millennials have little economic power, it could be theorized that they can trade on their youth in their relationships with older partners for economic support. However, none of the millennials here admit to engaging in such an exchange with older women, and while some millennials have dated older men, most seem uncomfortable with the assumption that they are trading on their youth/beauty/sexuality primarily for some kind of financial support. Yet at the end of the day, the stories of neither women nor men seem to challenge traditional gender power hierarchies more generally. While LGBTQ+ millennials arguably show a bit more resistance (or at least flexibility) when it comes to gender, their stories still convey the idea that older people tend to expect to have economic power and control over younger partners. These stories put into stark relief how gender, age, and class (via economic prowess) intersect in ways that still most commonly place older men, in particular, at the top of the power hierarchy.

Though this chapter explored gender, age, class, and sexual identity in the context of stories about dating older partners, race was notably absent here. While race/ethnicity did not emerge as a notable point of difference in regard to millennials' stories about dating older partners, this does not mean it isn't important in their stories overall. How millennials make sense of race and ethnicity in intimate contexts, and the intersection of race and ethnicity with other categories, is the primary focus of chapter 4.

4

The Color of Intimacy

•••••••••••••••••••••

Seeing and Not Seeing Race

While gender and age are two important categories of difference that millennials must navigate in their intimate lives and experiences, there are still other categories to consider. For example, racial/ethnic identities continue to factor into millennials' intimacy decisions.[1] Interracial relationships have not always been socially or even legally accepted in the United States. In fact, the nationwide abolishment of laws prohibiting interracial relationships and marriage—in 1967—is relatively recent (Steinbugler 2012). Yet as I mentioned in chapter 1, millennials are more racially diverse than older generations of Americans (U.S. Census Bureau 2017), and available polls and surveys also suggest that the vast majority of millennials support interracial dating and marriage (Rosentiel 2010). Thus, it may be reasonable to assume that millennials are better adept at navigating racial differences and inequalities compared to older generations. But do the accounts of the millennials in this book suggest that this is actually case? Do millennials seem to be skilled at navigating racial differences in the context of romantic and sexual intimacy, and in their lives more generally?

Examples from Oscar and Jamison add some insight into millennials' approaches. Oscar (twenty-five, gay/queer, Latino, upwardly mobile) acknowledges that his race has sometimes been important in shaping his romantic and sexual experiences:

> [My ex] never dated White guys. He was all about darker—I always said he had beaner fever[2]—and he was just all about that. . . . Hey, whatever works! [*laughs*]

It works for people like me! So, but sometimes it doesn't work, 'cause there's a guy who's been after me literally since I came to college. So he's been doing it for about six years, but he does it to the point where it's objectifying. Like, everything he says about my physical appearance has to be tied to being Latino or Hispanic, and that's just super unattractive to me.

Oscar's story highlights a tension around interracial dating that is present in the accounts of other millennials I interviewed as well. Due to the history of racial inequality and racism in the United States, the exoticization of racial differences can raise awkward questions related to the significance of race and racial differences in intimacy. Although Oscar seems slightly amused (saying "It works for people like me!"), his account also reflects discomfort around the possibility that a romantic interest is attracted to him because of his racial identity. This dynamic may bring up uncomfortable confrontations with racial inequalities and power differences in his relationships.

The account of Jamison (twenty-four, White, straight, class-advantaged) illustrates how some other millennials are thinking about racial differences in intimacy. Jamison has shoulder-length hair and a youthful look despite also having the beginnings of a full beard. Compared to Oscar, he is more reluctant to discuss how racial differences might matter in intimacy, although he does share a little about how race has (or has not) factored into his intimacy decisions: "I haven't really thought about [race], nope. [*laughs*] I will start though! . . . I don't think [race has made a difference]. That's a good question. I've never really been attracted to African American women. I did date a girl who was Hispanic in high school . . . not intentionally, that's just kinda how that went!" Rather than highlight the potential importance of racial differences, Jamison tries to downplay the salience of race in his intimate partner choices. However, his quote also gives away that he is sorting potential intimate partners differently based on his perceptions about their racial identities. For example, he claims he is less interested in "African American" women as potential romantic partners, although he tries to avoid appearing racist by stating that he did have a Hispanic girlfriend in the past. Even though race should not matter according to Jamison's logic, he reveals that he seems to be thinking about race and what racial differences mean.

Both Jamison's and Oscar's accounts may be unsurprising to those already familiar with sociological work on racial and ethnic difference in the United States. Nearly twenty years ago, Eduardo Bonilla-Silva (2003) introduced discussions of "color-blind racism," a concept that argues that the belief that race is no longer significant actually perpetuates racial inequality by obscuring the extent to which race continues to matter. Despite their reputation as more open and knowledgeable about race, many millennials came of age prior to mainstream conversations that problematized color blindness, and may thus be just as susceptible to using color-blind logic as older generations (Allen and Harris 2018; Cox 2017; DeSante and Smith 2019). At this point, the idea that color blindness is a barrier to greater racial equality and justice has entered mainstream vernacular, and it seems millennials would likely know—and be able to articulate—the understanding that color blindness can be counterproductive in their discussions about race. However, anyone following current events could confirm that racial inequality and tensions persist in the United States on a larger scale.[3] Even if millennials are aware of continuing racial inequalities and issues related to color blindness or downplaying the ongoing importance of race, do their stories about navigating racial difference in their intimate relationships suggest greater awareness around how to navigate and challenge racial inequalities?

The following stories highlight these millennials' experiences and understandings of the significance of race in romantic and sexual intimacy, particularly with regard to dating outside of their own racial groups. The stories in this chapter mostly focus on relationships between White individuals and people of color—itself an indicator of the importance of ideas about racial Whiteness in structuring these millennials' understandings and experiences around race in intimacy. In addition to showing how race intersects with gender, sexual identity, and class, this chapter also speculates what millennials' stories mean for their ability to traverse racial differences more generally. Millennials' stories are both reflective of, and help perpetuate, larger ideas about intimacy across racial lines and differences across racial lines in general. Despite believing that race shouldn't matter in intimacy—and in some cases, vehemently denying that it matters for them personally—millennials' stories reveal several patterns that illustrate how racial hierarchies and inequities are subtly (or not so subtly) maintained in intimacy.

Navigating Race in Intimacy

Though the social acceptance of interracial unions is on the rise in the United States, as the quotes of Oscar and Jamison show, race remains a factor in the dating and marriage choices of millennials and other young adults (see McClintock 2010; Vasquez 2015). Younger people in the United States are more likely than older groups to pursue interracial relationships (Barroso et al. 2020; Joyner and Kao 2005), and most U.S. millennials support interracial relationships (Rosentiel 2010). Yet when compared to older adults, young people are actually only slightly more likely to marry across racial lines (Kent 2010; Tsunokai, Kposowa, and Adams 2009; Vasquez-Tokos 2017). Though percentages differ by race and gender, most people in the United States still marry within their own racial groups (J. Lee and Bean 2004; Vasquez-Tokos 2017; Wang 2012, 2015). While certain factors—such attending a racially diverse school, for example—may increase the likelihood that young people will pursue interracial relationships (Strully 2014), research by scholars such as Joyner and Kao (2005) and McClintock (2010) finds that relationship choices based on race also vary according to levels of commitment. For instance, McClintock (2010) found that among college students, interracial relationships are usually more common in casual dating than in committed relationships.

One reason why interracial relationships are seemingly less common in more committed relationships may be due to the long-term work involved in negotiating racial differences in intimacy. The pre-existing race-based experiences that partners bring to the union impact the day-to-day lives of those in interracial relationships and can put additional strain on individuals or their partners (Steinbugler 2012). Oscar's story about eventually growing tired of being pursued due to his racial identity illustrates one example of this. In addition to the interpersonal challenges of interracial relationships, scholars have found that persistent physical and/or social segregation (Kalmijn 1998; McClintock 2010), social or familial pressure (DeSantis 2007; Vasquez 2015), and the persistence of ideologies that naturalize racial difference all support the persistence of homophily, or the tendency of people to seek out those like themselves in terms of race or class (McPherson, Smith-Lovin, and Cook 2001). Thus, there are both systemic/structural and interpersonal challenges involved in making an interracial relationship "work," which might explain why change is slower than we might expect. However, if millennials can overcome segregation and the racist legacies of the past, they might still be more adept at navigating racial differences.

Despite indications of (or hopes for) change, scholars have also found evidence of persistent racism in intimacy—even in the relationships of young people. This is apparent when we look at online dating patterns, a realm with which millennials are frequently engaged. For instance, research on internet daters indicates that many of those looking for partners online generally prefer racial similarity (Hitsch, Hortaçsu, and Ariely 2010; K. Lewis 2013). Further, other research has found that even when considering partners of a different race, both men and women engaged in online dating tend to sort and rank prospective partners according to race (Feliciano et al. 2009; Robnett and Feliciano 2011). Recently, the language of "personal preference" has emerged among individuals on the dating market, which obscures racist interpretations of potential partners (Robinson 2015). Among the millennials interviewed for this book, many have experience dating across racial lines or indicate that they are open to the idea of doing so. Simultaneously, many (especially White millennials) also try to emphasize that race shouldn't matter in relationship choices, even when their stories indicate that it does.

Based on their stories alone, I find that there seem to be several extant barriers to millennials' ability to more tactfully navigate race-based inequalities that show up in interracial relationships. I find that racial inequalities are perpetuated in millennials' accounts primarily in three ways: in stories about racializing partners (or potential partners) as exotic or as fundamentally different kinds of people based on race, in stories about the significance of external social pressures around interracial relationships, and in stories and comments that reinforce the idea that Whiteness is superior to other categories. Throughout this chapter, I also note where social class, sexual identity, and gender intersect with race. In general, millennials' stories about racial differences in intimacy help millennials make sense of themselves as belonging to racial groups, help them make sense of their partners as members of racial groups, and help them make sense of racial differences on a larger scale. These patterns persist even though many of the millennials here seemingly long to be well-informed when it comes to navigating race in their intimate lives. At the same time, similar to stories about gender, stories about solving issues related to racial inequities tend to be individualized. By framing racism, racial tension, and other race-related issues as personal, millennials tend to understand finding solutions to racial tension and racism to be an individual—rather than a structural—problem. Even those who better understand race and racial inequalities as structural (particularly millennials of color) sometimes convey feeling frustrated by their interracial dating experiences and (understandably) see careful selection of partners as their best recourse.

Exoticization and Othering: Constructing Partners as Different Types of People

One pattern complicating millennials' ability to navigate race in intimacy is a tendency to either exoticize or "other" partners based on race. I consider both of these processes to be intertwined, as both involve discussing race as imbuing potential partners with fundamentally different characteristics based on race. "Exoticization" and "othering" are two more examples of terms that have moved into popular vernacular, to the point where the terms themselves show up in millennials' accounts. Here, I use "othering" to describe the process of making sense of people as fundamentally different based on racial/ethnic identity (Jensen 2011) and exoticization to describe a related process of seemingly venerating intimate partners based on racial or ethnic stereotypes, albeit in a way that can objectify individuals and affirm, rather than challenge, racial status hierarchies. Ultimately, the effect of both othering and exoticizing can be—as Oscar put it—objectification, particularly directed at millennials of color. Both White millennials and millennials of color demonstrate evidence of these processes in their accounts; however, individual millennials' racial identities matter in different ways when it comes to the impact of these stories.

In general, White millennials take the stance that racial differences don't really matter for them personally—and their subsequent arguments are reminiscent of those Bonilla-Silva (2003) has described in the past. For example, responses such as those from Sam (twenty-six, White, straight, class-disadvantaged) are common. Sam wore a striped T-shirt to our interview and has a beautiful smile. When asked if race had impacted his dating life at all, Sam said, "I don't know. I don't think so. I've only dated White girls. But I think that's just how it's happened. I'm attracted to most races!" However, the more they discuss it, the more White millennials also reveal that they do indeed consider race when it comes to their intimate partner choices. Like Sam, Bridget (thirty, White, lesbian, upwardly mobile) emphasizes that race hasn't factored into her partner choices in the past. She works as a career counselor and has a friendly and cheerful demeanor. In her story, Bridget also stresses that she is currently open to dating people from racial backgrounds that are different from her own. However, despite her commitment to taking a racially neutral approach, it is clear that she does construct some important boundaries between Whiteness and other racial categories:

> I don't think [race has impacted my dating]. I was always really open. . . .
> I dated White guys, I dated Black guys. I've only dated White girls. I wouldn't
> mind a Latina. . . . From like a young kid my best friend was biracial. And so
> I think that was like the beginning because I used to, like, get mad at my mom
> because I wasn't biracial—because I never wanted to be White! I wanted to be
> like my beautiful biracial friend who actually had skin tone! [*laughs*] My mom
> tells me I literally got mad at her for it when I was little. She's like, "What am
> I going to do?"

Bridget's quote is revealing for a few reasons. By stressing that racial difference does not matter to her, Bridget tries to erase the potential social injuries of race and to reconstruct racial differences as cosmetic—although she also states that she is actually appreciative of these differences. Though Bridget doesn't indicate that her feelings were necessarily romantic, her comments about her friend having "skin tone," unlike herself, and that she "wouldn't mind a Latina" also help reify the idea that Whiteness is not a raced category and that the racial traits of individuals might reveal characteristic personality traits that make them different. Thus, race is simultaneously naturalized and cast as superficial in this excerpt; a reified marker of difference, otherness, and exotic beauty, yet also—in Bridget's view—ultimately inconsequential. This excerpt helps Bridget make sense of racial differences and make sense of herself as someone who is appreciative of difference and definitely not racist. However, in the process, she assigns meaning to race in a way that serves to place people into reified categories of difference.

The account of Brian (twenty-five, White, straight, class-disadvantaged) provides another example of constructing differences based on race and the racial identities of potential partners. Soft-spoken and blue-eyed Brian stresses his openness to dating partners of any racial identity. However, he also expresses the idea that racial identity reveals some innate truths or characteristics about potential partners:

> Yeah . . . [in the past] I associated women, and the type of women they probably were, by their race, you know? As funny as that sounds, 'cause my high school was a good percentage of Hispanic, or Chicano, and whatnot, and I felt like they were a completely different type of girl than a lot of, you know, formal and proper White females. And at the same time, I've had relationships with Black women, where I feel like those were different in their own sense, too. I feel like I've never chosen based on it, but I feel like they are slightly different, as rude as that may sound. . . . I've always been most open to whatever seemed attracted to me. [*laughs*]

Brian's account is interesting because even though he acknowledges that assuming things about women based on race is "rude" and "funny," he simultaneously voices the idea that there actually *are* some objective differences among women of different racial statuses. Like Sam and Bridget, Brian embraces being open and affirming when it comes to race and intimate partner choices. However, his account does have the effect of pointing out, and solidifying, race-based differences. Also notably, Brian contrasts different women of color to "proper White females," which helps cement the place of White women as the default category of femininity to which other women are compared. Similar to Bridget's account, Brian's quote reflects the idea that Whiteness in the United States is often considered an invisible racial category by those who embody it (Edwards 2008; McIntosh 1990). Further, Brian's comment about being "open to [whomever] seemed attracted" to him eases tension because it puts him in a position where he is *open* to women rather than actively choosing to *reject* any women due to race.

Millennials of color have stories about exoticization and othering as well, although these take a slightly different tone compared to White millennials' stories. For a few, exoticization causes ambivalence because while being "exotic" could be interpreted as partners thinking they were unique or special, it is also objectifying. Environmentally conscious Tamara (twenty-nine, mixed-race, queer, class-advantaged) said she has encountered exoticization while dating, but she tries not to let it bother her: "I think because people don't know what I am, off the bat, they tokenize it a little bit. My boyfriend that I had for three years thought I was half Black. [*laughs*] . . . I don't take it offensive or anything like that. So it doesn't really bother me." Tamara said racial difference generally doesn't cause problems for her, although as we will see later, issues around race sometimes do bother her.

Artistic and statuesque Leah (twenty-six, Brown [Middle Eastern], queer, upwardly mobile) is another woman who speaks about race and specifically references how racial/ethnic differences factor into her current relationship with her boyfriend Henry, who is White:

> As a young kid, I wasn't able to date boys because I was the Brown chick. And when 9/11 happened, I think I was in fifth grade, and kids made fun of my ethnic identity. . . . And so it manifested, as a kid, I was pretty self-conscious because I was so exotic. . . . But then in college I had this fucking recognition that everyone I was dating—and mind you, I ended most of those relationships because I was moving on to someone else. . . . But every person I would date, right after we broke up, they would find another Brown girl to date. And so I think to a certain extent, I mean, three of the guys I dated are now married to Brown women who look a lot like me. . . . So it has affected me to the extent that I think people exoticize me. . . . Last night Henry and I were hanging out, and he said to me, he's like, "You know, I just have always really wanted a Brown woman." He said that to me! And then he explained it further, he's like, "When I was little and saw myself grown up with a wife, she was always Brown, or Hispanic, or Indian or something like that." That was just kinda funny. So I think my racial identity definitely affects my life in multiple ways. And at first it was a huge problem, but now—not that I get off on being exoticized—but I do appreciate that the people I choose to share my time and body with love that I have curves, and that is bound to my racial identity.

Similar to Tamara, Leah likes to think she is mostly not upset by exoticization anymore despite past experiences in which she believes being Brown *prevented her* from dating. When Leah said she "wasn't able to date boys," she is referring to her impression that classmates and neighborhood boys found her unattractive rather than her parents having a rule against dating. Though she embraces her "otherness" (her term) now, Leah does admit that her racial identity is something that had a profound impact on her in the past, and it is something that she continues to think about even though her feelings about her racial identity have changed from discomfort to pride. Her story also affirms what White millennials' accounts imply—that Whiteness is thought to be "normal" in the United States whereas being something other than White is not.

Regardless of their own personal relationships to race or racial/ethnic identity, Tamara and Leah try to make sense of racial awkwardness or tension in their relationships as a thing of the past even though this may not entirely be the case. Seeing race-based issues as mostly in the past is a pattern that does not really hold among the other women of color interviewed. However, Tamara and Leah stand apart due to their queer sexual identities as well. As we have seen in chapters 2 and 3, claiming a queer identity is sometimes associated with more progressive and accepting views on gender and sexuality. The rejection of racial inequality as an issue in the relationships of Leah and Tamara might be an attempt at distancing from another oppressive social regime—racism—in addition to homophobia and sexism. These two thus paint racial tensions as largely a painful memory, and Leah frames her current relationship with Henry as appreciation of difference rather than exoticization. However, Henry's words could just as easily be read as insulting, since one could interpret his comments and his associated pursuit of "Brown" women to some kind of racial conquest or "experiment" (as Delilah puts it below).

Compared to Tamara and Leah, the stories of the straight women of color are more direct about their discomfort with experiences of being exoticized or othered. At the same time, consistent with the gendered patterns laid out in chapter 2, straight women of color also feel pressure to deal with racial issues in relationships on their own rather than to point out racial microaggressions to partners or ask their partners to change. Thus, women often use personal strategies such as the avoidance of certain partners (or entire raced groups of potential partners) in order to evade awkwardness or being hurt by insensitive, racially charged comments or actions.

The story of Delilah (twenty-four, Black, straight, class-advantaged) provides an example. Delilah shared that her fears and suspicions around White men's motivations for being interested in her have shaped her approach to potential partners. In this quote—an expansion of her quote from the introduction to this book—Delilah begins by talking about her general views on interracial dating and then moves to apply her beliefs to a specific experience she had recently with a romantic interest who is White:

> I've pretty much across the board stayed within my race. . . . I have had White males try to talk to me and things like that. I think that, I think I'm not comfortable with it. I'm interested in it. Like, I'll try anything. But I don't think I'm comfortable . . . with anyone that's not [Black]. I feel like I can't necessarily relate that well. . . . [With this] recent [White] guy . . . it's more subtle. Because he's kinda the hippie type, and open to everyone. So I'm like, maybe he's not [racist] but then, I don't know. It's hard to explain, but sometimes I just feel it! And I just feel like, sometimes, that I'm this experiment for him and he's trying to see where it's gonna go. But I mean, me and him only went out once. . . . And I think a part of me thinking that he might be exoticizing me made me apprehensive about the whole thing. So I was just kinda like, meh. [*shrugs*]

Though Delilah uses the same language of openness that is used by White millennials, her story diverges from there. Part of Delilah's fears around dating men who are not Black is that she worries she would be treated as an "experiment" rather than as a serious partner in the relationship. She even specifically refers to her fears about being exoticized by the White date whom she discusses in her example. This is not unfounded, as it seems consistent with some of the approaches that White millennials take when discussing people of color as potential romantic partners. Delilah keeps race in mind while dating due to suspicions about potential partners' motivations and her anxieties about how these motivations might play out if the relationships got more serious.

Priya (thirty-one, Brown [Indian], straight, class-advantaged) has also come to the conclusion that—based on her experience—dating men who share her racial/ethnic identity might be a better choice than dating White men. Priya is a speech pathologist with long, dark hair who likes to talk about pop culture. She identifies as Brown (Indian heritage) and has had issues with White partners in particular. She recalls that growing up, "I would just hear, you know, 'Oh, you're pretty for a Brown girl,' or, 'If I was into Indian girls I would date you,' [or] 'You're like a Black girl but spicier' . . . guys would say these things." Priya's experiences reflect being on the receiving end of the othering and exoticization that we have already seen in other accounts. Like Delilah, Priya also makes an explicit reference to being exoticized: "The second guy I dated also exoticized me. . . . And then on my birthday—and he should have known better—he went to this Indian grocery store and got me these Indian biscuits, or something, and I was just like, what is this shit? . . . It was just dumb." Priya said that even though she has always found White men attractive, she is on a Muslim dating website and is thinking seriously about specifically looking to date "Brown" men in an effort to avoid future incidents like those she has already experienced in her relationships with White men.

Overall, interviews with the women of color in this study challenge White millennials' insistence that race doesn't matter in the context of romantic and sexual intimacy. Responses to racial issues run the gamut from trying to downplay the importance of race to expressing frustration with the looming significance of race to just accepting that racial tensions are an unfortunate side effect of pursuing romantic relationships across racial lines (particularly with White partners). However, women of color clearly share that race matters and that being on the receiving end of awkward, race-based exoticization and othering from partners is a real threat. Simultaneously, women of color in particular seem to have accepted that they must put it on themselves to avoid racial tensions by choosing partners wisely, lest they risk spending time with partners who might turn out to be both casually racist and defensive about changing how they act and communicate.

While White women and men do not seem to differ much in regard to how they discuss exoticization and othering in accounts, and while White millennials discuss these processes differently than women of color in regard to their impact, men of color differ slightly from women of color. While some men admit to being bothered by exoticization and othering, rarely do they express fear over losing control in their relationships—or threats to their self-esteem—to the extent expressed by women of color. Masculinity seems to have something to do with this. For example, gregarious Christian (twenty-six, Latino, straight, upwardly mobile) indicates that romantic interests can be categorized based on their racial identities. However, rather than portray himself as at the mercy of partners' exoticization and othering, he participates in exoticizing women himself:

> [My girlfriend] looks White as a lark too. You could not tell [she's Latina]. Well, you can tell because she's got the body of a Puerto Rican. [*laughs*] It's one of those things. . . . I like White girls, don't get me wrong, but I do love Asian girls. And it's like, give me a good Black girl, I'm down. Spanish [girls]—I'm Spanish. Give me a Muslim girl, what's up? Japanese, and so forth. . . . And from my experience it's just like. . . . There is the physical aspect, and then if you bring race into it, there can be any number of outcomes depending on the actual individual.

Christian's masculinity factors into how he represents the importance of race in his account. In chapter 2, we saw that men tend to position themselves as agentic in their stories. Thus, while Christian is not White, he doesn't communicate that his racial identity makes him feel out of control in dating situations. His account also plays into the idea—similar to that expressed by White men—that women of different races may represent different "types." By participating in exoticizing women himself, Christian maintains masculine control even though he admits he has also experienced being judged for his own racial identity. For example, he mentioned being called a "wetback" by one girl's parents in the past, although he laughs this off.

Men of color shared that although race can cause issues, ultimately *men* decide themselves if racial tensions are a deal-breaker. Patrick (twenty-four, Black, queer, class-advantaged), the affable graduate student introduced in chapter 2, provides an example. He said when recounting his dating past, "Initially, I didn't discriminate in terms of who I was interested in. So there were a couple of White girls in my grade, one of them [I was in] a relationship [with], like kissing and everybody knew kind of thing. But then, when I transferred to high school and became more conservative, went through my Black Nationalist phase, you know I told myself I wasn't gonna deal with White women at all, or that I shouldn't or whatever. So then my focus was just—or, I had limited my options at that point." In this excerpt, Patrick communicates that it was his choice in high school to pursue intimate relationships exclusively with women of color even though he could have pursued anyone if he so desired.

Instead of seeing his relationship experiences as central to informing whom he should date, Patrick is the one who consciously decided to exclude White women as potential partners for political reasons. Compared to women, men generally place a greater emphasis on taking control of the narrative when faced with issues related to race in intimacy. Gender matters here since men cast themselves as able to make their own decisions about interracial intimacy even in the face of possible tensions.

Despite most millennials' admission that at the time of interview they try to be open to dating anyone regardless of racial identity, their opinions and accounts of past and present experiences around racial difference in intimacy complicate their claims. In particular, the persistence of exoticization and othering in millennials' accounts seems to counteract claims to racial neutrality in intimacy since these processes help reify the idea that different racial identities translate to individuals being different kinds of people. Regarding the impact of exoticization and othering, gender and—to a lesser extent—sexual identity can matter in certain cases. While the persistence of exoticization and othering has the power to further reify racial difference and inequalities, there are still other factors that contribute to these millennials' difficulty in being able to navigate race. Another persistent barrier relates to their perceptions of external social pressures.

Social Pressure around Interracial Relationships

Another factor influencing how millennials navigate and think about racial inequalities in intimacy is how they interpret social pressure from family and friends. Although several millennials in this project discussed fighting against social pressure discouraging interracial relationships, these interactions still matter for how millennials are thinking about—and how they traverse—racial differences and inequalities. At the very least, social pressures give millennials things to consider when it comes to racial difference in intimacy. This pressure could sometimes have material consequences for the directions that relationships take.

Like other millennials, professional photographer Stephanie (twenty-eight, White, straight, and class-advantaged) held fast to the idea that race shouldn't matter in her own relationships even while acknowledging that the idea people "don't see color" is "cliché" and not realistic. Despite this admission, she affirms that racial differences don't matter to her, even if she can't say the same about some of her relatives:

> I don't want to be like, "I don't see color," because it's so cliché. But no, I don't think [I do]. I've dated plenty of people that were not—that would not identify the same way that I do. I went to prom with a guy who was from Africa. Like,

my first boyfriend in high school was from India, which was right when 9/11 happened and I got a lot of shit from my grandpa who—God rest his soul and all—although he was a fantastic man, [he] was also like from an era that was very segregated. And he was also in the Navy and a service man, and 9/11 happened, and nobody liked people that were Arab. And even though [my boyfriend] was born in America, because of the way he looked [and] because his dad wore a turban, my grandpa almost lost his shit. But I don't think [race influences my decisions]. I don't know, I've never really thought race is important. I guess I was lucky when I was a kid to have influences that told me that race isn't important, so I never really thought about it or factored it [in]. I don't think so.

Stephanie provides the examples of her prom date and past boyfriend as evidence that race doesn't matter to her. However, Stephanie goes on to illustrate how race was important in her past relationship through the behavior of her grandfather. Even though she tries to emphasize that race doesn't matter, Stephanie admits that her grandfather was not shy about sharing his negative feelings when it came to the relationship. Stephanie also makes excuses for her grandfather, asserting that he was "a fantastic man" despite his dislike of her boyfriend, and sharing her belief that "nobody liked people that were Arab" (or who are stereotyped as looking Arab, even if they are not) in the years immediately after the September 11, 2001, terrorist attacks.[4] How Stephanie makes sense of this situation is important, as it affirms for her that racism is something for old people who are set in their ways and not common among young people like her who restrain themselves when it comes to racist remarks and behaviors. Yet Stephanie's own account—like the accounts of other millennials here—contradicts her claims to neutrality.

Bridget (introduced above), also had more to share about her mother's opinions on a past relationship Bridget had with a Black man: "My mom did tell me like if I ever dated a Black guy, she'd kick me out. That didn't stop me. It stopped me from bringing him home to meet her! . . . But yeah, I don't think [race] impacted it much at all really." While Bridget again stresses that race does not matter in the context of intimacy, she also admits to social/familial pressure to avoid partnering with certain raced groups of people and that this influenced her decision not to bring a Black boyfriend around her mother (see also Frankenberg 1993).

Additional comments from millennials indicate that Blackness in particular appears to be the most denigrated and stereotyped racial category in discussions about race. For example, Christian (introduced above) mentioned, "I know some guys who are just like, 'How can you like Black girls?' It's like, look at her. [*laughs*] How can you *not* like that? Come on!" Guidance counselor Molly (twenty-six, White, straight, and class-advantaged), who also considers herself open and socially liberal, mentioned that when she was going through puberty, "As my dad said, many of the young [neighborhood] Black boys had appreciated how far I had developed by the time I was ten [years old]!" In these examples, Christian and Molly recount interactions with others that send messages about Black women and boys. Christian's quote illustrates that he has had interactions with other men who voice the belief that Black women as less attractive than other groups of women because they are Black. Molly's quote draws on the idea of Black boys being more sexual and grown up than other raced groups of young boys (see P. Collins 2005). Even when millennials downplay the significance of race in intimacy decisions, racial stereotypes about potential partners and ideas about attractiveness based on race are revealed in recounting their interactions with others.

A story from Renee (twenty-six, Black, bisexual, class-advantaged), who works as a writer, illustrates how perceptions of other people's reactions to a relationship may help direct the outcomes of relationships. Renee's relationship with her White boyfriend had recently ended at the time of the interview, although she is unsure if the relationship is actually over for good. Renee is a bit upset that the relationship ended because she believes that her ex "fit[s] the bill" for everything she wants in a partner: "He had everything—like, before I even met him, I had a clear understanding of what I wanted in a relationship. . . . Oh, I had a whole little checklist, and he fit the bill for that." However, despite getting along well, Renee believes their demographic differences—and her ex's own insecurities around what other people think about their relationship—contributed to his decision to pull away from her:

> When we would go out, he would say things, make little comments that let me know that he was a little uncomfortable in the situation. Like, whenever we were hanging out and it wasn't in a public setting, it would be cool. But as soon as we went in public somewhere he would just, I dunno, start freaking out. [*laughs*] It was a lot of different things. I think it was a racial thing—racially, because he's Caucasian. . . . . And it was, like, we just didn't look like we matched. [*laughs*] . . . He knows a lot of people in town. And I think he was just trying to protect his reputation [and] his business as well, yeah.

Though Renee is still hoping for a reconciliation, she also believes the conflict around race that she imagines her ex is having seems difficult to overcome. In this example, class (and the intersection of class and race) may be a factor as well. Renee's ex comes from a position of affluence, and her comment about their relationship being awkward for his "reputation" and business suggests that much of his social circle and clientele are probably White (or at least not Black). Even though Renee comes from a middle- to upper-middle-class family herself, she still doesn't believe they "matched" as a couple. It seems that racial differences and social class differences influenced his decision to end the relationship, although Renee's emphasis on their physical appearance as a couple calls into question just how important her class position would be if she were White like her ex.

Though most stories about social pressure involve White individuals' avoidance of some racial category considered to be different from White, the story of Gabriel (twenty-five, Latino, bisexual, upwardly mobile) provides one interesting exception. Gabriel admits that his (Mexican and immigrant) father disapproved of his ex, Veronica, because she is White (non-Hispanic). However, Gabriel also points out that while race matters in intimacy, it is not going to stop him from going forward with any relationship that he wants. He said about navigating his father's disapproval, "[My father] did not like that she was White. He didn't like her *customs*. It was a cultural thing—she didn't know how to say hello, be proper. Hispanic culture is very—you have to almost humiliate yourself, kiss the ground in front of people, to show them respect." Despite his father's feedback, Gabriel went on to have a long-term relationship with Veronica. Though I discuss more about Gabriel's father's input in chapter 6, for now it is interesting to point out that even though Gabriel does not listen, his father sets up boundaries between Whiteness and being Latino (specifically Mexican-ness). While it is unclear why Gabriel's father does so, speculatively, he may be driven by experiences of racism with non-Hispanic White people or by a motivation to protect racial boundaries (see Vasquez 2015). Though Gabriel decided to move forward with the relationship, it did cause his already strained relationship with his father to become more hostile for a time.

While older generations may have been more likely to avoid interracial relationships (Joyner and Kao 2005), most of the millennials here attest that they don't want racial differences to come between them and their partners. However, regardless if millennials chose to listen or not, outside criticism of interracial unions can still loom over their relationships past and present. These criticisms matter for how millennials approach and navigate interracial relationships themselves.

Besides millennials' interpretations of external feedback, the third general pattern that I find gets in the way of millennials being able to navigate race and racial inequalities is statements that construct, and uphold, Whiteness as superior to other racial categories. Though an overall privileging of Whiteness might be observed or implied more generally in quotes throughout this chapter, millennials' stories also contain specific examples of statements that reflect a continued dominance of Whiteness in the United States as the normalized racial category against which all other categories are compared. Millennials' accounts also reveal that this comparison reifies a racial hierarchy with Whiteness at the top in terms of social power.

Privileging Whiteness

Though none of the millennials here consciously admit to believing that Whiteness is somehow inherently superior, many of their comments suggest that Whiteness maintains a place of privilege when it comes to intimate partner choices. A number of the quotes above have already hinted at millennials constructing Whiteness as the category against which all other racial groups are compared. Some millennials directly communicate that White people may be more desirable in terms of temperament and attractiveness. For example, recall Brian's quote in which he is discussing different raced groups of women and contrasts them to "formal and proper White females." Brian's quote also conflates Whiteness with class advantage, politeness, and upper-middle-class feminine values—all ideas about White femininity that have historically been used to justify elevating White women's status above women of other groups (Bettie 2003; P. Collins 2005; Strings 2019). At the same time, it seems White millennials often consider these opinions and comments to be outside the realm of offensiveness because they are under the umbrella of personal preference (see also Robinson 2015).

For example, even though tousle-haired Jeremy (twenty-six, White, straight, class-advantaged) is one of the only White participants to acknowledge that racism might be an issue in relationships *particularly* for people of color, he also takes issue with the defensiveness that he believes people of color sometimes bring to interracial relationships (and in life more generally). In thinking about his personal experience in a past relationship that he had with a Black woman, he shared:

> Being in the position of being a White human being in the United States, it's hard to really relate to someone who's of a different race. . . . I mean, you could guess, but at the end of the day you can't really understand that. . . . I feel like I'm pretty Anne Frank about shit, which means I think people are all pretty good at heart, and I think people who are discriminated against, if I had to guess—because look at me [*laughs*]—if I had to guess, I would say they get closed off. They build up walls, which—I don't agree with those walls—but I can't tell them how to live their lives. And so, maybe she interpreted a situation where she thought someone was being racist towards her. I think this is kind of—if I had to pinpoint a certain thing and just us getting into a conversation about race, just, [she should] quit assuming that this person is being racist towards you. Don't assume that.

Even though Jeremy tries to understand how race may have factored into the dissolution of his past relationship, ultimately he individualizes the problem as something to do with the racial hang-ups of his ex-girlfriend, who he believes may have "built walls" and seen racism where there was none. Jeremy's story implies here that he was the rational one in the relationship and that his ex was being illogical and argumentative. Although this is an example of one relationship, Jeremy links this experience to what it means to be a "White human being" in the United States who has not experienced racism. Even though he is able to acknowledge his lack of experience with racism, he also conveys that he believes his calm approach to addressing racial tensions is superior.

Examples from Oscar, Tamara, Leah, and Priya—all people of color introduced earlier in this chapter—also illustrate subtle (or not so subtle) examples of White racial identity being in a privileged position when it comes to intimate partner choices. For example, both Oscar and Priya discuss preferring exclusively White partners in the past, although today both say they are more open to dating different races. Oscar shared,

> I used to be bad, and just all about sexual needs. And [partners] had to be hot, and they had to be this archetype, skinny White boys, honestly. . . . My type, for sure [was] light features, very skinny, a little on the feminine side, but not super feminine. I actually used to be really constrained by masculinity and femininity in men, but honestly I think being educated in that has changed [me] a lot. Um, skin color was the biggest thing. I never wanted to date anybody my skin color or darker, and it's still kinda like that, but my horizons are opening up a little bit.

Though trying to broaden his horizons now, Oscar admits that in the past he refused to date anyone who had either the same skin tone as he or anyone who was darker. Even though he's changing and opening up, he admits his past preference for White skin still influences him in his search for partners.

Like Oscar, Priya was also attracted almost exclusively to White men in the past. Also like Oscar, she believes that since growing up and learning more about what is culturally praised as attractive, she is more open:

> I had grown up with images, almost exclusively, of White males being attractive. And on the flipside, growing up in these suburbs, any time I saw a male who was South Asian, it would be, like, my dad, or my brother, or my cousin, or the uncle from the masjid who has smelly feet! . . . And again, it's one of the things that in my thirties, I recognize that thinking is wrong and a product of pop culture. Here's these attractive men on television and in the movies, and here's your dad and your brother. If your family is literally your experience of your color, you're not gonna think that's attractive! . . . [And] I think I do hold South Asian men to a different standard than non-South Asian men. It's almost like, if they trip up, I'm like, "No, you should've known better." I just hold them to a higher standard.

Priya says she still holds South Asian men "to a higher standard" and she expects them to be more understanding—and less condescending—when it comes to matters of gender and race norms because they are from a similar background as her family. On the other hand, she has let White men get away with saying some offensive things to her in the past. For example, Priya shared one instance of a White partner whom she let get away with more condescension than she believes she should have in retrospect. Her story also reflects being on the receiving end of some "othering" discussed earlier in this chapter:

> Oh, he'd call me stuck-up because of my upbringing. Then he'd be like, "We need to break down these hang-ups you have because of how you were raised." You know, to loosen me up or whatever. And he felt the need to say these things. And he felt the need to take on this educator role. Like, "Oh look at this innocent Muslim girl who doesn't know anything. I'm gonna teach her everything there is to know about being in a relationship and the sexual [aspects] that go along with it," you know? Yeah, he was [*scoffs*], oh God!

In retrospect, Priya is angry about how she has been treated by previous (White) boyfriends. At the same time, she admits that even though she is interested in dating more South Asian men currently, she "still struggle[s]" with her ideas about attractiveness as well as trying to navigate the possibility of more partnerships with White men who do or say hurtful things. Priya is still attracted to White men but is suspicious of White partners based on her past experiences.

Lastly, Tamara and Leah—who previously reported that though they have experienced exoticization, they try not to let it bother them—also both have past, or current, examples of White standards of beauty impacting their dating lives. For example, discussing her ex, Tamara shares that it still "bothers" her that her ex dated a "big-breasted blonde woman" just before her. She said, "My ex, for years this girl he was in love with was, like, this big-breasted blonde woman. So I'm like, why do you want me? Because I'm obviously not that. So I think that's the only thing where it is weird." Even though she is past the relationship at this point, Tamara admits to feeling suspicious about why her ex would be interested in her after dating a "big-breasted blonde." She questions why her ex would "want" her since she does not fit this type, and her quote suggests some fear around being a dating experiment—a fear we have already seen reflected in other women's accounts.

Similar to Tamara, Leah compares herself to the "blonde" archetype and considers the significance of her appearance in her own intimate experiences:

> [In the past], I got picked on a lot, not only for being Brown but for being tall, for having curves, things like that. So my embodied race was definitely a thing. Whether or not it was extremely overt all the time, I don't know. But I think

I made the reference earlier, all the little boys who want the blonde cheerleader. . . . They wanted a girl that sort of looked normal, and I didn't. I didn't look normal. . . . I used to fantasize about being [White]. . . . And now, I'm like, thank God I am different, 'cause I don't wanna be average! And now I embrace my otherness, [but] I've been grappling with my race a lot the past few years.

Unlike Leah, Tamara, and the other women of color quoted previously, the White women I interviewed for this project did not report having to come to terms with their own racial identities in light of either not fitting in (racially) or in dealing with partners of a different race. In contrast, the accounts of Priya, Tamara, and Leah demonstrate that they spend a large amount of time and energy thinking about race. However, ultimately their accounts and experiences also show that Whiteness continues to enjoy a venerated position in the United States when it comes to millennials' dating lives. Indeed, the subtle—and not so subtle—privileging of Whiteness seems to transcend race, class, gender, and sexual identity categories. Even Patrick's decision to not date White women was fueled by an attempt to intentionally make a statement about decentering Whiteness. Millennials' stories about race and navigating racial difference in intimacy are synonymous with their stories of grappling with racial hierarchies and inequalities while making sense of themselves as racialized people. Unfortunately, millennials make sense of their stories within a system that provides messages about racial hierarchies and privileges Whiteness. These messages are often reaffirmed in millennials' accounts even if they individually attempt to disavow White supremacy.

Conclusions

At the beginning of this chapter, Jamison shared that he'd "never really been attracted to African American women" while also saying that he doesn't really think about race too much in his relationships. Interestingly however, one of Jamison's most significant relationships (from the amount of time he spends discussing it in his interview) was with a biracial Black and White woman whom he met online. The two carried on a long-distance relationship since she lived in California and he lived in the Mountain West. However, he insisted that he did not see her as racially different from himself, and instead focused on characteristics and experiences they shared together: "My girlfriend from California was half Black, half White . . . [and we were] the same social class, yeah, I think so. . . . The girl from California was the girl I lost my virginity to, and apparently she lost her virginity to me as well. . . . She's really gorgeous. I think she's sort of a model right now." Though Jamison and his girlfriend eventually broke up (she broke up with him), his account suggests that they had an intense relationship, and he flew to see her once or twice a month while they were together. Despite his girlfriend being biracial, Jamison claims that racial differences were so insignificant in their relationship that he never even thought about them and they were barely worth mentioning. They were so insignificant that he seemed to forget he dated a Black woman when I originally brought up the topic of race in our interview. However, based on the accounts of the women of color interviewed in this chapter, his girlfriend may have a different story to tell when it comes to the importance of race in their relationship. From Jamison's White perspective, there is little to discuss nowadays when it comes to race. Yet when the details are examined, the stories of both White millennials and millennials of color *both* belie this claim.

For these particular millennials, dilemmas around navigating racial difference often arise in stories of relationships between White people and people of color. Their stories reveal several important points. First, the stories told by White millennials and millennials of color are usually different: while White millennials attempt to avoid nuanced conversations about both racism and the continued importance of race seemingly to avoid looking racist, the accounts of many millennials of color (and often White millennials' own accounts) illustrate the ongoing significance of race and racism in society and in intimacy. Second, in these millennials' accounts and across racial identifications, Whiteness is revealed to occupy a privileged place in the millennial dating market, whereas Blackness in particular is devalued. The persistence of racial inequalities and hierarchies in intimacy continue to be affirmed through off-hand, and direct, comments as millennials recount their own experiences.

Further, although some millennials recognize that race continues to be a structural problem, potential solutions to racial tensions tend to be individualized. Since White millennials generally disavow color blindness while simultaneously failing to recognize the ongoing importance of race, millennials of color are left with limited options when it comes to the prospect of relationships with White millennials: they can either risk having to endure White ignorance around matters of race and racial inequality or avoid relationships with White partners in order to protect their own emotional well-being. Even if people of color make sense of racism as bigger than individuals (and many here appear to do so), the persistent individualized, color-blind approach of White millennials undermines the structural significance of racism and race in society. This conflict seems an issue in relationships between White millennials and millennials of color especially, but understanding racial categories as hierarchical can loom over relationships that do not involve White people as well. For instance, recall Latino-identified Christian's comments about what other men he knows say about dating Black women (see also Vasquez 2015). While Whiteness is privileged, Blackness is especially stereotyped and denigrated according to these millennials' stories.

Of course, this chapter still leaves stories untold. For instance, I was not able to interview any East Asian millennials, and the experiences of all "people of color" in the United States are by no means uniform. While I have touched on these differences ever so slightly here—such as the finding that Black participants, especially Black women, appear to face some of the harshest treatment on the millennial dating market—interview studies that include larger samples of individuals from different groups would likely reveal more nuance. Further, I was unable to capture much about millennials' interracial relationships that do *not* involve White people. Nonetheless, that most stories here focus on relationships between White millennials and millennials of color indicates the ongoing significance of Whiteness as a socially privileged category in millennials' dating lives. Not unlike older generations of Americans, millennials struggle to navigate racial differences and inequalities in their relationships and to overcome ideas about Whiteness as superior.

My impression through these interviews is that millennials (especially White millennials) are sometimes cagey when discussing race. However, I found that they were surprisingly not as shy about discussing social class and their class expectations for both themselves and their intimate partners. Discussions of class bring to the fore once again the importance of both identity and social category origins and expectations in millennials' intimate lives. It is these stories about social class that I turn to next.

5

No Compromise on Class

• •

Expectations and Limitations

In the United States, defining social class and delineating social class divisions are notoriously messy tasks. Social class divisions are both continually in flux and can be determined in a number of ways, be they economic, social, cultural, or some combination of these (Bourdieu 1993). For example, the measurement of socioeconomic status—which is sometimes used as a proxy measure for social class—determines a given individual's class standing by evaluating their level of education, occupation, and income (American Psychological Association 2020). According to this measure, a high income itself is not necessarily an indicator of prestigious social class status—more is needed in order to enter the top rungs of class in the United States (Currid-Halkett 2017). Simultaneously, perhaps due to its messiness, issues of class inequality sometimes arguably fly under the radar in discussions where we might expect to find them. For instance, even famous left-leaning millennial Taylor Swift has come under fire for perpetuating stereotypes about poor and working-class people in one of her music videos at the same time that she champions gender equality and social justice for LGBTQ+ people (Bustillos 2019; R. Lewis 2019). Famous people aside, what do other millennials make of social class, and how do they negotiate class and class differences in the context of romantic and sexual intimacy?

The story of Adelle (twenty-eight, White, queer, class-advantaged) adds some insight into how millennials are thinking about social class differences and how class matters in intimacy. Like some others interviewed, Adelle did not grow up in the Mountain West but moved there as a young adult. She's a dog lover and seems to have found her niche as a social worker. In our discussions about her desires and expectations for her partners, social class emerges as important even though Adelle never actually mentions the word "class":

> I [have] a list in my head. . . . [Someone] around my age range. I always—and this is a little pretentious—but I always thought, I want somebody with a college degree. I want somebody with a solid job, or at least a student. I want somebody sort of on a career path. Somebody who's practical—not over-the-top spontaneous, I don't tend to be that way. Somebody who is like-minded in terms of social politics and values, and sees the world like I do, and can engage in that intellectual level about whatever it is. . . . Somebody who gets along with my family, those are the big ones.

Like other millennials interviewed, rather than explicitly mention class, Adelle uses signifiers such as "education," "values," and "sees the world like I do" to indicate certain classed sensibilities (see also Cherlin 2014; Currid-Halkett 2017). Adelle's discussion of her expectations for partners is very revealing in terms of her own class background and goals. The class status she hopes to embody herself is also the status she looks for in potential partners. Further, even though she mentions that her criteria might be "pretentious," Adelle doesn't shy away from being open about her class preferences for her partners. Her expectations are what they are, take them or leave them.

Interestingly, Adelle's current partner does not fit with her own list of expectations and specifications, and tensions seemingly rooted in class differences have proven to be a cause of concern for Adelle in this relationship: "When I first got together with my current partner, right off the bat I thought, this is short-term. This is not the person I wanna end up with—I'm looking for qualities A through Z and he doesn't have them—and we'd argue about certain things, and we're very different in certain ways. . . . And so that was tough. He didn't initially see the world the same way that I do. . . . In all these areas there's certainly been improvement, but yeah that doesn't line up on my list." Though still together at the time of the interview, Adelle is unsure about the longevity of the relationship due to the couple's ongoing communication issues. Her boyfriend is working-class, doesn't have a college degree, and has some different views when compared to Adelle. To make matters worse, Adelle's mother is critical of the relationship, which conflicts with Adelle's criterion that her romantic partner "gets along with [her] family." Despite Adelle's feelings for her partner, conflicts seem to be getting in the way of the relationship. Adelle's stated class expectations loom over the relationship and seem to influence her understanding of the reasons why she and her partner sometimes have issues.

In these millennials' stories, like in much of U.S. society, social class occupies a place of ambiguity. These millennials' accounts reflect the belief that class is not static. Rather, they communicate the view that class determinations are fluid and depend on individual choice based on one's goals, values, and worldviews. In other words, the millennials here often communicate that individual actions, choices, and personality—rather than structural constraints or chance—are what determine class. This is consistent with larger U.S. ideologies, which suggest that class position is a result of individual work ethic, personality traits, and decision making (Khan 2011). By this reasoning, anyone can move along the class ladder as they so choose—and not doing so favorably is a personal failure. In the context of intimacy, the class position of a potential partner is important since partner choice itself can be a reflection of an individual's own class status. However, millennials' actual experiences traversing class differences in dating and relationships reveal the continued importance of background as well. Upwardly mobile millennials in particular face an interesting conundrum, as their poor and working-class backgrounds conflict with their goals of class advancement. Due to disparities of background, communicating with partners who grew up class-privileged can sometimes prove difficult for this group.

This chapter focuses on how millennials navigate social class issues and inequalities in intimacy and how other factors (such as gender, age, and race) are also important in stories about traversing class. Stories about navigating social class are revealing of millennials' own class concerns for themselves as they move into the future. These stories also reveal how millennials deal with issues related to discrepancies in class backgrounds and/or goals when it comes to dating and intimate relationships. Lastly, millennials' stories provide insight into how they are thinking about social class more generally. Similar to chapters 2–4, which explored gender, age, and race, respectively, I wonder to what extent millennials are challenging ideas related to *class* inequalities, and/or to what extent they are perpetuating persistent ideas about class divisions. Based on reports of millennials' intolerance of inequality when compared to older adults (Arnett and Fishell 2011), as well as their own economic struggles as a group (Harris 2017), we might expect them to be less concerned when it comes to the class statuses of their partners and more incensed about economic inequalities at the societal level. However, we do not have strong evidence that millennials challenge social class hierarchies and inequalities in their own lives. Although millennials differ in their approaches to other categories of difference, I find a surprising amount of agreement when it comes to these millennials' understandings of class, although their *experiences* with navigating class in intimacy are not uniform. I argue that these millennials' accounts do not suggest widespread change when it comes to making sense of social class hierarchies and inequalities, and in this chapter I explore why.

Social Class in Relationships

Social class divisions and inequalities have fascinated sociologists since the early days of the discipline. Yet even though stories such as Adelle's illustrate the importance of class in sexual and romantic bonds, a great deal of the research on the intersection of class and intimacy is relatively recent (see, e.g., Cherlin 2014; Streib 2015b). In Western nations like the United States, individuals often choose partners who hold social class positions similar to their own (Bennhold 2012), and this trend is holding strong. For example, educational homogamy— or the tendency of people to marry others with similar education levels—has actually increased since the 1960s (Swartz and Mare 2005). Currently, education level is a marker of social class status (Currid-Halkett 2017), which suggests that social class concerns may be at least related to educational homogamy trends. At the same time, there can be structural and interpersonal barriers to sustaining relationships across categories of class difference. For instance, exposure to certain classed groups of people through social and educational activities may determine one's dating pool, and exclusionary boundary maintenance practices may also narrow down the pool of eligible partners for those on the dating market (Dalessandro 2020).

To complicate matters further, even though background is an important predictor of where young adults will eventually land when it comes to class, social class status *can* be fluid throughout the life course. Additionally, individuals' social class goals may not always line up with their class backgrounds (Bettie 2003). The flexibility and murkiness of class itself thus has the potential to complicate the study of class. However, even though class is flexible, class background still matters both inside and outside of intimacy. For example, Streib's (2015b) research on class-diverse marriages finds that, regardless of the class position of a given couple, the disparate class backgrounds of partners are related to divergent approaches to everyday decisions around childcare, money management, and even planning for the future. While these differences can be useful or complementary in the context of a marriage, as we see with the quote from Adelle above, differences in class background can also sometimes cause conflict. As Streib (2015a) has additionally pointed out elsewhere, more generally, the ways that people negotiate class differences in intimacy are not well understood. We need more information regarding how people negotiate class issues in dating outside of the context of marriage. The findings that follow, which profile millennials' experiences, shed some light on extant questions about how class matters in intimacy outside of a marital context.

In the coming pages, I first begin by examining how millennials approach social class in romantic and sexual intimacy. How do millennials make sense of class, and to what extent do class expectations inform their search for partners and intimate relationships? Second, I examine how millennials negotiate class-based differences and inequalities in intimacy. How do millennials respond when they find themselves in relationships with partners who have dissimilar class experiences? In answering both of these questions, I also illustrate how class backgrounds and future class expectations are important in millennials' experiences negotiating class in intimacy.

The Importance of Social Class and Classed Expectations

Though the term "class" is uncommon in these millennials' accounts, many had little trouble discussing their own expectations for their classed futures. Since intimate partners are an important part of creating those futures, discussions of desired partner traits utilize class-coded language. Unlike discussions about race and ethnicity, which for this group were sometimes restrained, I found discussions about class to flow more freely in interviews. Among these particular millennials, it seems that understandings of class as a choice encourages more open conversation. Class is about one's values, attitudes, and goals, according to many of their accounts.

Though I find that women and men both have things to say about their class expectations for partners, women are slightly more detailed. This may have to do with ongoing gender inequality as well as the persistent link between men's careers and their ability to live up to expectations of masculinity (Rao 2020; Wong 2017). Women who plan to partner with men might have more to say since the class status of their boyfriends or husbands could still be considered integral to the achievement of their own class goals (Hamilton 2016). However, men did have things to say as well. The account of Dylan (twenty-four, White, straight, class-advantaged) provides an example. Like some of the other White millennials discussed in chapter 4, outdoor enthusiast Dylan claims that race doesn't really matter in his considerations of intimacy. However, Dylan is more open to speaking about his expectation that potential partners subscribe to certain classed sensibilities. This excerpt from his interview shows that he clearly has class expectations of the women he dates:

> I think I have a tendency towards more intellectual, educated people . . . yeah, generally. I mentioned I lived a little ways north of Baltimore, and there's a lot of people in Baltimore that aren't so fortunate. And it's abundantly evident! The level of education that a lot of people get in the city, I'm inclined to say regardless of race, you know if you went to a city school you probably weren't getting as much out of it as if you went to a county school or a private school. So, that certainly played a part in my relationships.

Like Adelle, Dylan uses "education" to signify his class preferences and to set boundary expectations. Though educational pursuits and privileged economic status aren't necessarily interchangeable, many participants understand interest in—and the pursuit of—education to be a signifier of middle-class status and/or of middle-class goals. It is also interesting to note that even though Dylan's explanation is racialized, he also goes out of his way to say that his preferences are not about race. Baltimore is heavily segregated, and many of the "city" residents that Dylan talks about in his account are likely people of color. Nonetheless, while Dylan goes out of his way to say his expectations are not about race, he has no trouble admitting that he has class expectations for potential partners. Class options are ostensibly open to anyone regardless of race.

Madeline (twenty-eight, White, straight, class-advantaged) provides another example of using coded language to signify her own class status and the kinds of partners she and those in her friend group seek out. Madeline has a straightforward communication style and seems to have little tolerance for superficial small talk. She says that dating among the people in her friend group can be tough sometimes because they all have high expectations for themselves and their partners: "I'm in a very active, educated crowd. . . . We want to be the best that we can be! Surrounded by the best! Work really hard, or whatever. But it seems like there's this mentality of, you can always do better [in relationships]." Madeline describes her friend group as "active," "educated," and concerned with working hard and being "the best"—all traits and terms that other researchers have identified as being associated with class-privileged people (Farrell 2020; Jenkins 2020; Khan 2011). Though Madeline, like Dylan, doesn't explicitly mention class, her quote signifies that she and her friends are interested in partners who embody these classed traits as well and that she sees a lot of people who are always on the lookout for a "better" partner.

Speech pathologist Priya (thirty-one, Brown [Indian], straight, class-advantaged) also uses class-coded language to signify her expectations, and she is arguably even more direct than Dylan and Madeline when it comes to outlining her class expectations for potential partners. Yet again, the word "class" does not appear in her account. In reference to a discussion about what she looks for in a partner, she shared, "I want somebody to be passionate about something. I want them to be educated and somewhat successful in what they do—not complacent. I want somebody who doesn't just sit and watch Netflix all day every weekend—not that there's anything wrong with doing that one day, but [not every day]. Somebody who's in shape, has good style—you know, kind of just somebody who's the male version of me, except maybe less feisty! . . . Somebody who's cultured and has knowledge on things, cares about things." While Priya's standards for a hypothetical partner don't necessarily stipulate that they must be class-advantaged, her language suggests it is probably more likely that this will be the case. For example, she discusses an ideal prospective mate being "passionate" and "in shape" and "cultured," which are all words that are reminiscent of Madeline's previous discussion about her class-privileged friend group. Further, Priya's admission that she wants someone who is "the male version" of herself also provides another clue as to her expectations since Priya is highly educated and is on a professional career track. Further, she shared that she does not want to partner with "somebody who hasn't traveled the world, somebody who just takes everything at face value." Her expectation that prospective partners have "traveled the world" might exclude working-class partners who haven't had the means to experience international travel. Though Priya's expectations don't explicitly rule out working-class partners, prospective partners would likely need to have some class-privileged resources to live up to her expectations.

Like other class-advantaged millennial women, master's student Delilah (twenty-four, Black, straight, class-advantaged) voices her belief that she sometimes has trouble connecting with partners who aren't educated. Like Dylan, Madeline, and Priya, she uses "education" as a way to make sense of why she just seems to get along better with certain people over others: "I do find myself, like, if I'm on a date with someone and they don't have a bachelor's degree— I'm not gonna write them off—but I do find myself being better able to connect with someone that does have at least a bachelor's degree. . . . So it's really just a matter of the person's intellectual capability [regardless of] whether they went to college or not. But the pattern is, most of them have [gone to college] that I'm attracted to." While Delilah says that college isn't necessarily a requirement, she seems to gravitate toward other people with college degrees. She goes on to say more about what she expects in a mate: "I want him to be able to support himself, and to have some sort of vision. . . . You need to have something going on. . . . I don't perceive money as being the end all, be all, so it's not really, you need to make this [amount]. [But] you need to be able to support yourself, 'cause if we are gonna be together you need that support if you're gonna have a family or anything like that." Delilah's account on the surface downplays the importance of making money, but income is just one component of class. Her account also reveals the extent to which the markers of class privilege— including education, enough wealth to comfortably support a family, and the ability to do creative or entrepreneurial work—are important qualities to her.

The class-advantaged millennials here are often not shy about their class expectations for partners. However, upwardly mobile millennials have similar middle- to upper-middle-class expectations for their own lives. Due to the importance of partner choice in helping achieve privileged class status, upwardly mobile millennials sometimes use similar class-coded language when talking about expectations for partners. For example, Saul (twenty-two, White, straight, upwardly mobile) says he is attracted to "intelligent types" of women and that, concerning his future, "I definitely don't wanna bring up a kid, like, rich and snotty, but definitely not scraping by month to month. I definitely would like to have enough money to treat people and all that." In this scenario, Saul sees himself as the breadwinner, so his future wife's earning potential might be secondary to his own even if he expects her to be intelligent and educated. Vanessa (thirty-two, Latina, straight, upwardly mobile) also uses lack of "intelligence" to explain why she is uninterested in most of the working-class men she met during her time in the military—an institution she participated in "for the college money." She said, "They aren't even intelligent, they're just opinionated, and they equate opinions with intelligence. No." Others were even more forthcoming regarding class expectations.

Oscar (twenty-five, Latino, gay/queer, upwardly mobile) is very open about his social class goals and expectations for partners. Despite being from a poor background, Oscar has strict standards that the people he dates conform to his own middle- to upper-middle-class expectations:

> Education is the biggest thing for me—like, if a guy's not college-educated, that turns me off. And that's so, like, elitist of me. But honestly, it freaks me out when I meet someone in their thirties and they're just working a management job somewhere—which is cool, if that works for you. And I'll date someone like that casually, but I haven't been able to get to a more serious point from that.... There's that, and also, I kind of judge them for not wanting to do more with their life . . .'cause education wasn't guaranteed for me, I [really] value higher education.

Instead of explicitly using the vernacular of class, Oscar also relies on "education" as a shorthand to signify middle- to upper-middle-class sensibilities (Bettie 2002; Currid-Halkett 2017). Oscar makes the leap that he would be disappointed if a potential partner is content with working a job that does not require a degree and may have limited opportunity for advancement since that serves as a signal to him that they have different values.

Oscar's strong views are interesting, especially given his own class background. Similar to Dylan, Oscar also makes a connection between race and social class, although Oscar is more explicit in making this connection: "[My hometown is] a big town with a small mind. Like, if you think of any small town—and I'm gonna stereotype for a second—when you think of a small town, you think of small, southern hicks, where the men are men and the women are women, and they very much adhere to those roles.... I don't know what to attribute that to. I trace it back to race, honestly, 'cause I would say personally—I don't know any statistics or anything—but there's very few Hispanics who are in the higher-middle or upper class." In addition, as we saw in chapter 4, Oscar admits that he usually prefers to date men with lighter skin tone. Though Oscar's preference seems to be about race, it also seems that this may in part be related to his class preferences, since he associates being Latino or Hispanic with being poor or working-class. Oscar's case also further illustrates the importance of gender in stories about class, since he plans to get married to a man in the future. Compared to Saul's account, for instance, Oscar's account highlights the intersection of gender and class expectations for his prospective partners.

The story of Danielle (twenty-four, White, straight, class-advantaged) also provides an interesting example of how class expectations extend to decision making about the potential viability of a romantic relationship. Much to her parents' irritation, Danielle sees herself as a free spirit who doesn't care as much about class or social standing. Her current boyfriend comes from a working-class background and, somewhat unbeknownst to him, she is planning to end their relationship in the near future. Even though she says she doesn't care about class as much as her parents, Danielle does admit that differences in social class backgrounds and expectations are dooming her relationship with her boyfriend, who is an unemployed tradesman:

> I grew up in a cookie-cutter town. You know, everyone looks like an Easter egg, going to and from the country club. . . . Everyone in my town was wealthy. . . . His background's very different. His family is all in the line of construction workers, welders. So, and their town is, just some crap, like, podunk[1] town, that like, I never wanna go back to! [*laughs*] . . . I think it probably does cause tension, maybe on my side. Just because—and I would like to think that I don't judge people that way at all—money is not actually a big factor in my life. Or, maybe I'm just trying so hard to think it's not, and maybe it actually is? But after seeing his town and stuff, I was like, dude, I don't wanna grow up like that. I don't need to be in a mansion, but I don't want [my future kids] to grow up in just a rundown town, you know?

In this excerpt, Danielle tries to communicate that she believes pursuing wealth in and of itself is not a noble goal. However, in visiting her boyfriend's hometown, her expectations around social class for herself, her partner, and her future children begin to sink in. While Danielle says that she doesn't "need" to live in a "mansion" in order to be happy, she also admits that living in a small town and leading a working-class life will not fulfill her desires and expectations. She finds her boyfriend's positive feelings around his hometown to be alarming since she suspects he would try to encourage them both to relocate there if the relationship continued to move forward, which somewhat horrifies Danielle.

Yet in addition to differences in *both* class backgrounds and goals, Danielle's gender and age seem to factor into her desires to end the relationship. After learning about her boyfriend's background, Danielle's parents tried to intervene and provide gendered and classed reasoning for their expressions of concern. As I have written about elsewhere (Dalessandro 2020), middle- and upper-middle-class millennial women in particular share that their families often voice concerns over boyfriends who come from working-class or poor backgrounds. Danielle's parents also use aged, classed reasoning that encourages young people to explore themselves before settling down in a committed relationship when explaining to Danielle why she should break up with her boyfriend:

> Like, my dad, when I told him that my boyfriend didn't need to work because he was collecting unemployment, my dad was just like, "DON'T marry him!" And I was like, "Well you don't know anything! You barely know him, you only met him once, that's just wrong of you to say." But then subconsciously I'm like, but maybe he's right. . . . [My mom] did tell me a few days ago, she doesn't, she thinks I need to move to Florida by myself. She thinks I need to go out and meet more people . . . She doesn't want me to settle down early, yeah.

In addition, Danielle shared that her father advised, "[I]f you marry a rich guy, you can do whatever you want whenever you want." Though Danielle's decision to end her relationship seems partially based on her parents' advice, aged and gendered class concerns also fuel her decision. For example, Danielle wants to move out of state and explore career options—including what it would take to start her own business—while she is still young: a classic sign of the emerging adult exploration in which many class-advantaged young adults partake (Arnett 2004; Hamilton and Armstrong 2009). She has already started hinting to her boyfriend that she is going alone if she moves out of state: "No, he's not coming. . . . It's understood between the two of us that I'm gonna do my own thing, and he's gonna stay here." Further, Danielle's gender seems to be a factor. Previous research has found that many affluent parents expect their daughters to find similarly affluent, professional spouses (Hamilton 2016). This finding matches up with the quote from Danielle's father. Ultimately, economic and class expectations (that are also structured by gender and age) seem to influence Danielle's decision that her relationship is not tenable for much longer. Yet beyond differences, Danielle and her affluent parents also go one step further and disparage her boyfriend for his supposed lack of career motivation and his seeming lack of shame around his "podunk" roots. Similar to Dylan and Oscar, Danielle not only constructs her boyfriend's working-class life as different, but as *undesirable*.

For both upwardly mobile and class-advantaged millennials, class expectations for partners include living up to middle- and upper-middle-class sensibilities and goals. *Not* living up to these goals is understood as largely a personal shortcoming. This understanding helps construct middle- and upper-middle-class status as desirable and poor and working-class status as undesirable, an idea bolstered by the societal-wide notion that definitions of "success" in the United States closely align with being able to "accomplish" a middle- or upper-middle-class lifestyle (Contreras 2012). These classed constructions are important because as class status is thought to be malleable and the result of personal choices, the people associated with poor and working-class lifestyles can also be constructed as undesirable through association. Interestingly, I found that the class-disadvantaged millennials here do not discuss class expectations for potential partners in the same ways as their upwardly mobile and class-advantaged peers, although associations with poverty and being working-class sometimes force millennials to engage with class in uncomfortable ways.

Often, as Danielle's case also illustrates, class differences manifest in these millennials' stories as tensions, insecurities, and judgments around class difference. Yet interestingly, millennials' own class backgrounds help structure how they discuss approaching awkwardness around class in romantic and sexual intimacy. Upwardly mobile millennials are especially interesting to examine in this regard, since they must both reconcile their disparate backgrounds and goals *and* decide how to deal with the uncomfortable feelings that arise from dealing with partners who have similar class goals, but who come from more privileged backgrounds.

Navigating Class-Based Tensions and Issues in Intimacy

It is perhaps not surprising that some millennials make distinctions between desirable (middle- to upper-middle-class) and undesirable (working-class and poor) class statuses, since these distinctions are also found in much of the Western world, including in the United States (Contreras 2012). Given the importance placed on being class-advantaged both in millennials' stories and in U.S. society, the class-disadvantaged millennials (or those from poor and working-class backgrounds) interviewed here sometimes find themselves on the receiving end of slights. In addition, awkward communication around class can sometimes be lethal to cross-class relationships. For example, Lee (thirty-one, White, straight, class-advantaged), who was introduced in chapter 3, discusses a past experience dating a woman who lived in a low-income neighborhood and came from a working-class background. One night, Lee published a social media post related to an incident in his girlfriend's neighborhood, which elicited comments from some of his friends that made fun of where his girlfriend was living. This incident led to the end of their brief relationship since Lee's girlfriend understood the posts to be disrespecting and disparaging her and where she comes from:

> I was staying over at this girl's house, who I'd been seeing a couple of months, [at] her place, and in the middle of the night I heard gunshots out the window. . . . So the next day I posted [online], "Oh, what happened?" This is what happened. I wasn't judging. I was in the more southern part [of the county] which

is a little more—again, I don't wanna be cliché—but it's ghetto. It's less affluent, a lot more crime, poverty. So I posted [online], "Oh, I heard gunshots last night in this town called Woodland City." And she saw it, and all my friends were like, "Oh, of course you heard, it's called 'Hoodland City.' Of course you heard gunshots in Hoodland City!"[2] Blah, blah, and she got really offended by these people talking about her hometown like that, and she was like, "Fine if you feel this way then you don't ever have to come back here again!" . . . After that weekend, she wasn't responding to my calls and stuff, so I emailed her like, "What's going on? Can we talk about this?" type of thing. I wasn't judging where you're from, please don't blame me for what my friends are saying. And, she went off, like, "You don't get me! You're not from where I'm from, you're from [the northside], you're from the money!" Of course she's implying, you'll never understand the struggles I've been through, and stuff like that. So that, definitely, it was spat in my face, like, "Oh, I'm too good for you" type of thing. I kinda thought it was ridiculous, but that's how she felt, you know? 'Cause you know, where she came from, her struggles, I've never seen a girl, or a person, that has struggled that hard.

Though this story is from Lee's perspective, his ex-girlfriend's reaction seems to communicate that she was angry at Lee's friends for making her feel bad about her class position. At the same time, Lee is angered by the incident as well because he believes his ex-girlfriend unfairly accused him of joining his friends in making fun of her. Rather than lead to a moment of clarity or more understanding for Lee, this incident seems to have just brought out anger and defensiveness.

Regardless of their class goals, other millennials from poor and working-class backgrounds have similar stories of being on the *receiving end* of awkward or hurtful interactions around class as a result of dating partners from more privileged class positions. For example, Marissa and Brian are two millennials with cross-class dating experience. Brian (twenty-five, White, straight, class-disadvantaged) has a story about a past relationship that is relevant here. When he was eighteen, Brian had a girlfriend who came from a wealthy family. His girlfriend's mother was actually supportive of the relationship, although over time Brian came to believe that her support stemmed from a place of wanting to take on a charity project: "Kinda like, with Lindsay and her mother—the one that was just really fond of me—she bought more clothes for me just going into college than my parents ever had my whole life! You know, it was a really interesting thing, but I also felt like she felt sorry for me. But I didn't wanna take it as that, but at the same time, I just saw the difference of what it would be like, you know, if my class had been different." Though Brian tries to reason that his girlfriend's mother meant well, her generosity did bother him because it felt patronizing. Rather than see him as their equal, Brian thinks they felt bad for him: "They couldn't see or understand where I might have been coming from." Even though the situation was superficially benevolent, Brian sensed the awkward power differential between himself and his girlfriend's family. He also said that for a long time, he had anxiety around interacting with more affluent people.

Unlike Brian, quirky and friendly Marissa (twenty-two, White, straight) qualifies as upwardly mobile. Yet Marissa also recalled a past relationship in which she felt she was being judged by her boyfriend's wealthy family due to her background:

> Oh gosh, I remember I had to go over to his parents' house for Thanksgiving, or Easter, it was one of those [holidays]. And you know, you go in there, and you straighten your back up, make sure you have your fancy clothes on, [*laughs*] and I've always used manners growing up. My parents were always really harsh on me for that. But like, I felt like I was being critiqued, because I was! [*laughs*] But, you know, they wanna make sure [their son's] not with some cheap, silly girl. So, it makes sense. But yeah, I definitely think any time I got around his parents, I needed to impress them or put on a show, and you know, be the best me I could be! I definitely felt that with parents growing up—friends' parents and I guess relationships. But it's a different feeling when you feel like you are being judged in that aspect—like, your social standing.

For Marissa, being judged for her class or "social standing" was a new level of embarrassment or stress beyond just being judged more generally for her behavior. Despite feeling bad, she also said, "I guess I could see that from a parent's perspective, like, protecting their child and making sure he stays on track—this track—and making sure he doesn't go off track with some girl who doesn't—you know, who is not like him." Despite her own background and the fact that she was the "girl" who was the subject of criticism, she seems to accept in her story that working-class women are less appropriate partners for class-advantaged men compared to women from more privileged class backgrounds.

Statuesque and artistic Leah (twenty-six, Brown [Middle Eastern], queer) also qualifies as upwardly mobile, and her working-class background has similarly had an impact on her relationships with men from more affluent backgrounds. Like Brian and Marissa, Leah's sense of the social power differences between herself and partners have made some of her relationships difficult. For example, Leah perceives that her college boyfriend, Rex, had an uncomfortable hold over her due to not just class differences, but gender and race differences (Rex is a White man). She shared:

> Rex was one of those rich boys that I grew up with in town. Of course, he didn't know who I was [growing up]. And he was a year older than me, and

totally hot, and I was, I think, qualitatively and quantitatively—and I put this in air quotes for the record—I was "not as good as him." I was someone who was *lucky* to be dating a guy like him. And that was something I felt within myself. That was something he imposed upon me in subtle ways. That was something my friends saw. That was something my family even said—like, "You know, he's a rich boy. You can't keep up with him. We're not gonna be able to take you guys out to fancy dinners like you do with his parents." There were all these differences between us, and so I felt that I had to do a little extra work to *earn* my spot in his life, you know? And that's pretty manipulative, 'cause I never felt good enough, you know, ever. And he made me feel [bad] about my body. I remember I got a gym membership. . . . I would still have to pay, like, seventy dollars a month for this shit, but I was somehow linked to his account, so he would go and, like, check to see how often I'd gone to the gym and how long I'd stayed—things like that. He was fucking crazy. And he just made me feel like shit about myself. It was a really emotionally exhausting relationship, and probably abusive, emotionally. So that's how that manifested.

Although as a college student Leah was already on an upwardly mobile track by the time this relationship came along, her working-class background set up an uncomfortable power dynamic in the relationship. Though Leah's story is reminiscent of some of the unequal gender power dynamics discussed in chapter 2, the power dynamics here are also about social class and may be linked to racial differences as well. Leah said part of the appeal of being "Rex's girl" was the opportunity to be associated with someone whom she perceived was socially above her. However, ultimately the emotional toll became too great for Leah and she ended the relationship by moving out of state for graduate school despite Rex's desire to keep the relationship going.

In addition to Leah, several other upwardly mobile millennials have stories of awkward interactions between themselves and partners due to differences in class background. For example, April (thirty-two, White, straight, upwardly mobile) recalls a few experiences with partners seemingly unable to recognize their class privilege. She shared about one man in particular, "I was really frustrated with him. He was really unhappy with his life, and yet he had two degrees, bilingual, White, male, um hey—guess what, you can pretty much do what you want with your life, cause you're like, on top of the chain! Stop complaining, I can't deal. You know, you're SO privileged, and you're SO unhappy, I can't deal." Similar to Leah, April makes a connection between not just social class and privilege, but gender and race position as well. April ended up cutting ties with her boyfriend because his own annoyance with his seemingly privileged life became too irritating to April, who has had to overcome numerous obstacles just to obtain a college degree. For women like April and Leah, these experiences are both disheartening and disappointing. In the process of pursuing relationships with those whose class goals are similar to their own, both came across partners who could not—or would not—acknowledge their privilege. In Leah's case especially, her ex-boyfriend used his raced, classed, and gendered privilege to overpower and try to control her in the relationship.

Upwardly mobile men relate similar experiences of having difficulty managing their annoyed feelings in relationships with partners who are seemingly unaware of their class privilege. For example, small business-owner Tommy (twenty-eight, White, straight, upwardly mobile) shared:

> One girl I dated for about a year and a half—super attractive, and was a model, did that for a living—and you know, pretty well put together person, I suppose. . . . So [I wondered,] how [isn't she] in a relationship, at thirty years old, that's serious? You know what I mean? That type of thing. And I look at that particular person's background: came from a foreign family, very well to do, came to the states and really didn't have to work for a whole lot. And I just don't see people who never had to work for anything really putting any effort into relationships, 'cause they're not used to working, if that makes sense. . . . If your parents are paying for your stuff, don't tell me about how hard you work and how rough life is. I don't wanna hear it!

Though Tommy's case differs by gender, he makes a similar assertion to the women quoted previously in that he constructs his ex-girlfriend's approach to life as difficult to deal with given the struggles he has overcome himself: "I've seen poverty . . . I've actually been hungry, I've actually been to a food bank, stuff like that, and it's not a good feeling." Comparing his own experience to his ex-girlfriend's, differences in class struggles make Tommy feel annoyed. Recall also the example of Oscar's cross-class relationship discussed briefly in chapter 1. Oscar remembered in his relationship with his ex-boyfriend, "I was putting myself through school, and . . . he was just loaded—never had to work a day in his life. Still to this day, actually, he's graduated and still living off his parents' money. So that caused a lot of problems." Similar to April and Leah, even though Oscar and Tommy are upwardly mobile, their past experiences growing up poor and/or working-class have shaped their experiences with, and reactions to, intimate relationships with partners who grew up more privileged. Perceived disparities in the work involved to access social class privilege and status seems to be one source of discomfort, although social interactions that communicate a ranking of class positions are also a source of uneasiness.

While cross-class relationships might not always end badly, at the very least, class differences can be difficult to overcome. For example, Sam (twenty-six, White, straight, class-disadvantaged), introduced in chapter 4, had a recent experience with cross-class dating that didn't go exactly as he'd hoped. In a college town with high rents, Sam ended up leasing a "disgusting" basement room in a house filled with university students. He was the only one paying his rent on his own—all of his roommates got rent money from their parents. Nonetheless, Sam ended up in a relationship with his roommate Marina, who is from a wealthy family. Although they are now broken up, they are still friendly, and so Sam talks in the present tense about his experiences visiting her family in Los Angeles: "The girl Marina, she came from a really wealthy family in LA. Both her parents are lawyers. . . . When I go and visit her parents there's these giant houses and they always take me out to sushi and all these really nice restaurants and spend all this money. And I always feel kind of weird when I take her back to Nebraska and like my mom cooks like meat and potatoes and we just hang out at the house and go for walks in the woods. It's completely different than going to her place." Though Sam still seems to have feelings for Marina, the way he tells it, Marina is in the thick of the self-exploration that is typical of women with her class orientation (see Hamilton and Armstrong 2009). He said, "I feel like she's just kind of lost and trying to find what she wants to do," and thinks getting back together romantically probably would not happen because "we went our different ways." Though personalized, Sam's story communicates that—similar to what other millennials shared—class differences are a factor in why he and Marina went their separate ways.

While obviously cross-class relationships can—and do—work in the United States, it is also worth wondering to what extent class differences cause problems for millennials' relationships or influence millennials' partnership decisions. As Streib (2015b) has shown in the case of marriages, differences of class background require ongoing work between spouses *even after* they have reached economic/class parity. Millennials must ask themselves whether this work is worth it. Though only speculation, it might be that some millennials find themselves compelled to seek out others more similar to themselves after discouraging experiences such as those profiled earlier in the chapter. Some make the decision to prioritize shared background over goals. For example, though some of the millennials quoted here are not in committed relationships, Brian and Leah (who are class-disadvantaged and upwardly mobile, respectively) are in relationships with partners who have working-class jobs.

Compared to past cohorts, statistics do show that millennials are most likely to partner with others who hold similar levels of education (Barroso et al. 2020). However, education—though often a potential ticket to upward mobility—is just one component of social class, which doesn't on the surface account for background. Thus, more research is needed to explore how upwardly mobile people negotiate class background and goals when it comes to partner choice, especially when making long-term relationship or marriage decisions.

The story of Bridget (thirty, White, lesbian, upwardly mobile), who was introduced in chapter 4, provides an example of partnering based on class understandings that are structured by background, but not necessarily by goals. Bridget's ex-girlfriend Jill was from a "very wealthy" family, and even though Bridget was attracted to the financial security associated with having Jill as a partner, she sometimes felt guilty about it and definitely noticed "differences" based on their disparate backgrounds:

> Jill is from a very, very wealthy family. I am from a very, very unwealthy family—beyond [unwealthy]. And so we used to say we were from like such far sides, like different sides of the track that I couldn't even see the tracks! [*laughs*] Like very, very different. And I think that's part of what kept me around too was it was comfortable being comfortable—financially—and I know that's bad. . . . But it was [nice] knowing if anything happened, her family would be there for us, so I didn't have to worry. . . . We were very, very different though. Very different views of money, very different like—when she would want to make decisions, she would want to ask her dad. She was used to that and he knew stuff, like, he's been there. And I didn't really have anyone to ask. So very, very different in a lot of aspects.

However, Bridget's current girlfriend Katie—with whom she is planning marriage—is from a working-class background like her. Compared to her ex, Bridget believes that she and Katie just "get" (or understand) each other better:

> I feel like I connect with Katie a lot better [compared to Jill] because we are from very similar areas and we understand the mindset from those areas and we understand how we grow up. . . . And [Katie] makes fun of me because I'm all educated now. [*laughs*] And she hates school. Like, she didn't go to college, she wants nothing to do with it and that's fine. But it's interesting because she gets it. She gets that like, on the outside, I'm like all educated and stuff like that but on the inside, I'm still like the country girl that I grew up as. And I don't think Jill understood that because she grew up in suburbia and so just very, very different. It [made] it hard to kind of get each other sometimes—with Jill.

Although Bridget and Katie are not necessarily on the same class trajectory, ultimately part of the attraction to Katie for Bridget is a shared understanding based on similar class experiences they had growing up.

Though not upwardly mobile like Bridget, barista Chelsea (twenty-six, White, queer, class-disadvantaged) also had some cross-class dating experiences that caused her to gravitate toward potential partners from backgrounds like her own. At one point, she got to know some exchange students and formed a romantic interest in a few of the men. However, her experiences with them put her off to richer partners:

> They all seemed to come from very wealthy backgrounds, and I found that very grating. Like, they take a lot of things for granted that I wouldn't necessarily think of to take for granted. Like, they didn't understand when I was like, "Oh, I gotta go to work!" And I mean—I'm totally serious when I say this and not in a stereotypical manner—these are guys who . . . their dad was like, "Yeah, I'm gonna just buy you a car while you're in the states, and if you don't want it you can sell it, or we'll just get rid of it or give it to somebody else, and you can come back and drive your car here" . . . And my experience is I like to date people who are in my similar situation, or who are worse off, 'cause I feel like they have a better grasp of reality in some aspects. And I do find it grating if you're out with somebody or talking to somebody and they're just so, completely, completely different levels of understanding of how people work—and arrogance! And I don't like that.

Chelsea is now engaged to be married to a man from a working-class background similar to her own. While of course not every millennial—or even every upwardly mobile millennial—will make marriage commitments with partners from similar backgrounds, it is worth thinking about how shared background can make a difference when it comes to marriage or partner choices.

Ultimately, what the examples presented here show is that despite identity and status goals, background experiences continue to be important in shaping how millennials navigate class differences in intimacy. In short, both backgrounds *and* goals are important. Class differences might translate to concrete problems that are seemingly solvable by gravitating toward partners who have similar experiences of either class privilege or struggle. In fact, of the seven participants here who had ever been married (three men and four women), regardless of their class goals, their partners came from socioeconomic *backgrounds* similar to their own. Class experiences and class goals work together in complicated ways regarding how intimate partner choices are informed by class. Though ideals are important, practical concerns also inform decisions. As Isabel (twenty-four, Latina, queer, class-advantaged) put it, class differences doomed one of her relationships because of differences in "economic means and opportunities and family structure and education—it was clearly different. So yes [class] did make a difference because at one point, the things that I wanted to do she was not able to do at all. . . . It shouldn't be a problem, but sometimes it plays a role." While class differences shouldn't be a problem, because class resources are an important part of crafting class identity, the cultural and economic capital of potential partners seemingly play a significant role in informing these millennials' intimate partner choices and experiences around social class.

Conclusions

At the start of this chapter we saw that though Adelle really cares about her current partner and would like to see the relationship last, she worries that their upbringings have led to too many differences when it comes to how they relate to each other. While Adelle thinks that she has seen "improvement," it may not be enough to counteract their communication issues:

> My current partner doesn't have a bachelor's degree—God forbid, I know! But, he has a solid job and is excelling. Um, initially—like, I went to a very small, liberal college and grad school, and so I just have more education around feminism, and queer politics, and racism, and all the isms, and I've read about those things and have engaged in discussions and activism, and he hadn't. So he was starting in a different place with his, sort of, intellectual development. . . . [And] he does not like to talk about his feelings, and that's hard for me. . . . And when he's angry, he's like, transported to this different world where he's very black and white, and he's very quick to jump to conclusions, and doesn't wanna talk things through, and pulls away. And he sort of catastrophizes a little. So in the moment, he will go into this, "Well maybe this isn't going to work out" place—and then the next morning, or later that day, he comes around. It's almost like a temper tantrum from a toddler! [*laughs*] You're just not thinking clearly, you're just not.

Though Adelle has extensive education around inequalities and "all the isms," she also seems to have trouble understanding where her boyfriend is coming from. Throughout their relationship, she has tried to bring her boyfriend around to seeing things her way, but still encounters frustration and difficulty when he doesn't always live up to her expectations. Adelle interprets his reactions, communication style, and "intellectual development" as immature, helping to reinforce the idea that her own class-advantaged approaches to the world are comparatively better. It seems the class issues in Adelle's relationship might eventually lead to a breakup if she and her boyfriend cannot find a common ground.

As the example from Adelle demonstrates, many millennials here believe that sharing common class-based understandings (including aspirations, goals, and communication styles) is important for compatibility in a relationship. However, both the value judgments placed on social class categories themselves *and* the lack of willingness to see class as something bigger than individuals sometimes get in the way of millennials' ability to successfully navigate class differences. Many millennials are not shy about their class expectations, even if these expectations might be exclusionary. However, there are side effects that result from drawing these class boundary lines. Millennials' coded language helps construct poor- and working-class partners as undesirable. Millennials also convey the belief that landing in a disparaged class category may be the result of some personal failing or personality flaw rather than a result of social structures.

These findings are particularly interesting, especially given the economic precarity that characterizes many U.S. millennials' lives. Both researchers and the popular press lament the economic status of millennials, often highlighting issues such as overwhelming student loan debt, the stagnation of incomes, and millennials' status as financially worse off than many of their parents were at the same age (Harris 2017; Hobbes 2017; Kalish 2016). Yet despite these lived experiences—or maybe, because of them—millennials seem to care a lot about social class and the class statuses of partners. Notably, many millennials seem to believe that affluence is better not only from a financial security standpoint, but culturally as well. This could be due to the association of affluence with both respect and security in U.S. society. At the same time, compared to those from more privileged backgrounds, millennials who are class-disadvantaged or upwardly mobile more often recognize that class differences can lead to uncomfortable and hurtful interactions in intimacy. Yet these millennials' awareness of the class inequalities they've experienced does not always prevent them from feeling badly about themselves *or* from rejecting the idea that having a more privileged class position makes someone a different—possibly, better—kind of person.

Thus, outside of millennials' own personal stories about navigating class, this chapter demonstrates something about constructions of class more generally. In looking for intimate partners, class-advantaged millennials especially communicate that partners who embody the coded markers of class-privileged status (such as education, world travel, and so on) are desirable. This helps construct class as not only a personal choice, but also a choice that says something about an individual depending on which choices they (ostensibly) make. Thus, despite the idea that millennials are more open-minded and less tolerant of inequality than other groups of adults (Arnett and Fishel 2011), successfully navigating social class seems to remain a challenge, at least for the millennials interviewed here. These millennials' stories indicate that class is still today an extremely powerful indicator of both difference and inequality in the context of intimate relationships. Further, while cross-generational comparisons of class or economic status (such as between millennials and baby boomers) are popular, conversations around class inequalities *among* millennials don't seem to be happening as much. These millennials' stories indicate that until we decenter the idea that affluence relates to how good, talented, special, and worthy people are as individuals, it will be difficult to get to a place of valuing intimate partners—and people more generally—more fairly regardless of class.

While I speculate a bit in this chapter on what millennials might do in the future in terms of decision making around social class, I did also ask millennials more directly about their future intimacy plans. The research on intimate partnerships, after all, suggests that the landscape of intimacy is changing, with younger generations leading the charge (Bogle 2008; Sassler and Miller 2017). Yet despite these changes, I found that many millennials still see marriage as the obvious future outcome when it comes to their fully mature intimate lives. Many whom I talked to envision marriage as an important part of their intimacy futures; however, not all millennials see marriage equally. Millennials' approaches and to, understandings of, marriage are influenced by their unique identity locations, and decisions about future marriage are sometimes shaped by their ongoing identity concerns. In chapter 6, I discuss millennials' own predictions of their intimacy futures, and further explore what millennials' stories about their future plans reveal about what we might expect from them going forward. Since most millennials in this study either expect, or must engage with, the prospect of marriage, I now turn to millennials' stories about marriage and their marriage views.

6

Millennial Marriage

● ●

Not a One-Size-Fits-All

Historically, marriage has served as one of the proxy measures signifying the full transition to adult status (Settersten and Ray 2010). However, given that marriage rates are down more generally in the United States—and that divorce, cohabiting without marriage, and remaining unpartnered are all seemingly acceptable options for millennials (Santos and Weiss 2016)—the standing of marriage as *the* marker of "adult" intimacy is uncertain. At the same time, these developments regarding marriage are somewhat new, and millennials—just like older generations—may be compelled to engage with the topic of marriage when considering their intimacy futures and their full transition to maturity, even if marriage is not something they see for themselves. Since marriage does not seem to be a given for millennials, their views on marriage can tell us much about their own identity goals and how different those goals might be from those of older generations. Millennials' views of marriage can also indicate whether marriage remains the most socially accepted way to essentially "do" mature adult intimacy, or whether there is increasing space for alternatives.

In terms of how some millennials are thinking about marriage, the account of Adrian (twenty-eight, Latino, straight, class-advantaged) provides clues. Adrian is a teacher whose real passion is playing music. He also cohabits with his girlfriend, Julie. Though Adrian and Julie are doing alright financially, Adrian admits that he wishes that they had a bit more money saved up. To Adrian, his financial goals are ideally something he would like to accomplish before Julie and he make their relationship official in the eyes of the state. He shared, "I mean, we've talked about [marriage] a little bit. We're kind of at the point where, right now, it doesn't really make sense in terms of, neither one of us are really set up, like, financially . . . we know it will happen, but it will happen when it does." Interestingly, Adrian and Julie have already talked about marriage and have pretty much agreed that it is going to happen for them. Cohabiting is not their last stop. However, Adrian, Julie, and other millennials with similar concerns agree that financial stability (as well as other factors, such as self-exploration) should precede official marriage commitments. Once they get their other goals in order, they can take the next step of commitment through marriage.

However, not all millennials approach marriage as Adrian and Julie do. For example, rather than consider marriage a worthwhile pursuit, victim advocacy worker Colleen (twenty-five, White, queer, class-advantaged) takes issue with the very essence of what marriage represents. At the time of the interview, the Supreme Court had not yet ruled on *Obergefell vs. Hodges*—the case that made "gay marriage" legal nationally—although gay marriage was already legal in certain states.[1] Even though Colleen would have been able to marry her girlfriend due to state laws, she rejected this option as well:

> I don't plan on getting married, I don't believe in marriage as an institution. . . . Marriage is fucked, and heterosexist, and is just convenient for a capitalist society that wants little worker bees and someone to stay home. . . . I do see myself with a life partner. I do wanna have kids, but I don't see—OK, I just want a little house, and everything to be the same. Like I want a life partner, and I want kids, but I would be happy for my life to look alternatively. I don't wanna be normal, at all. Being queer is the best thing that ever happened to me, and being normal sounds like hell.

For Colleen, agreeing to a state-sanctioned marriage would be unfavorable because she is against the oppressive characteristics that she believes marriage advocates. Colleen isn't against relationships and bringing children into committed relationships, or even monogamy (although she is open to nonmonogamy). Rather, she finds distasteful the normativity and inequalities that she associates with the institution of marriage. For Colleen, agreeing to marriage is also agreeing to live a "normal" life, and thus getting married seems to contradict some of the values she associates with her queer identity, including a rejection of potentially oppressive normative standards. While Colleen has thought a lot about what getting married actually means to her, straight millennials' accounts do not necessarily indicate a similarly drawn-out thought process with regard to marriage. As we'll see in the coming pages, millennials' approaches to marriage are not one-size-fits-all, but are instead complicated by their gender, race, class, sexual identity, and even age statuses and identities.

Given Adrian's and Colleen's seemingly inconsistent views, it's worth asking if millennials generally want marriage. Despite projections that marriage could eventually become obsolete (see, e.g., Cherlin 2004), many millennials in the United States are still getting married. Just under half of the millennials in the United States are married right now (Barroso et al. 2020). However, gender, age, social class, sexual identity, and race are all important to millennials' understandings of marriage and its place in their lives. Given millennials' diversity as a group, we need to ask how they negotiate whether or not they believe marriage will work for them, and why. How might marriage help millennials reach their identity goals? Do millennials understand marriage as the final step that makes them fully mature? Do millennials have issues with marriage?

While previous chapters have mostly explored millennials' stories about their past and current relationship experiences, and their attempts to navigate inequalities that they've encountered in their intimate lives, this chapter engages where millennials believe their intimate lives are going in the future and how their unique identities and status positions help structure their ideas about that future. Though marriage is still popular among millennials according to the statistics, their approaches to marriage are not uniform. Gender, race, class, age, and sexual identity all work together to create a complex web of divergent ways that millennials understand marriage and their intimacy futures. Further, millennials' thoughts on marriage can reveal how they see their intimacy options, and whether these options feel broad or constrained.

Marriage and Millennials in a U.S. Context

Though change is happening slowly, recent research suggests that most young people in the United States (including millennials) continue to privilege monogamy over other relationship choices (Conrad 2014; D'Emilio [2006] 2014; Duggan 2003; Sizemore and Olmstead 2018). This is reflected in existing literature on the topic, which tends to divide intimate relationships into two types: either hooking up/casual sex relationships or committed, monogamous relationships (see, e.g., Bogle 2008; Freitas 2013; Stepp 2007). Research studies—and the participants featured in those studies—often make sense of hooking up and casual sex as immature, youthful, and irresponsible forms of intimacy (Bogle 2008; Dalessandro 2019a; Glenn and Marquardt 2001). Conversely, committed monogamy and marriage maintain their position as mature, moral, and healthy, with marriage in a particularly venerated position (Heath 2012). Even those who aren't married sometimes idealize marriage as the ultimate symbol of love, happiness, and personal life success (Edin and Kefalas 2005; Ingraham 2008; Koontz and Norman 2018). For example, Adrian's discussion of his marriage plans above hint that marriage will signify the culmination of his relationship with Julie. Once married, they will have made it.

Yet despite the hold of marriage ideals on U.S. society, marriage is in a state of change. For example, while 81 percent of those in the "Silent Generation" (born between the mid-1920s and mid-1940s) were married by the time they reached the same ages the millennials are now, only 44 percent of millennials are currently married (Barroso et al. 2020). Marriage is increasingly becoming most common among middle- and upper-middle-class people (Carbone and Cahn 2014; Cherlin 2014). Further, for most demographic groups in the United States, age at first marriage is steadily increasing (Carbone and Cahn 2014; Cherlin 2014; Santos and Weiss 2016). The growing economic constraints felt by millennials and other young adults are consistently offered as an explanation for these trends, since economic stability is often idealized as an expected precursor to marriage in the West (Santos and Weiss 2016; Settersten and Ray 2010; J. Silva 2013). We saw this idea play out in Adrian's account of his marriage plans above.

At the same time, support for monogamous marriage among same-sex couples has ascended rapidly during the first part of the twenty-first century (Whitehead 2011), culminating in the 2015 U.S. Supreme Court decision in favor of marriage equality (Frank 2017; Margolin 2015). Yet it may be surprising to some readers to learn that marriage equality actually has its critics not just among those who are socially and politically conservative, but among some of those in queer circles as well. These latter critics question whether the Supreme Court decision signifies the coming of greater divisions among LGBTQ+ individuals in the eyes of the state, separating the "good" who are willing to get married from the "bad" who either intentionally or unintentionally live their lives outside the bounds of normative expectations (Bernstein and Taylor 2013; Conrad 2014; Orne 2017). Colleen's account above reflects these tensions since she critiques marriage as a capitalist endeavor that only exacerbates social inequalities rooted in traditional gender expectations. Broadly, legal changes have forced LGBTQ+ people to grapple with what it means for them to be granted access to a highly normative social institution that was historically hostile to their relationships. In sum, the history of marriage in the twenty-first century has endured controversies and shifts, and millennials must sift through these changes to situate the place of marriage in their own lives.

Questions about marriage also extend beyond those related to sexual identity and economics or class. In addition, gender and race matter to millennials' and other young adults' approaches to marriage. For example, Gerson (2010) has found that young women and men expect gender to influence their roles in marriage, with women especially in fear of prevailing gender inequality and its impact on their ability to maintain their own livelihoods and identities. Colleen's account illustrates this fear too—that making a marriage commitment signifies compliance with a normative division of (gendered) labor. In terms of race, many people of color in the United States have seen their intimate lives closely scrutinized and regulated by the government and social institutions regardless of their willingness to conform (Coontz 1992). In short, parsing out exactly how millennials and other young adults approach marriage can be complicated due to past, and ongoing, inequalities in intimacy. In the pages that follow, I explore millennials' views and speculate on what their stories might reveal about how history and recent changes have shaped their expectations around marriage and their intimacy futures. I first begin by discussing the ways that straight women and men discuss marriage, noting how gender and age matter as well in their accounts. I then move on to in-depth discussions of the importance of social class and LGBTQ+ identity in millennials' approaches to marriage.

Straight Women and Men on Marriage

Strikingly, nearly all of the straight women and men interviewed assume marriage will happen for them, see marriage as worth pursuing, or both. Very few participants in general (four women and three men) had ever been married, so the millennials here very much discuss marriage as they discuss their future plans. Those class-advantaged and upwardly mobile millennials *especially* assume that marriage will be in their futures. Yet these assumptions about marriage as a goal worth pursuing belie another curious pattern. Rather than voice excitement around the prospect of future marriage, many of these millennials display anxieties around marriage, although these anxieties differ by gender.

One marriage-related anxiety that is seemingly unique to straight, upwardly mobile and class-advantaged millennial *men* is financial pressures. As the example of Adrian demonstrates, upwardly mobile and class-advantaged men put tremendous pressure on themselves to achieve financial security prior to marriage. This indicates the continued importance of financial stability to class-advantaged constructions of masculinity. Paul (twenty-four, White, straight, class-advantaged), a redheaded fitness instructor and trainer, illustrates this financial expectation as well: "Before I marry someone I want to make sure I have myself figured out 100 percent—[my] career path, being able to support a family, before I would [marry]." Connor (twenty-six, White, straight, class-advantaged) has a similar opinion regarding his readiness to commit to a marriage:

Yeah, I'm ready to commit to someone, but I'm not ready to commit with, like, marriage or children. I was maybe more so like that in college . . .'cause I'm working on my PhD which is, like, six years, or more. [*laughs*] And yeah, I dunno, depending on what career trajectory I follow after that—like, my friend, he just graduated and now he's a postdoc. And you can't really have children on a postdoc salary. That's rough, unless I had a wife that was, like, making bank! So yeah I think career plays in it for sure. There's not gonna be money for a while. [*laughs*] And I think it's common in academia, actually. Most of the faculty at my school, I feel like they do have children, but it's like one or two. And they're young children, and the faculty are, like, forty-five [years old].

Similar to Adrian, Paul, and Connor, other men have stories about how financial goals shape their intimacy plans. These men do plan to marry. However, establishing themselves financially is a priority to take care of first. This suggests that many millennial men are still seeing themselves in a breadwinner role. Ideas about financial stability being a precursor to marriage aren't necessarily new (Coontz 2006). However, what is interesting is that I found millennial men, but not women, discuss these worries. Being a married man—to upwardly mobile and class-advantaged men—is a sign of not just financial accomplishment, but of gender and class accomplishment. Marriage is a sign that men are living up to mature masculinity expectations.

Simultaneously, the millennial men interviewed here seem comfortable taking their time in getting ready for marriage and finding marriageable partners. For example, Luke (thirty-two, White, straight, upwardly mobile) shared, "If I wait 'til I'm forty to get married—are there forty-year-olds that marry twenty-year-olds? You know, nowadays it's not that socially uncommon. . . . Yes, one day I will get married. . . . Where's that little angel? [*laughs*] She's definitely out there floating around!" Luke's comments probably aren't surprising given men's approach to age in intimacy outlined in chapter 3. Recall that in discussing older women as partners, men acknowledged that while women's reproductive capabilities are time sensitive, men have more time to spare. Also similar to men's stories in chapter 2, Luke's account communicates the view that men's internal process of change is what ultimately drives relationships forward.

Unlike men, millennial women do not express worries about finances before marriage. For women, among those who are upwardly mobile and class-advantaged especially, gendered age concerns emerge as a paramount marriage-related anxiety. April (thirty-two, White, straight, upwardly mobile) broke up with a former fiancé in her early twenties when she realized that instead of getting married, she wanted to pursue a bachelor's degree and be single for a while:

The way I remember myself, was, this person who's here now—actually, this person wasn't conceived yet. I was, let's say, when I was twenty-four, that woman [who I am now]—she was in a closet underneath a blanket, you know? And this other person was on auto control, kind of going through the motions.

And, when I told [my ex] I needed to leave, it was hard because I couldn't really put my finger on why it needed to change. It's just, I had a vision of myself living in a really sunny house, with a girl [roommate] my age, and you know, having those experiences and being really free. . . . It was a really painful experience, but it was the right thing to do, for everyone.

While April has no doubt that she made the right decision, at thirty-two and single she is now a little worried about her marriage prospects. She believes that she gets less attention from men now than in the past due to her age, especially compared to her younger friends, and this worries her:

And what's funny is, my roommate Monica—she's twenty-six, little, petite blonde. . . . Guys throw themselves at her all the time—aaaaalllll the time. . . . [We went to a] four-day festival . . . [but] not a single guy hit on me the whole weekend! And you know, people are drinking, and I'm half naked. . . . So I'm making peace with [my age]. It's been kind of frustrating, like, oh—are my maiden days over? Like, is that, you know, done? I'm not—I mean—I'm cute, I'm smart, I'm nice—so it's really frustrating. And my friends have been so precious, you know, telling me these things, which is good to hear as a lady. And, I feel like I have a really good source of self-confidence and self-respect, and you know, I don't wanna source my happiness or my confidence from a dude or from, you know, a response from strangers. I don't need that. I think I'm at that place in my life where I'm pretty happy with where I am. But it would be really nice to get some play!

Previous research has pointed out that unlike men, women sometimes struggle to balance their commitments to intimacy and self-development—the former of which is a gendered ideal, the latter a classed and aged ideal (Hamilton and Armstrong 2009). April's account provides an example of women grappling with these standards. Thus, predictions from chapter 3 seem all the more plausible: if women's "worth" in romantic and sexual contexts is partially based on age, and marriage is a sign that women are properly transitioning to maturity in intimacy, then increasing age without marriage potentially translates to both decreased power on the romantic market and increased anxiety for millennial women. April's use of the term "maiden" is also telling. Despite being a strong, feminist woman, she uses an old-fashioned term to describe what she believes she has lost by aging. April fears that at thirty-two she is already beyond her most valuable years on the dating market and is veering into "old maid" territory (to continue the analogy).

Like April, science fiction fan Kara (twenty-nine, White, straight, class-advantaged) also ended an engagement in her early twenties because she wanted to pursue more education before settling down. Though it was rare for class-advantaged women to be engaged in their early twenties, Kara comes from a socially and politically conservative state where earlier marriage is more common regardless of social class. However, as she is now twenty-nine and single, she also admits that she sometimes feels regret over her past decision: "I freaked out, and just broke up with him out of the blue, and I'm not really sure why. I kind of regret it sometimes. . . . I [thought back then], 'Oh fuck, I'm twenty-one years old and I'm gonna get married—that's way too young!'" Given her past choices, Kara is now worried about finding a marriageable partner:

> Based on what I grew up with, you know people get married and they have kids. Twenty-five is late in my family. You know, now I'm twenty-nine and I'm single [and] I don't know if I'm gonna meet somebody, then have to move, get a job, then I get all angsty. And there are times when I succumb to the angst. You know, watching *Grey's Anatomy* and I'm like "I'm never gonna find somebody!" [*fake cry*] Um, and so I'm a little bit scared, you know, but it's also—you know there are times I worry about it, but there's nothing I can do about it now. . . . My four-year-old niece has started asking me, "Why aren't you married?" Because she doesn't know anybody else my age who is not married!

Though Kara expresses in other parts of her interview that she is more confident and sure of herself now than she ever was in the past, when it comes to the subject of marriage, she admits to feeling a bit insecure due to her age and the fact that she is not currently partnered. However, the age of marriage that is considered appropriate for upwardly mobile and class-advantaged women is also murky. For instance, Molly (twenty-six, White, straight, class-advantaged) said about her recent engagement, "I think if you would have told me [years ago] I'd be getting married at twenty-six—well, twenty-seven—I would have said, 'Really? No, it will probably be closer to thirty!'" For women, the ideal age to get married seems confusing since it is a tug-of-war between time and accomplishing classed self-development goals. The acceptable time period seems to be in the mid- to late twenties, although women must have everything in order *and* have someone they want to marry at that precise time in order to do things "right" according to normative expectations.

Though gender differentiates upwardly mobile and class-advantaged straight women's and men's accounts, neither millennial women nor men seem particularly excited about marriage. Instead, marriage is both expected and a cause for anxiety since millennial women and men have much opportunity to critique themselves where they believe they fall short of expectations. The concerns of these women and men have to do with class expectations, but their expectations are also gendered. While men worry about supporting a family, women worry about balancing self-development (including pursuing education) and holding on to the social and erotic power that they believe diminishes with age (see also Kessler-Harris 1990; Mears 2011). For these women and men, marriage is a marker of both classed and gendered success, since marriage serves as a signal that self-development and financial stability are accomplished. Further, marriage is a gender accomplishment because it signifies that men have economic prowess and that women's (ostensibly time-sensitive) erotic value (as judged by men's approval) is confirmed. Getting married validates these millennials' classed and gendered goals, even if their goals are predicated on expectations rooted in gender inequalities.

While there is good reason to believe that class-advantaged and upwardly mobile millennials will reach their marriage goals eventually, it does often take time for them to do so. As the time and credentials needed to access economic resources are seemingly always increasing, millennials must also spend more energy building up their careers before marriage if they want to build a financial cushion first. Even though only 44 percent of millennials are married, it's worth thinking about how many more millennials on class-advantaged tracks would be married now if they could reach their economic goals faster. At the same time, while the patterns I just described seem to hold for class-advantaged and upwardly mobile millennials, the class-disadvantaged millennials I talked to have a slightly different take on marriage.

Marriage and the Importance of Class

One factor differentiating class-disadvantaged women and men from others interviewed is their orientation to marriage. While the women and men just discussed have a longer timeline for marriage and a clear idea of other things they should accomplish first (self-exploration and financial stability), the class-disadvantaged millennials interviewed for this project are more likely to take everything—including marriage—in stride (see also Dalessandro 2019b). Thus, if the opportunity for marriage presents itself, by their own admission these millennials are more likely to act on it. This finding is consistent with some studies and contradictory to others. For example, it is consistent with findings that show that lower levels of education (a proxy for class status) can be associated with a lower age at first marriage (Yau 2007). On the other hand, it is somewhat inconsistent with the findings of Edin and Kefalas (2005) and Edin and Nelson (2013), who conclude that lower-income individuals can be cautious of marriage. At the same time, the millennials profiled here are a bit different from those profiled in these latter studies, which focus on women and men in a large city in the eastern United States. While the class-disadvantaged millennials here sometimes approach parenthood in a flexible manner when it comes to timing, they also take a flexible approach to decisions around getting married.

For example, barista Chelsea (twenty-six, White, queer, class-disadvantaged) agreed to plan a marriage with her fiancé in the spirit of living life in the present rather than trying to strategize about the future too much. Chelsea identifies as queer and is in a relationship with a cisgender man. Despite her ambivalence around marriage—which is similar to the other LGBTQ+ participants whom I discuss below—Chelsea agreed to get married. She shared:

> Everyone I know seems to have kids, and families, and jobs, and graduating, and I'm kind of—I feel like I'm kind of lagging behind in a really weird sort of way. Like, I don't really want kids. I'm fine with my timeline for marriage. And I have no real rush to get into any sort of particular career anymore. . . . I actually don't spend as much time anymore thinking about the future as I used to. The furthest I've got is wedding, which is in October. And then after that, all the good stuff that happens is sort of, like, extra awesomeness! You know, I've stopped trying to micromanage and plan every aspect of my life. Now I just kinda let things happen as they will, and just have a general goal of, survive and be happy. That's kind of where I'm at.

Due to her life experiences, Chelsea came to the conclusion that trying to plan too far ahead is maybe not realistic. Instead, she resolves to enjoy her life now. In light of this, Chelsea decided to get married and enjoy herself rather than worry that everything should be absolutely perfect first.

Like Chelsea, Brian (twenty-five, White, straight, class-disadvantaged) also had to change and adjust his plans for his life due to financial constraints. Brian has a daughter with his fiancée, and despite his past fears about marriage, he now scoffs at the idea that everything should be flawless before making a marriage commitment: "I told myself [in the past] that was the one thing I actually didn't want to do, was get married. . . . But finally it's become a choice. . . . The last thing that someone you love wants to hear from you [is], "Oh, I can't get married to you until I own my own house and my own business." It's like, wow, that's only OK when? . . . [It's] OK to get married and not feel bad about it. [*laughs*]" While upwardly mobile and class-advantaged men express worry about their ability to provide, Brian makes peace with letting go of the idea that financial or economic accomplishments need to be achieved before marriage. The other class-disadvantaged men approach marriage similarly.

Noah (thirty-two, mixed-race, straight, class-disadvantaged) had been married at age twenty but is currently divorced. Troy (twenty-six, White, straight, class-disadvantaged), as I discussed in chapter 2, was engaged in his early twenties and the relationship broke up only when his fiancée ended it. Sam (twenty-six, White, straight, class-disadvantaged), the only class-disadvantaged man who had not been engaged or married, expressed surprise that he was not married yet: "I remember I went back [home] to one of my friend's weddings and I said I'd been dating this girl for like three years and all my friends were like, 'You're not married yet? That seems so weird.' Because they date someone for maybe a couple years and then the guy usually proposes." However, the woman whom Sam was dating at the time of his friends' surprised reactions came from a more privileged class position than he and wouldn't entertain the idea of getting married at a young age. As I discussed previously in chapter 5, Sam shared that he felt his ex, Marina, was "just kind of lost and trying to find what she wants to do." Men with more privileged class expectations put pressure on themselves to be breadwinners. However, for class-disadvantaged men this task could be difficult given their work prospects, and so rather than worry about their financial readiness, they seem to prioritize emotions and commitment to intimate relationships and children (if applicable) as an indication of their ability to be good partners.[2]

As far as the willingness to become parents and get married at young ages goes, most of the class-disadvantaged women share this trait with men. Faith (thirty, White, straight, class-disadvantaged) was married at a young age but is now separated. Katelyn (twenty-two, White, straight, class-disadvantaged) is younger among study participants but is expecting to get engaged in the near future. The only exception is Jasmine (twenty-seven, Black, straight, class-disadvantaged), who shies away from marriage despite the father of her children begging her to marry him on multiple occasions. More similar to the women in Edin and Kefalas's (2005) study, Jasmine fears that getting married might make her life more complicated, and she is holding out until it feels right. Intersections of gender and race may be a factor here, since Jasmine is Black while Faith and Katelyn are both White. Geography may also be a factor, as Jasmine grew up in a large city while Faith and Katelyn are both from suburban and rural backgrounds. As recent reports have shown, marriage tends to be slightly less common among those who identify as Black (regardless of geography) and those living in urban environments (regardless of race) (Barroso et al. 2020; Livingston 2018). One needed avenue for future research would be to gather more information on how, when, and why millennials' lived experiences square with these aforementioned quantitative trends.

In millennials' divergent approaches to marriage, both class origins and expectations matter. Despite a shared background, upwardly mobile millennials stress that they have other tasks to accomplish first when compared to most class-disadvantaged millennials. Interestingly, I do not find that most class-disadvantaged millennials here are overly apprehensive about marriage. Instead, most class-disadvantaged millennials welcome marriage and take it in stride if the opportunity presents itself (see also L. Rubin 1976). Given that class-disadvantaged millennials live less secure lives than their peers, it makes sense that they might welcome the opportunity to experience positive emotions—such as those promised by marriage or parenthood—rather than delay them for the unforeseeable future.

However, experiences such as those of Noah, Faith, and Troy (who featured in chapter 2 as well) show that sometimes, youth and financial strains get in the way of marriage or marriage intentions. These three all cite young age and/or economic stability as barriers to making relationships work. For example, recall from chapter 2 that Troy's fiancée left him when they were in their early twenties. Though upset at the time, Troy later said, "[The breakup] was actually probably the best thing that could have happened to me at that age because I had not known myself, and neither did she." Though Troy says this now—and sounds similar to more class-advantaged millennials in his acceptance that self-exploration should come before marriage—if his fiancée would not have decided to leave, he would have been married and the relationship may have fallen apart given the financial constraints that were already taking a toll on their relationship.

Faith, who got married in her early twenties, wonders in retrospect about her choice given she believes that she missed out on an opportunity for greater self-exploration: "I never really figured out who I was—what I believe, what I want. That sounds really selfish. [*laughs*] But yeah, I just went from high school, to living with my parents, to this weird [social] group, to marriage. And then I was like, 'Wait a minute . . . who am I? What's going on?'" Despite their more accepting approach to early marriage, class-disadvantaged millennials still understand that *ideally* marriage is something entered into by full adults who know themselves completely and have a comfortable financial safety net (see also Dalessandro 2019b). While class-disadvantaged women and men don't voice the same gendered concerns as those on more class-advantaged trajectories, it seems that they are also aware of the expectations for what millennials should accomplish before marriage, and if they see themselves as not quite living up to these expectations, it could potentially cause issues later. As other work has shown, conventional understandings of success in the United States are the same across class categories (Contreras 2012). Access and opportunity structure how individuals approach the decisions in their lives both inside, and outside, of intimacy. Thus, even if class-disadvantaged millennials take a different approach to marriage timing, these choices are conditioned by class realities, and these millennials are still aware of broader expectations and social norms that seem tailor-made for more privileged individuals.

Although the normative way to progress to marriage—self-exploration and financial stability before marriage commitments—aligns best with middle- and upper-middle-class opportunities, this path is also specific to straight, cisgender people in heterosexual relationships. Historically, the relationships of LGBTQ+ individuals were generally considered outside the bounds of normativity and not recognized by the state. However, now that access to marriage has opened up, how do LGBTQ+ millennials negotiate the place of marriage in their lives?

Marriage and LGBTQ+ Identity

Though social class adds a layer of complexity to millennials' approaches to marriage, another factor matters for their understandings of marriage as well: sexual identity. While straight millennials more or less accept that marriage is something they will pursue, LGBTQ+ millennials are divided regarding how, and if, marriage fits into their lives. Some LGBTQ+ millennials' generally ambivalent, or critical, views of marriage seem directly related to exposure to "queer critiques" of marriage (Conrad 2014). According to queer critiques, which were heavily discussed and debated leading up to the 2015 Supreme Court decision, marriage has the potential to further normalize government control over intimacy and concentrate social and economic resources among the class-advantaged, since marriage, as it currently stands, provides some rights and resources that are inaccessible to unmarried people (Conrad 2014).[3] Those LGBTQ+ millennials who articulate this argument often feel conflicted about marriage for themselves, and as Colleen's quote at the start this chapter shows, not all LGBTQ+ millennials agree that marriage is a worthwhile goal (Conrad 2014; D'Emilio [2006] 2014). Compared to their straight cisgender counterparts, the LGBTQ+ millennials here demonstrate more thought when it comes to considering marriage as something they should do. Most of the views expressed in the following pages also come from either upwardly mobile or class-advantaged LGBTQ+ people—the demographic who ostensibly benefit most from the expansion of marriage rights (see Conrad 2014).

Ambivalence, such as that found in the story of social worker Adelle (twenty-eight, White, queer, class-advantaged), rings true for some of the LGBTQ+ millennials interviewed: "I have a love-hate relationship with marriage as an institution. It doesn't feel very important to me, but at the same time I know it's important as sort of a legal contract and the rights that come along with it. And, I like the idea of what it symbolizes." Adelle believes that marriage has its problems. She also doesn't feel particularly excited about marriage. However, she says that marriage can make sense from a practical standpoint—it grants access to certain civil rights. Though she seems to be more forgiving than Colleen, she also communicates that the status of her future vis-à-vis marriage is uncertain.

Artist and art director Aaron (twenty-six, White, queer, upwardly mobile) expresses similar sentiments. Like Adelle, he has an ambivalent take on marriage and doesn't assume that it is something he will pursue for himself. Though Aaron said he doesn't have a problem with other people getting married, he's not sure if it is in his own future: "I'm really supportive of people getting married. But for whatever reason, it doesn't appeal to me so much. . . . I don't know. Marriage is so rooted in Christianity, and these traditions that I don't feel particularly connected to right now. And so, unless I was, you know, really with someone that I knew I would be with for my whole life, and our accountant, someday, was like, 'You really should get married for this [financial] reason,' then I'd be like, OK." Similar to other LGBTQ+ millennials, Aaron has a complicated relationship with marriage due to its association with religious and social "traditions" that he doesn't feel attached to at this time in his life. However, he also mentions that there might be practical reasons to get married despite his conflicting feelings about it. Though Aaron and Adelle are more on the fence, some other LGBTQ+ millennials are not so forgiving of marriage.

Tamara (twenty-nine, mixed-race, queer, class-advantaged) voices a critique of marriage that is arguably harsher than those voiced by Aaron and Adelle. Namely, Tamara is not in favor of the politics that she believes marriage exemplifies:

> Politically, I'm not for marriage. I'm not even for gay marriage. I don't think that the government should be sanctioning our private lives like that. They shouldn't have control over who I can be in a relationship with. That, to me, is ridiculous. And so when we get married, we're saying it's OK, government, for giving me a break because I'm saying I'm gonna have sex with only one person for the rest of my life. . . . To me, that's wrong. You should get tax breaks when you're sharing your space with somebody, whether you're married to them or not. When they tell you, "You can get married," now they can control who you can get married to. So they're like, "Oh now gays can get married." But what about nonmonogamous [people], can they get married to several people? You know, it's just too much control that I don't agree with. And it is completely and inherently sexist. You know, it's about property and ownership, and I just don't agree with any of those things. . . . And my sister got married when I was twenty-two, I think, and she asked me to be a bridesmaid. Which, for her it was like, [groans] "Do you wanna be a bridesmaid?" . . . And so I called her up and was like, "I totally support your commitment to a partner. I think it's beautiful. But I have some questions because I'm having some conflicts." And this is exactly what I said to her: "I'm having some internal conflicts. So why are you getting married?" And that's when she said, "'Cause that's what you do." And I was like, OK. [laughs] OK, wrong answer.

In Tamara's view, marriage is an example of the government overstepping its boundaries by getting involved with people's intimate lives. She echoes the queer critiques of marriage in her excerpt, since she mentions that certain "tax breaks" only available to married people are unfair. Tamara reasons that marriage might be OK for other people if it signifies an authentic emotional commitment, but she is generally critical of marriage as an institution.

Personal trainer Eddie (twenty-six, Latino, gay, upwardly mobile) is also critical of marriage since he believes most people, irrespective of sexual identity, treat marriage as not much more than a "status symbol": "I feel like marriage has just become this status symbol. People aren't getting married because, oh, 'I love you and I wanna spend the rest of my life with you.' It's just kinda, like, 'I'm getting married because my parents want grandchildren.' It's like, OK, that's great. . . . I don't really agree with [that]." For Eddie, marriage today doesn't signify what it *should*; instead, it is merely a way to access social status and privilege. Gabriel (twenty-five, Latino, bisexual, upwardly mobile) holds a similar disdain for choices people might make out of a desire for social status or in the name of chasing "convention": "It's just such a well-navigated path to be hetero, and to be, um, married with kids—done deal in your twenties, and to traverse the advertised way of life—the way that Lowe's, and Home Depot, and Chase advertise life! It's kind of sad. It's incredibly sad what people will chase in the name of convention." Coincidentally, Gabriel himself is engaged. However, he justifies his own interest in marriage with emotional language: "The short answer to how I found out [my fiancée] was what I wanted. . . . I had essentially done everything, in my opinion. I had run myself ragged, both with liquor and tattoos, and pain, and chasing ass in bars." For Tamara, Eddie, and Gabriel, marriage either for the sake of going through the motions or as a social status power play is not acceptable. Rather, making a marriage commitment for reasons other than an expression of emotionality can be a barrier to authenticity and personal truth. For these millennials, marriage should be an expression of authentic and deep emotional commitment and not simply a conformist agreement that one makes with the state.

Many LGBTQ+ millennials also seem to have an ambivalent or critical orientation toward marriage due to the association of marriage with normalcy and conformity. LGBTQ+ identities have historically been marginalized in U.S. society, and because marriage is a highly normative, conventional, and heterosexualized social institution, it can stand in contrast to what LGBTQ+ identities represent (Bernstein and Taylor 2013). For some LGBTQ+ millennials, a rejection of marriage as an institution can be, in a way, an affirmation of LGBTQ+ identity. However, these LGBTQ+ millennials do make a concession for marriage if it is based on authentic expressions of emotions and love. Incidentally, the language of emotions was a large feature of the pro-gay marriage movement (Moscowitz 2013). Thus, for some LGBTQ+ millennials, marriage is complicated. It is conventional, yet also a vehicle for accessing civil rights and having one's relationships officially recognized by the state. These contradictions are present in these millennials' accounts, and don't necessarily point to a uniform resolution. However, they do at least point out the potential institutional constraints of marriage, while straight millennials' accounts seldom (if ever) do.

At the same time, not all LGBTQ+ millennials in this study are ambivalent about marriage. Some see marriage as generally a good thing and want it for themselves. For example, Spencer, Oscar, and Taylor admit that they don't really have problems with marriage. At the same time, none of these three men reject marriage on the principle that it is conformist. Instead, all three actually see themselves as nonconformist relative to LGBTQ+ peer groups since they believe nonmonogamy and a rejection of marriage is actually more normalized among their own LGBTQ+ peers. Spencer and Oscar see themselves as sexually conservative relative to other gay men. For example, Oscar (twenty-five, Latino, gay/queer, upwardly mobile) shared: "I've always envisioned myself married, with a family—which sucks, 'cause there's not a lot of gay people my age who are thinking about those things at this moment, as well as just the gay community itself. It's a little more—I don't wanna say encouraged—but it's not scrutinized as much to be single or to be in a nonlegal union without children. And I do understand that that's not for all people, but a lot of people are into that single, social kind of lifestyle, rather than wanting to build a family and a home." Oscar perceives that among his peers, marriage is less popular, and he sees his own interest in it as actually making him an outlier in his own LGBTQ+ friend circle.

Similar to Oscar, animated and inquisitive Spencer (twenty-five, White, gay/queer, class-advantaged) also sees himself as relatively conservative compared to some of his gay peers. For instance, he said, "I would say compared to some of my friends, I'm kind of more of a prude. . . . I've never had a one-night stand [and] I never want to!" His story about convincing his mother that being gay in 2010 (the year he came out) shouldn't be considered "scary" is also revealing:

> I had to give [my mom] time to come to terms with [my sexual identity], and have her little shitshow and pity party, then move on and be like "OK, my son is gay, that's fine." But a lot of it had to do with her expectations as far as, like, a traditional life trajectory that you would want for your child—to, like, go to college, get a job, get married, buy a house, that whole thing. You know? The thing that people *think* is the path to happiness but really isn't at all. She wanted that for me. She was kind of expecting that from me. . . . And then I told her that, and yeah, it really bummed her out that I was gay. And I told her, "I don't think you understand what it means to be gay—especially in 2010!" That's what I told her. . . . You can adopt, there's artificial insemination. It's fine, and normal, for gay couples to be married, and have children, and own houses, and do all the things straight people do. And I think her thought of what being gay was, was so tied to this eighties cliché of a dude in leather in a basement somewhere, like, having sex and getting AIDS. [*laughs*] You know, this scary picture of what it meant to be gay. It's not that way at all anymore. Our generation of gay people fight for, and want, the same things—we just want to be treated the same as everyone else! That's why we're fighting so hard

for marriage, when the institution of marriage is in shambles anyway! It's because we wanna be committed to each other, love each other, and have the same life trajectory that straight people do, and for it not to be an issue. So, I think once I explained that to her, it was a little bit easier for her to come to terms with it.

Spencer makes the argument that opening up marriage is a good thing: since the institution of marriage is already in trouble among straight people, why not let gay people take a shot at forming normative families if that is what they want to do? Spencer emphasizes that many gay people—himself included—want "the same things" as straight people, even if marriage and monogamy aren't the ultimate goals for everyone.

Taylor (thirty-one, White, queer, upwardly mobile), a somewhat shy man who works in tech, is also planning on getting married to his girlfriend and having a family. Further, he sees himself as more sexually conservative than other men: "It makes me uncomfortable even when people joke around like with one-night stands. It's not what I want in a relationship or what I want for myself for an [intimate] experience." Among the LGBTQ+ men, a desire to make a normative family life is related to seeing marriage as a positive thing. Even though they share gay and queer identities with other men interviewed, their views on marriage are not necessarily the same.

Additionally, four LGBTQ+ women interviewed see marriage in their futures or are already married. However, unlike the LGBTQ+ men, associations between creating a normative family life and desires for marriage do not come through as strongly. Chelsea and Morgan, coincidentally, tell similar marriage stories. In both cases, the women said that marriage was their partner's idea. While both agreed to marry, they both also asked partners to be open to nonmonogamy, which they did not see as incompatible with marriage. For example, Chelsea (twenty-six, White, queer, class-disadvantaged) shared: "I have actually talked a lot about polyamory, and we both agree that it's probably a better way to have a family in a certain sense, especially if you have kids. 'Cause then you can have two adults who are working, or more [than two people working], and you [can] have somebody who stays home and they stay home because that's what they wanna do, and there's not as much stress." Chelsea's quote indicates that polyamory (in this case, a romantic and sexual relationship that involves more than two partners) might be a good option for her and her fiancé because her impression is that rather than have one couple struggle with all the household and paid work duties, people in a polyamorous relationship have more options as far as whether they want to stay home or work outside the home. More people will be contributing to the household income and care duties, taking some pressure off the other adults in the house.

Interestingly, Morgan (thirty-one, White, bisexual, class-advantaged) made a similar deal with her husband: "I told my husband, before we got serious, that [my desire for polyamory] is something he should know 'cause that's important. [Too bad] if he has a problem with it! And I think that's one of the cards that has to be on the table if you're going to be bringing it to another level . . . yeah. It definitely will be brought to the table at some time." Chelsea and Morgan both shared that their partners' openness to nonmonogamy is an important part of their agreeing to their respective marriages. Although Chelsea's reasons for nonmonogamy also seem rooted in class concerns, both ultimately assert that their marriages will not be like other normative marriages between straight women and men. Renee (twenty-six, Black, bisexual, class-advantaged) could imagine herself married but asserted that she saw having one partner for the rest of her life as unlikely. Lastly, Bridget (thirty, White, lesbian, upwardly mobile) is the only LGBTQ+ woman whose desire to create a normative family life (with a monogamous partner) seemingly drives her desire to marry.

Partner choice may be a factor for some of the women here, since three out of the four women who were married or planning marriage all saw themselves with cisgender men, whereas Bridget planned on marrying a cisgender woman. Since Chelsea, Morgan, and Renee were all interested in both women and men, their interest in nonmonogamy could be a way to assert their queer and bisexual identities despite having relationships that may appear normative to outsiders. Gabriel—who as we saw above is a bisexual cisgender man engaged to a cisgender woman—also saw nonmonogamy in his future. Thus, for those individuals who were planning on entering into a marriage contract that would look like a normative, cisgender, heterosexual union in the eyes of the state, flipping expectations of monogamy on its head seems to be important.

What the stories of LGBTQ+ millennials show is that among these millennials, marriage views and opinions are far from uniform. Queer critiques of marriage compel many to either reject marriage or have ambivalent feelings about it. The desire to create a middle-class and/or normative family life inspires some to pursue marriage, while others insist on marriage only on their own terms. The stories of LGBTQ+ millennials complicate the meanings attached to marriage, while also illustrating both potential issues with marriage as an institution and potential ways to reimagine it.

Race/Ethnicity and Marriage

Though I do not have strong evidence for racial differences among millennials regarding their willingness to enter into marriages, race/ethnicity does seem to shape approaches and understandings of marriage among some participants. For example, specific stories about marriage, marriage plans, or relationships that might progress to marriage from Delilah, Priya, and Gabriel illustrate the significance of race. Similar to stories about relationships in chapter 4, stories about how race/ethnicity might matter in marriage or in the future come from millennials of color. Though race likely factors into the marriage decisions of White participants as well, it is generally absent in their accounts.

One example of a discussion about how race matters in possible marriage decisions comes from Delilah (twenty-four, Black, straight, class-advantaged). Delilah grew up middle-class with a professional single mother. However, in regard to her own plans for the future, Delilah wants marriage and doesn't want to be a single parent. She talked about how a former boyfriend helped shift her views toward believing that marital monogamy is the best setup for a family: "When I met his family, it all made sense, because his parents are older and they've been together the whole time living in the same house, same street, and they seem really happy. And that changed something in my mind like, oh, this is possible. Because that's just not my reality, from my upbringing. Most of the women in my family are single." However, in explaining further, it seems that both race and class concerns structure her views:

Yeah, [my mom] kinda drove home, "You don't want a kid before you're married." . . . Luckily she had my grandma and great-grandma to watch me while she went to college. But what she constantly told me is that, "You're not necessarily gonna have the same support system that I had, so don't do it." And it stuck with me. . . . So I was kinda always in the back [of my mind], like, I don't want that. It's not gonna be fine. . . . If I [ever] had a son I would be extra, extra cautious with the males I bring around, and making sure there's positive images of males in his life especially as a Black boy, if it's a Black boy. . . . I feel if I had a husband that I knew was gonna be there, I would feel a lot more at ease. I know that it would still be some work, but I would be a lot more at ease if I had a husband.

Delilah's background with her single mother, her ex-boyfriend's family, and her experiences as a middle-class Black woman seem to have influenced her views on marriage and parenting. Delilah wants marriage and children, but would rather not have the two separated. Delilah dislikes "the strong Black woman label" and doesn't want to have to parent by herself.

In a different context, Priya (thirty-one, Brown [Indian], straight, class-advantaged) discusses how race has influenced her approach to marriage as well. Priya's Indian parents are immigrants, which is rare in the sample. Priya said that her parents gave her the following option: "It was either go to college or get married at seventeen." Though she chose to go to college, her parents ask her every time they see her how her search for love is coming along. Priya's efforts to reconcile being an American with the expectations associated with her parents' Indian background have been front and center in her negotiations of romantic intimacy all her life:

> So there was this big dichotomy between what I grew up thinking was attractive and then the reality of, oh, if I have an arranged marriage I'll probably end up with a Brown guy.... I'm on this Muslim dating website, but it's more, like, marriage-geared ... which is interesting, in all of this. I'm kind of hoping maybe I'll come across that one guy who's my soulmate, you know? But, I've been on it for about a year, and I don't check it as often as I should. I don't try as hard as I should, probably. And I have met some cool people ... [but] it's harder when the conversation is intent on marriage from the outset, so ... I think I feel more pressure on me because my sister's married and settled.... Like, I feel a little bit of pressure just because my sister's settled, and my [younger] brother probably won't get married, culturally, until I do.

Priya's experience is different from other millennials' experiences due to her parents' Indian roots. All the same, in her case, the differing marriage norms and expectations held by Priya's family connect her experiences and understandings of marriage to racial/ethnic identity.

Gabriel's parents are also immigrants—from Mexico—and their opinions, in particular those of his father, on proper courtship have influenced his experiences in intimacy. For example, Gabriel's father disapproved of Gabriel's (non-Hispanic) White ex-girlfriend, and the fact that Gabriel was considering marriage with his girlfriend made the situation more tense. As I discussed previously in chapter 4, Gabriel ties his father's dislike of non-Hispanic White women more generally to cultural differences: "I was having issues with my father.... He didn't like her customs, didn't like her influence on me.... And yeah, he's just a very controlling man—always has been." Though Gabriel's account is consistent with a gendered approach to race differences in intimacy (see chapter 4), he does share a commonality with Priya in that both have immigrant parents.

Though she is not from an immigrant family, Chelsea had been friendly with some exchange students at one point in the past. Though interested in them romantically, she remembered that they communicated to her that their families (who were outside the United States) would not approve of them getting serious with her: "For some guys that I've kind of been interested in, they've been interested in me too, but they didn't wanna date me 'cause they didn't think their parents would approve that I was White—or, that they couldn't marry me eventually. Not that they were thinking of marriage, but just like, if this turned into something really serious, they couldn't think that they could really commit to it because of their parents or traditions." Though not an exact comparison with Gabriel's and Priya's experiences, Chelsea's story adds further evidence that racial/ethnic differences are definitely pronounced in intimacy when potential intimate partners have families with deep roots outside the United States.

Priya and Gabriel are the only two millennials who shared coming from families with two immigrant parents living in the United States. Therefore, the immigrant experience could be a factor in why race/ethnicity shows up so strongly in these millennials' discussions of marriage and marriage decisions. Yet beyond this, and though I show only a few examples, the stories of those represented here demonstrate that just like decisions in dating (see chapter 4), race and ethnicity can play a part in shaping experiences and opinions on marriage and marriageable partners.

Conclusions

As we saw at the start of this chapter, although Colleen has strong feelings about her dislike of marriage, her opinions have only come about after much thought. The first turning point revolved around her decision to start dating women after spending her teenage years exclusively dating men. She came to this conclusion after some soul-searching and after assessing her personal experiences: "I just saw it as, I know I'd be happier if I woke up in the morning and a woman was there, and I went to bed at night and a woman was there. Guys annoy me so much, like with [my ex-boyfriend], I would go to bed . . . and wake up wishing he was gone." However, making the switch to dating women produced even more revelations for Colleen. She began to seek out other gay and queer people, "read a lot of books" and, in the process, began to question not just heterosexuality but the social customs and expectations associated with it (including marriage). She then saw her goals for how she wanted her life to look begin to change:

> No, not at first [did my goals change]. Now, yes, three years into being queer—being out and being queer—but at the time [of first coming out], no. It was like, OK, "I still wanna have a wife and kids." . . . [Now I'm] more political. Like even hearing myself say, "I knew I wanted a wife" is like, ugh! Like, I don't plan on getting married, I don't believe in marriage as an institution. . . . You know, for a woman to say she doesn't wanna get married [is big]. For me that's, like, only happened in the last few years. . . . In my friend group, I'm one of the few who do see myself in a like, marriage-type thing. But, I don't think I would get married—but a life partner? Sure!

Colleen also said that learning that there are entire groups of people—including those in her queer friend group—who eschew marriage in favor of creating relationships outside of state-sanctioned recognition "blew [her] mind." For Colleen, how she structures her intimate life—both now and in the future—is important because it sends a message about who she is to the world. How she approaches marriage conveys important messages about her beliefs as a queer woman who understands marriage to be an institution rooted in, and contributing to the perpetuation of, intimate inequalities. Colleen's identity and interest in partnering with women place her as a member of a group historically marginalized by marriage laws in the United States. Due to this, Colleen has thought a lot about marriage and believes that how she approaches it is important and political. However, this is not true only for Colleen and other queer women; all the millennials here engage with marriage in ways that help them make sense of who they are in life, where they are going, and how they present themselves to the world. Classed, raced, gendered, and aged concerns and understandings are wrapped up with these millennials' approaches to marriage. This is the case for those who might take marriage for granted as well as those who have thought about marriage a great deal.

While marriage is, perhaps surprisingly, an expectation among straight-identified millennials, their approaches to marriage are also gendered. The main concern of straight, upwardly mobile and class-advantaged millennial men is establishing financial stability before marriage. On the other hand, straight, upwardly mobile and class-advantaged women are largely concerned about successfully balancing concerns about aging and class-based self-development imperatives. For both women and men, marriage is a classed and gendered accomplishment—getting married marks a successful transition to class-advantaged maturity since it implies that financial and self-discovery prerequisites have been accomplished *first*. While the class-disadvantaged millennials here also see marriage as worthwhile, there is sometimes less room to meticulously plan beforehand. Instead, many express the feeling that marriage should be pursued if the opportunity presents itself and feels right. However, this doesn't mean that class-disadvantaged millennials are immune to broader cultural messages about the *normative* ways to transition to maturity via marriage, which currently seem to encourage establishing a career and financial cushion *prior* to "tying the knot." Of course, these normative expectations often don't square well with class-disadvantaged realities, since these standards are most easily accomplished by class-advantaged people.

Overall, one surprising factor was largely absent from these millennials' accounts: religion. Given the intense relationship between religion and marriage in the United States especially (Heath 2012), this is an interesting omission. Only one participant—Faith—mentioned that she was affiliated with a Christian religious group at the time she got married, and that her religious friends encouraged her marriage plans. While the general absence of discussions of religion could be due to the area of the country where I conducted these interviews, this absence also indicates that many millennials seem to be finding meaning in marriage beyond its religious significance. While undoubtedly there are millennials out there who see marriage as a religious vocation, the millennials I interviewed discuss marriage more so in terms of a vehicle that helps them accomplish their classed, gendered, and aged goals. These millennials do not want marriage because they believe it is a religious vocation; rather, they accept (or reject) marriage based on their own personal identity aims (which, for these millennials, are overwhelmingly not religious). Though the personal identity goals for these millennials are not religion-centered, interviewing millennials in a more religious community or part of the country may yield different results.

As far as connecting to larger trends, what might these millennials' stories about marriage tell us? The first thing they reveal is that straight millennials—similar to older cohorts—don't appear to be rejecting marriage. The dominance of marriage seems to be unchallenged by these millennials, although increased agency and choice does mean that getting and staying married may not so much be about living up to tradition as it might have been in the past. Instead, millennials use marriage as a means to make sense of themselves and their class, gender, and age expectations and goals as they come into their own as mature in intimacy.

At the same time, it is also worth thinking about how millennials' approaches reflect ongoing social inequalities related to the venerated place of marriage in United States society. The moral conflicts of the LGBTQ+ millennials outlined here illustrate some of the issues with marriage as it stands. Simultaneously, the ways in which marriage is considered an accomplishment help maintain inequalities of gender and social class. That many millennials seem to still consider marriage—which is, as their accounts indicate, an institution still connected to ideas about heteronormativity and class power inequalities—to be the ultimate achievement in intimacy may give us pause. Why is something so supposedly private, such as marriage, also seemingly so important in millennials' stories about where they see themselves going in the future? Millennials' choices are significant to both their private *and* public lives because marriage decisions send important messages about who they are to those watching. Deciding to accept, or reject, marriage says something about these millennials themselves and how they situate themselves socially and politically in society.

7

Relationship Goals

• • • • • • • • • • • • • • • • • • • •

Millennials, Inequalities,
and Intimacy Futures

We've now reached the conclusion of this exploration into a group of U.S. millennials' negotiations of inequalities by examining their intimacy stories. In synthesizing what millennials' stories tell us about their propensity to navigate inequalities in intimacy, it is also worth highlighting more generally the uniqueness of millennials compared to other generations of U.S. adults. In this regard, I think it would help to return to Whitney—the twenty-eight-year-old ski instructor introduced in the preface to this book. As I wrapped up the interview, our conversation turned to her future goals and plans. I asked Whitney if she had any ideas about where she saw herself ten years down the road, and she let out a laugh: "I can't [imagine]! Yeah, marriage, kids, and I guess some sort of job security, but I guess I'm learning more it's really about me being happy in my job. Like, for example, I'm not really that happy in my current job. I guess now I'm geared more towards [finding fulfillment] than the money. . . . When you're younger, there's so many heavier pressures, peer pressures, and whatnot that influence you to the bone, and finally there's that aha moment of, I don't really care! [*laughs*] This is my life, I'm gonna do what I want!" Whitney uses the phrase "do what I want," which—taken out of context—feeds into the charge that millennials are, at their worst, selfish and disorganized, disengaged, or don't know what they want out of life.[1] Yet in looking closer, Whitney's account is more complex.

On the positive side, Whitney seems to communicate that she feels empowered to create the life she wants without worrying about chasing someone else's ideas about what she should do. Simultaneously, her intimate desires and ultimate goals—marriage, parenthood, but also a fulfilling career—are not all that different from what many Generation X and baby boomer women seem to have wanted when they were Whitney's age. Some social observers fear that millennials are fundamentally changing what adult life looks like in the United States through "killing" various social traditions and institutions.[2] Yet it may be less that millennials are rushing in a new era and more that they are simply adapting to the increasing constraints happening around them.

Millennials in the United States arguably enjoy more civil and political freedoms than past generations. Yet social stagnation and even reversion persist right alongside these changes. For instance, as the 2020 protests in Minneapolis (and across the United States) have made clear, rampant racial tensions and inequalities persist. Certain freedoms, such as LGBTQ+ millennials' right to marry anyone regardless of sex or gender, currently feel fragile and at risk of being revoked contingent upon the personal preferences of the politicians in power (Baumle and Compton 2017). Even during pre-COVID-19 times of low unemployment, salaries were not high enough to alleviate the financial strains that many millennials face (Harris 2017). As the economic impacts of the pandemic take hold, it is becoming apparent that millennials' economic vulnerability will likely worsen still further. There is widespread precarity and a seeming one step forward, two steps back dance of progress that characterizes most millennials' lives. There is a continual battle between the social changes many millennials would like to see and the continued threat of not just stagnation, but increasingly dire and unequal social circumstances.[3] These social conditions influence millennials' intimate lives as well.

Yet despite sweeping changes (some good and others challenging), many millennials' intimate desires, goals, and approaches to social inequality in intimacy seem not so different as we might expect. Sharing similarities with older generations also means that traditional ideas about social divisions, hierarchies, and inequalities in society that pervade older adults' relationships can loom large for millennials as well. For example, in the preceding chapters we saw many millennials voice understandings of women and men that draw from outmoded ideas about gender—for instance, that caring for partners while having to put up with their bad behaviors simply comes with the territory of womanhood, and that men need to make as much money as they can in order to best live up to the expectations of masculinity. We saw White millennials discussing racial power dynamics in ways that obscure the importance of race and largely put the burden of solving racial inequalities on the people of color who are on the receiving end of racism in society. We saw how many millennials here (especially those with classed power) do little to challenge ideas about social class hierarchies, and the social value assigned to different class statuses. Based on these interviews, we might conclude that, with some exceptions, millennials continue to struggle with intimate inequalities in their lives.

At the same time that many millennials struggle, many are also trying to make sense of structural issues and inequalities using personal experiences—a task that makes addressing intimate inequalities (which are rooted in structures beyond the individual) inherently difficult. While it is my view that this process is not exclusive to millennials, it is important to parse out how it works specifically for millennials as they are rapidly ascending into full adult territory and will replace older people in positions of power in the coming decades. We should take heed if it seems that millennials are understanding the world—both inside and outside of intimacy—in ways that are not radically different than the generations that have come immediately before. Even if we might empathize with millennials for having trouble recognizing the structures behind their individual experiences of inequality in intimacy, the individualization of structural inequalities still has implications. Examining intimate inequalities is not just about looking at how millennials navigate social and identity differences in their relationships, it is also about how millennials form relationships in the first place and how they make sense of themselves and others not only as intimate partners, but as different kinds of people. Conclusions about navigating differences and inequalities that millennials come to in their private lives can have implications for how they deal with others in more public settings and how they think about entire categories of difference (and the people attached to those categories) as well.

I initially set out in this book to explore three big questions related to the current state of millennials' intimate lives. First, I wanted to explore what millennials' intimacy stories reveal about how they are making sense of themselves as gendered, classed, raced, aged, and sexual people. In light of social and cultural shifts—including widespread uncertainty—I argue that stories about experiences are a valuable resource that millennials can use to garner meaning and make sense of themselves. Second, using millennials' own intimacy stories as a guide, I wanted to investigate how millennials navigate issues of inequality in intimacy. Do they communicate and solve problems effectively and tactfully, or do we see more tension related to social and identity differences and inequalities than we might expect (or hope) to see? Third—in keeping with the ultimate goal of intersectional scholars and thinkers to not just identify inequality, but to think about ways to alleviate oppression—I wanted to consider what millennials' stories might tell us about where they are headed in the future and how they might deal with harmful and hurtful inequalities in both their private *and* public lives. Thus, to finish out this book, I explore what millennials' stories have revealed regarding each of these questions. I also discuss how we might think about lingering intimate inequalities that are getting in the way of millennials being able to have the relationships they want and take constructive steps toward addressing inequalities in their lives.

Making Sense of Identity: Why Is Intimacy Important?

Throughout this book, I have argued that millennials' stories about their intimate lives and experiences are an important resource via which they can come to understand themselves and their identities. Yet this argument only makes sense given the cultural context of the West, in which individuality, emotions, and personal identity are considered important. Even popular sayings, quips, and refrains, such as "live your truth," "self-care," "live, laugh, love," or "to love someone else, you must first love yourself," reflect the significance placed on centering the individual and honoring each individual's own personal "truths" in order to "live your best life." For example, recall Paige's story from chapter 2 in which she said that all of her negative experiences in her relationships led her to take some time away from intimacy and reflect on herself: "I just kind of needed to go through this, all this crap, really, to just be like, I want to work on myself." Shortly after doing so, she said she met her fiancé, which confirmed for her the importance of her self-reflective period for finding a healthy relationship. Yet curiously, despite the intense importance of personal exploration and identity in the contemporary romantic and sexual experiences of individuals, with few exceptions (such as Swidler's *Talk of Love* and Riessman's *Divorce Talk*), links between broader cultural trends, intimate life, and the process of coming to terms with questions about identity and one's place in society have been underexplored. This is a startling omission, since millennials' intimacy stories show how important their experiences are to the project of making sense of themselves as people coming into their own as full adults.

The previous chapters demonstrate that millennials take cues from their intimate lives to make sense of their various personal identities—and the experiences that accompany those identities—in myriad ways. Throughout each of the chapters, I also explored the importance of identity and status *intersections*. In lieu of focusing on how one or two categories intersect in millennials' lives and intimacy experiences, I attempted here to examine how a number of different categories—race, class, gender, sexual identity, and age—contribute to millennials' understandings and experiences with intimate inequalities. Since personal identities as a vehicle for making sense of one's place in the world show no signs of becoming obsolete, it is vital to consider identity and status intersections in millennials' stories about their relationships. Had we not considered these intersections, our knowledge about millennials would be less revealing. The importance of intersections can sometimes be subtle. The use of stories helps bring forth the importance of these intersections to show where they matter a great deal.

While I spent time in the preceding chapters mapping intersections where they appeared, it is also worth noting that I did not observe as many differences in some cases. For example, I documented fewer obvious differences among millennials in chapter 5, wherein I profiled millennials' discussions about navigating social class. Although intersections are obvious in some cases, in other cases they do not come through as strongly. Chapter 5 demonstrates this latter point well, as it shows how the denigration of poor and working-class status is, at best, mostly unquestioned, and, at worst, openly supported by millennials who belong to various gender, race, sexual identity, and even class groups.

Stories—and intimacy stories in particular—are important because in a world in which individuality (rather than social tradition) seems increasingly central, stories give millennials a way to make sense of themselves. In their stories, millennials make sense of their interactions with intimate partners in ways that tell them about who they are as individual people, and they come to conclusions about who their partners are as people. Individualization can be positive, as it opens up the possibility for people to live their lives the way they want rather than be compelled to do what's always been done. However, individualization can also have a downside because when centering the individual, it may be more difficult to understand how experiences of inequality, oppression, and privilege are connected to larger patterns. Further, perhaps without realizing it, the patterns in millennials' stories indicate that their stories both draw from, and help preserve, larger ideas about categories of difference that in many cases help maintain unfair social inequalities. Even so, there are examples of resistance, or partial resistance, among some millennials.

Inequalities in Intimacy: How Do Millennials Measure Up?

As far as being able to navigate inequalities in their intimate lives, millennials' stories indicate mixed results. There is evidence of progress in some areas at the same time that there is stagnation when it comes to millennials' ability to successfully navigate inequalities in intimacy. In my view, being able to "successfully" address inequalities in intimacy means approaching inequalities in such a way that challenges the structural basis of the potentially harmful inequalities at hand in order to try to overcome them. In this sense, some millennials seem slightly better equipped than others to deal with certain intimate inequalities. However, in other areas, many of the millennials interviewed demonstrate a lack of knowledge around how to tactfully navigate inequality. For example, while gender inequalities are both challenged and upheld by different millennials, many millennials here generally do less to question hierarchies around social class—even those whom we might expect to be more critical. Recall how Oscar, who grew up poor himself, looked to individual—rather than structural—factors to explain poverty. He said, "I don't understand why there isn't more of a drive [for people] to rise above [their background] . . . but a lot of people don't." Class-advantaged Adelle, whose educational experiences taught her about being conscious of racism, sexism, and other social issues, struggled to reconcile her expectations with the perspectives of her working-class partner. In short, even among those with some understanding of how social structures perpetuate inequalities and impact individual lives, there are still struggles when it comes to navigating intimate inequalities and no millennials here demonstrate a perfect formula for how to do so.[4]

Yet despite evidence of continued roadblocks, it is important to acknowledge that there is some evidence of progress. For example, having an LGBTQ+ identity is associated here with a greater likelihood of being able to challenge gendered stereotypes in intimacy. For gender in particular, resistance actually seems related to queer critiques of both gender as a strict binary and heteronormative social institutions. This more systemic view poses a challenge to approaches to gendered expectations that obscure structural patterns. Thus, even though LGBTQ+ millennials still experience—and must navigate— issues around inequalities of gender, the greater understandings of systemic forces that some LGBTQ+ people here have seemingly helps them understand gender differently than their straight peers and may—in the long run—result in more equitable experiences when it comes to navigating gender with intimate partners.

Other millennials understand the importance of systemic forces to their personal experiences as well. For example, having a racial identity that is not White is associated with a greater knowledge and awareness of how racial inequality matters in intimate relationships. However, while many millennials of color here express an understanding of the importance of race in intimacy, they are also in something of a bind because many White millennials continue to demonstrate a level of illiteracy when it comes to race and how race matters. Further, even millennials of color sometimes struggle with race. For instance, this research found that those millennials of color who are not Black hint that anti-Black bias informs intimacy decisions. Racism in U.S. society is prevalent and is a problem for White millennials and millennials of color alike. However, as a racially privileged group, White millennials in particular may fail to grasp this (and grasp it in ways that lead to productive change). Similarly, LGBTQ+ millennials' approaches alone cannot solve issues around gender inequality if cisgender, straight millennials continue to individualize gender inequality issues using ideas about gender predicated on the idea that women and men are fundamentally different and always have radically different experiences in intimacy. No one here "solves" intimate inequalities because individuals are always embedded in a web of interactions with others who bring their own identities and understandings to relationships. Further, those millennials with relatively more social power—such as those who are White, masculine, and class-advantaged—sometimes show the least evidence of taking steps to make relationships better for their partners (and, I would argue, also for themselves).

This discussion brings me to where millennials seem more stuck when it comes to intimate inequalities. Unfortunately, again, the individualization of millennials' stories means that the problems, and solutions, to intimate inequalities are situated within the individual. When individuals are responsible for solving problems, they draw on what they know. For many millennials, what they know are the prevailing ideas about race, class, gender, age, and sexual identity differences already circulating in society. These prevailing ideas don't necessarily encourage equity, even if millennials themselves want to be and do better when it comes to intimate inequalities. As a result, for example, millennial women and men downplay gender issues and talk about how issues of gender might be solved by simply growing up—although narratives of age suggest this may not turn out to be the case. White millennials ignore race because they want to see themselves as nonracist. Millennials use coded language that suggests that failing to ascend the social class ladder is a personality flaw rooted in a lack of talent and drive. Lastly, when considering the future, many millennials assume that they will get married without necessarily considering what marriage means and the broader implications of marriage's continued dominance for those who can't, or don't want to, get married.

While many millennials might have progressive values in principle (as popular surveys suggest), negotiating differences and inequalities in intimate life can prove difficult due to the conflict that arises when millennials use a personalized lens to make sense of experiences that are rooted in complex webs of systemic inequalities. Yet at the same time, it also seems that the solution to the individualization conundrum is not for millennials—and other young adults—to ignore their own emotions and individuality. The alternative—a restriction of choice or relying on tradition to make decisions—is not ideal for most. The question then becomes: How do we preserve and protect the good things that come along with more choice, freedom, and emotional authenticity while also addressing complicated patterns of systemic inequality that individualized accounts are often slow to challenge?

Thinking about the Bigger Picture: Where Do We Go from Here?

Before attempting to answer the question of how to balance personal emotions and systemic forces, I should also point out that millennials' lives and negotiations of issues in intimacy do not end at full adulthood, and it would be misguided to assume that their twenties and thirties are the *only* chance millennials will ever have to sort out their approaches to intimate inequalities. However, how millennials handle intimate inequalities in their relationships *now*—as they come into their own as mature adults—can provide clues as to how they will approach intimate inequalities going into the future. Millennials use broader ideas about difference to understand themselves, their experiences, and their partners. Yet this sense-making process has implications beyond individual millennials' relationships. Millennials' stories reveal insight into *both* how they are faring with navigating inequalities in intimacy *and* the extent to which there may be larger social progress when it comes to millennials' ability to navigate, and overcome, social inequalities. Given all we have learned throughout the book, we can now better assess more generally where millennials are at—and where they are going—when it comes to dealing with inequalities in intimacy and more broadly.

Throughout the book, I have focused on analyzing millennials' stories. Stories are very useful and powerful—they help individuals make sense of their lives and identities. As we have seen, social or identity backgrounds do not solely determine where people will end up in the future (although they certainly have much sway over these predictions). Millennials can change their ideas about their own identities as they move through life. There is much power in being able to control one's story. While this control is a positive thing, issues can potentially arise when stories obscure ongoing intimate inequalities and issues related to those inequalities. So, what is the best way to move forward?

If we are interested in addressing intimate inequalities in the United States, it seems that the main task is to ensure that individualized experiences do not drown out the importance of social patterns and systemic forces. In focusing on individualized experience as we have done in the past (a practice that I think actually predates millennials),[5] not only is an understanding of the systemic potentially lost, but the opportunity for understanding the individual experiences of *others* is in danger of being lost as well. This is certainly something that applies in intimacy, and yet it applies outside of intimacy too. Because we're dealing with complicated, systemic issues that have formed over time, there is really no quick fix to addressing inequalities either inside, or outside, of intimacy. To see shifts on a broader scale will likely mean bringing about larger cultural changes that encourage people to understand themselves, their emotions, and their individual lives as embedded within a larger system.

How do we bring about cultural (and structural) change? I do think there are things individuals—millennials and those of other generations—can do in the immediate future that can bring about the more equal, just, and peaceful environment in the United States that many millennials say they want. To me, the best avenue to systemic change is for individuals to focus on policy—whether that be at the organizational, state, or federal level. We need to preserve the civil rights we do have, to fight against those who would restrict those rights, and to work on expanding rights to those who lack them. That the intimate realm is so often a site of political contention is proof, to me, of the continual flow between public and private life. What we do in private is connected to our public lives and vice versa. Policies that protect rights when it comes to both public and private matters have a synergistic relationship. In the coming years, millennials will only have greater power and ability to bring about the kinds of changes they want to see. They must use that power wisely. Cultural conversations and tangible change also work in tandem, although words without actions are empty. For example, conversations about supporting parents in the workplace are empty without actual policies that allow for parents (regardless of gender) to support their children and still keep their jobs. The introduction of gender-neutral workplace policies that support parenting could relate to change in how care work is divided in many households and help precipitate the achievement of a more equitable gendered division of household labor that many millennials want in their lives.

While policy change may be a longer game, I do think there are other things each of us can do today in our own lives in order to move forward. For instance, if you are reading this book and have recognized yourself in some of the stories—perhaps in some of the more unsavory ones—one exercise might be to ask your partners how they really feel about what's going on in your relationship and then listen. Though an individualized approach to addressing intimacy inequalities may cause problems, as we've seen, it can help solve them too if deployed a different way. I would argue that using our understandings of what we need and want—rather than predetermined maps or social pressure—to navigate life and relationships is a positive thing. However, especially for those with more social power, it is important to remember that personal concerns should not distract completely from either how others are feeling or the larger systemic forces at play. Many millennials want change, and there is a tremendous opportunity at the moment to make a better world that transcends both the public and private. However, millennials won't be able to accomplish this task without communication and without understanding that other people's perspectives are important too.

At the end of the day, what is also needed to address inequalities is for those with relatively more social power (through class, race, gender, and sexual identity positions) to also get on board. This seems easier said than done, and indeed could be a tall order—not every millennial wants, or cares, about addressing intimate inequalities. Some are content with power imbalances either because these imbalances give them a disproportionate amount of control over others or because of personal beliefs around gender, class, and race hierarchies and roles. However, many millennials and young adults *do* care about building more equitable relationships (Dalessandro and Wilkins 2017; Gerson 2010; Lamont 2017; Parker, Graf, and Igielnik 2019). Among those who care, millennials must remember that addressing intimate inequalities is an ongoing project that is far from complete. Especially for those with raced, classed, gendered, sexual, and aged power, millennials should remember that their individualized experiences do not occur in a vacuum; their experiences with others are always conditioned by a landscape that privileges some and disadvantages others. If an individual's growth experiences come at the expense of others, those experiences aren't so much ones of growth but, rather, of solidifying power imbalances and social boundaries that will only perpetuate inequalities.

Concluding Thoughts

To circle back to the question posed at the beginning of this chapter, based on the stories throughout this book I would caution readers against seeing millennials and other young generations as categorically different from older adults. Many of the problems and issues that older adults faced as young people continue to bother millennials as well. Yet I would also caution against seeing younger and older generations as the same. Even if they have similar dilemmas, millennials are making their transition to full adult life during unprecedented times in the United States. If nothing else, millennials' experiences seem to be exposing in real time the foundational cracks in many social systems and institutions. Perhaps this era is paving the way for long-term change. However, we cannot assume this just yet.

It is also important to keep in mind is that while social change is possible, it can be slow, and there is always backlash to progress. For instance, take gender. Baby boomers participated in calls for gender equality during the second wave of feminism in the mid-twentieth century, and there is no denying that these calls brought about historic gains. However, baby boomers did not solve gender inequality issues either at work or at home. Similarly, though they have pressed for *even more* gender progress, equality, and justice, younger generations have not solved the issue of gender inequality either. In fact, the most recent research on the division of labor in households in the wake of COVID-19 shows that we're backsliding toward even greater gender inequality (C. Collins et al. 2020). The pandemic is exposing the cracks in our social systems and exacerbating pre-existing inequalities in both public and private. Further, while gender equality has ostensibly expanded in the last fifty years, there are continuing threats to gendered freedom both legal (such as through changing laws) and cultural (such as through select media representations, discussions, and interactions). If we are continually marching toward progress and greater access and equality for all, we should not in theory have to deal with these struggles; and yet, here we are.

Since my research doesn't suggest that millennials have widespread mastery when it comes to their ability to challenge intimate inequalities at this time, the knee-jerk reaction might be to focus on a younger generation as our potential saviors: the group of people called Generation Z or even younger, as-yet-unnamed groups. However, it would be hasty to assume that Generation Z or future generations will be better adept at challenging intimate inequalities. In fact, recent polls and reports suggest that millennials and Generation Z share many of the same views when it comes to political and social issues (Parker, Graf, and Igielnik 2019). Progressive views on social issues—such as those related to gender equity—don't automatically translate to being able to skillfully navigate inequalities. Further, it would also be unfair of us to task Generation Z with leveling the playing field once and for all. Knowing what we now do about inequalities, it's up to millennials and other older adults to work through their own issues with inequalities by confronting them, and to also help younger generations work through their intimate inequalities as they arise.

Navigating intimate inequalities can be complicated, and challenging inequalities on a large scale is a slower and a more incremental process than many of us would like. There is hope for the future, but what these millennials have shown us in this project is that there is still much work to do when it comes to addressing and navigating intimate inequalities and the social power hierarchies to which they are intimately connected. I hope millennials and younger people in the United States can indeed ultimately make a better world inside and outside of intimacy, although doing so will require that we stay educated and consider how our actions, thoughts, and words have implications beyond just ourselves.

Appendix A

●●●●●●●●●●●●●●●●●●●●●●●

Participant Demographics

Table A.1
Demographic characteristics of the men

Pseudonym	Age	Race/ethnic identity	Social class	Sexual identity
Troy	26	White	Disadvantaged	Heterosexual
Noah	32	Mixed-race	Disadvantaged	Heterosexual
Brian	25	White	Disadvantaged	Heterosexual
Sam	26	White	Disadvantaged	Heterosexual
Tommy	28	White	Upwardly mobile	Heterosexual
Hunter	24	White	Upwardly mobile	Heterosexual
Luke	32	White	Upwardly mobile	Heterosexual
Christian	26	Latino	Upwardly mobile	Heterosexual
Saul	22	White	Upwardly mobile	Heterosexual
Aaron	26	White	Upwardly mobile	Queer
Oscar	25	Latino	Upwardly mobile	Gay/Queer
Gabriel	25	Latino	Upwardly mobile	Bisexual
Taylor	31	White	Upwardly mobile	Queer*
Marcus	31	Black	Upwardly mobile	Queer*
Eddie	26	Latino	Upwardly mobile	Gay
Joel	24	White	Advantaged	Heterosexual
Rob	26	White	Advantaged	Heterosexual
Keegan	24	White	Advantaged	Heterosexual
Paul	24	White	Advantaged	Heterosexual
Reid	28	White	Advantaged	Heterosexual
Lee	32	White	Advantaged	Heterosexual
Adrian	28	Latino	Advantaged	Heterosexual
Connor	26	White	Advantaged	Heterosexual
Jamison	24	White	Advantaged	Heterosexual
Jeremy	26	White	Advantaged	Heterosexual**
Patrick	24	Black	Advantaged	Queer
Elias	24	White	Advantaged	Queer
Spencer	25	White	Advantaged	Gay/Queer
Dawson	29	White	Advantaged	Gay
Dylan	24	White	Advantaged	Heterosexual

* Also identifies as a trans man.
** Also identifies as a genderqueer man.

Table A.2
Demographic characteristics of the women

Pseudonym	Age	Race/ethnic identity	Social class	Sexual identity
Katelyn	22	White	Disadvantaged	Heterosexual
Jasmine	27	Black	Disadvantaged	Heterosexual
Faith	30	White	Disadvantaged	Heterosexual
Chelsea	26	White	Disadvantaged	Queer
Marissa	22	White	Upwardly mobile	Heterosexual
April	32	White	Upwardly mobile	Heterosexual
Vanessa	32	Latina	Upwardly mobile	Heterosexual
Ruby	28	White	Upwardly mobile	Heterosexual
Leah	26	Brown (Middle Eastern)	Upwardly mobile	Queer
Bridget	30	White	Upwardly mobile	Lesbian
Paige	22	White	Advantaged	Heterosexual
Kara	29	White	Advantaged	Heterosexual
Lucia	28	White	Advantaged	Heterosexual
Ellie	28	White	Advantaged	Heterosexual
Courtney	24	White	Advantaged	Heterosexual
Molly	26	White	Advantaged	Heterosexual
Priya	31	Brown (Indian)	Advantaged	Heterosexual
Delilah	24	Black	Advantaged	Heterosexual
Stephanie	28	White	Advantaged	Heterosexual
Danielle	24	White	Advantaged	Heterosexual
Whitney	28	White	Advantaged	Heterosexual
Hallie	27	White	Advantaged	Heterosexual
Zoey	25	White	Advantaged	Heterosexual
Madeline	28	White	Advantaged	Heterosexual
Adelle	28	White	Advantaged	Queer
Colleen	25	White	Advantaged	Queer
Tamara	29	Mixed-race	Advantaged	Queer
Isabel	24	Latina	Advantaged	Queer
Morgan	31	White	Advantaged	Bisexual
Renee	26	Black	Advantaged	Bisexual

Appendix B

•••••••••••••••••••••••

Methods

In the summer of 2011, I began working on a project with my dissertation advisor that focused on how college students navigate issues in their relationships (in particular, infidelity). However, we also wondered how some of what we saw in our interviews with undergraduate students might be applicable beyond a university setting. We found that beyond collegiate and college-aged samples, information on young adults' negotiations of inequalities in their romantic and sexual relationships was largely missing. Yet young adults in their twenties and early thirties might be different than both younger and older groups in important ways. For one thing, young and emerging adults are still arguably making the transition to full adulthood up through their late twenties and have more experiences when compared to college students. Surely, we thought, there must be more to know about the unique challenges faced by young adults who fit into this "in-between" group at the end of adolescence but before full-fledged adulthood. If nothing else, we thought they could provide a fuller picture of what it is like to navigate intimacy during late-stage emerging adulthood. As others have argued, without including the stories of people at the end of a life stage, we have an incomplete picture of that experience (see Martin 1996; Mollborn 2017).

With this rationale in mind, in 2012 I conducted pilot interviews with participants between the ages of twenty-two and thirty-two in order to explore how their experiences in intimacy might be similar to, or different from, the experiences described by college students in the literature. Besides being older emerging adults (in their twenties) in the United States, the young adults I interviewed for the pilot phase also belonged to the generation known as "millennials." Millennials are interesting in their own right. I decided it would be worth exploring the experiences of these young people and how their stories might compare to what we already know about both older and younger groups. Though the pilot interviews yielded interesting leads, it also became clear that in order to fulfill my own research goals about diversifying the literature on intimate relationships, I needed to look beyond just age. The overarching goal of the project then became not only to investigate how age and gender are essential factors in understanding older emerging adults' and millennials' intimate relationships and experiences, but also how age and gender intersect in important ways with race, social class, and sexual identity in millennials' intimate lives.

Sampling

In recruiting participants, I attempted to gather as diverse a sample as possible in order to compare the range of identities among millennials and differences in their approaches to intimate relationships. However, the qualitative, face-to-face interview method of the project called for a convenience sample that is not representative of all millennials in the United States. Nearly all of the recruiting for the project took place in two cities in the Mountain West. During the pilot phase of the project in 2012, I experimented with one Skype interview, but was unsatisfied with the quality of the call. Since the call quality could not match the clarity of a face-to-face interview at the time (in 2012), I elected not to pursue subsequent Skype interviews. Instead, the remainder of the participants completed their interviews face-to-face. During the pilot phase of the study, I recruited participants via existing contacts and snowball sampling (Biernacki and Waldorf 1981). The only stipulation during the pilot phase was that participants be between the ages of twenty-two and thirty-two. I set this age parameter to distinguish my participants from the "traditional" college-age population present in the area, and indeed, every participant who had collegiate experience had either graduated or was a nontraditional student removed from the predominant collegiate social scene.

Perhaps due to the fact that I am a millennial myself, recruiting participants through the pilot phase proved to be generally uncomplicated. I was able to draw on my social networks to find participants and was successful even though those in the pilot phase did not receive an incentive payment for participating. However, thanks to two research awards from my department, I began paying participants thirty dollars for their time in the second phase of the study (2014–2015). During the second phase, I began recruiting participants through advertisements that explained the research as a study about intimate relationships. I continued to use snowball sampling stemming from the participants who responded to the advertisements. Though I posted physical advertisements in high-traffic areas (such as gyms, community centers, and coffee shops), I ultimately did not find any participants through these means (see also Dalessandro 2018b). Instead, I found the most success through the classifieds website Craigslist. I posit that the reason why no one responded to the physical ads was that, by 2014, millennials were already looking for jobs and other opportunities primarily online. Since I found enough participants from the online advertisements alone, I decided not to pursue the physical ads further. In all phases of the project, I primarily recruited and interviewed participants during the summer and fall months. Due to my recruitment strategies in both 2012 and 2014–2015, I was acquainted with—or had preexisting relationships with—a few of the participants. However, I met the majority of participants for the first time on the days of their interviews.

Initially, Craigslist advertisements (and subsequent snowball sampling) yielded more variety in my sample when compared to the original pilot group. However, one group more difficult to recruit through Craigslist was LGBTQ+ millennials. For this reason, about halfway through the second phase of the study, I reached out to a local LGBTQ+ group, which allowed me to post an advertisement on their Facebook page. This resulted in the recruitment of more LGBTQ+ participants.

Though it was sometimes difficult to account for so many identity factors in recruiting, ultimately I was able to compile a diverse group. One unforeseen surprise was that although almost half (n = 25) of my final sample of sixty came from class-disadvantaged backgrounds, I found that seventeen of those participants were actually better categorized as "upwardly mobile," and were different from their class-disadvantaged peers in important ways. I had assumed based on prior studies that background would be the determining factor when it came to social class; however, this assumption proved incorrect. While I finished with fewer class-disadvantaged participants than I originally anticipated, comparing these millennials to their peers on more advantaged tracks also helped illuminate the importance of not just backgrounds, but also identity goals, to millennials' stories.

While this study provides an interesting snapshot of how a diverse group of millennials are navigating their intimacy experiences, their experiences aren't generalizable to the experiences of all millennials across the United States because I confined interviews to a specific geographic area of the United States. Millennials interviewed elsewhere would probably differ somewhat from the millennials interviewed here. Thus, it is useful to discuss the geographic location, or research site, where these interviews took place. The geographic location also might help explain the high number of upwardly mobile participants in the sample.

The Research Site

I conducted the interviews for this project in and around two medium-to-large cities in the U.S. Mountain West that are in close proximity to each other. Both cities differ from other places in the United States in important ways. First, job and economic growth in both cities is currently booming and shows no signs of halting in the immediate future, a pattern increasingly common throughout the region (Schmalzbauer 2014). Further, much of the job growth is in middle-class positions and industries, such as education, technology, and healthcare. Yet along with its economic prospects, the region's reputation as a cool place to be attracts young adults from all over the country. These changes *have* also led to various issues—such as gentrification and rising housing costs—that have caused tensions along classed and raced lines.

The social climate of the two cities where I recruited participants seems to have influenced my data in several ways. For instance, both cities are predominantly White, which is reflected in the sample. Also, as I alluded to earlier, I believe the large number of upwardly mobile participants is related to the trends I just described. Those from poor backgrounds who are either local, or coming from elsewhere, might have more opportunities for upward mobility than they would in an area of the country that is struggling economically or has fewer educational opportunities available. Though upward mobility anywhere in the United States is currently difficult, other research has argued for the influence of immediate social and educational environments on young people (Bettie 2002; Wilkins 2014). Local opportunities are by no means a guarantee of upward mobility, but they (ostensibly) open up more possibilities for upward mobility. It also makes sense that upwardly mobile millennials would be interested in participating in a university-affiliated research study, since most were involved with higher education already either as current students or as alumni. I did advertise myself as a graduate student when recruiting participants for the research study.

In-Depth Interviews

The data from this project come from face-to-face, semistructured interviews. Since I was interested in millennials' stories about their experiences and what their stories can tell us about their ability to navigate intimate inequalities, I elected to conduct interviews in the interest of receiving a "full report" from participants (R. Weiss 1994). Semistructured interviewing allowed participants to go into detail about their experiences and helped direct the conversation. This method also allowed me as the researcher to read body language and facial expressions, which influenced the tone and strategy I used to proceed through the interviews (H. Rubin and Rubin 2012). Though I did use a guide in interviews, I also allowed participants to veer from the set questions and topics if interesting leads or asides emerged in conversation.

Broadly, my interview guide covered questions on participants' sexual and romantic relationship experiences. I also included questions at the end of the guide that served as reflections on what it means to be an adult nowadays. Though my guide included specific questions, because the interviews were semistructured I also allowed participants a great deal of freedom with regard to which topics we discussed, or expanded upon (as long as the topic did not veer too far from romantic and sexual intimacy). I let participants choose the meeting places for interviews, and most chose public locales such as coffee shops, restaurants, or parks.

After each interview concluded, I noted the participant's overall demeanor, communication style, and other defining characteristics in order to differentiate among participants. I also noted the locations of each interview and assigned each participant the pseudonym that replaces their real name. Ultimately, the interviews lasted anywhere from just under an hour to around three hours. I also recorded each interview for later transcription, since none of the participants declined to be recorded. Out of the sixty interviews, I transcribed fifty-three and an experienced transcriptionist who signed a confidentiality form transcribed the remaining seven interviews. In total, single-spaced typed transcripts of the interviews came out to 1,237 pages of text.

My reasoning behind the use of in-depth interviews was to capture millennials' own stories and interpretations of their intimacy experiences. I sought to understand what millennials' stories accomplish for them, and how they make sense of their realities through their own stories (Holstein and Gubrium 1995). This sense-making process tells us what is true for the participants themselves and how their experiences shape (and are shaped by) their identities and understandings of the world. This goal seeks to understand how millennials make sense of their experiences, and how the messages they take from their experiences impact how they view and interact with the world and other people.

The initial analysis of data for this project began in 2012 with the pilot interviews. Early findings from the interviews focused on gender and gender differences. However, in both the first and second phase of the project, the process of analysis flowed similarly. I first read through transcripts and kept memos about emerging themes, treating each participant interview as its own case study (see Becker 2007; Dalessandro and Wilkins 2017; Lofland et al. 2006). These memos would serve as the basis for codes that would inform themes highlighted throughout the chapters of this book. In order to facilitate coding and keep track of codes, I utilized the qualitative analysis software NVivo.

Researcher Position

I was different from many of my participants in terms of race, class, gender, and sexual identity. However, I did find establishing rapport to be less complicated than I had feared. I primarily attribute this to two factors. First, one commonality that I did share with participants was age. Though I did not necessarily disclose my own age to every participant, most assumed that I was in my twenties and, thus, close in age to them. The average age of all participants hovered around twenty-six to twenty-seven, and I collected most interviews (the second phase of data collection) when I myself was twenty-six and twenty-seven. Many interview participants also alluded to age commonalities with their comments, such as references to people "our age." Thus, even though some participants had very different identities and experiences than me, I believe shared age facilitated rapport-building (see Dalessandro and Wilkins 2013; Mollborn 2017). The second factor that I believe smoothed the establishment of rapport was that even though the discussion involved a personal topic (intimacy experiences), participants came into the study knowing what we would discuss. Those potential participants who may have seen the advertisements or heard of the study but would be reluctant to discuss their personal lives were likely filtered out. One participant (Vanessa) even commented that she was surprised my questions weren't more intrusive!

With regard to how my own identity factored into the research process, I especially wondered how gender might influence the interview data. At the beginning stages of the project, I questioned if I should consider gender-matched interviews in which I conducted interviews with self-identified women while a man handled interviews with self-identified men in order to avoid the possibility that men would withhold information from me (see Martin 1996; Schwalbe and Wolkomir 2002). I ultimately conducted all interviews myself, and remain convinced that this was the best decision. I did not experience a reluctance of men to discuss their intimate lives with me, even though I did perceive differences between women and men in the level of detail and emotionality shared in accounts (see also Dalessandro and Wilkins 2017). As I discuss in chapter 2, the reluctance I initially perceived seems related to broader gendered, classed concerns, since patterns of emotionality in stories differed among men according to class trajectory. Further, after working on a separate project using gender-matched interviews (see Dalessandro, James-Hawkins, and Sennott 2019; James-Hawkins, Dalessandro, and Sennott 2018), I am convinced that men's limited emotionality in accounts has more to do with classed, gendered approaches to relationships than an actual withholding of significant amounts of information due to the gender of the interviewer. Thus, while interviewer identities are important (see Ray and Rosow 2010), in this project, I believe—and argue—that participants' stories do more or less reflect their understandings of identity and navigating difference in intimacy. I also argue that disparities between my identity and those of participants do not discount the validity of interviews. If anything, that I conducted all interviews is an argument *for* validity since the questions and communication style of the interviewer (me) remained consistent throughout the study.

Outside of gender and age, the other identities I brought to the interview space were those of being specifically cisgender, middle-class, and White. Though my class presentation was ambiguous, because I was affiliated with a well-known research university I assume that most participants thought of me as middle-class or upwardly mobile. I also identify as White and cisgender, and am usually read as such by strangers. Sometimes being cisgender is read as being "straight" in terms of sexual identity, and I'm sure that many participants probably read me this way even though I rarely, if ever, disclosed my sexual identity. While I stand by my data, it is of course possible that if I had another race, class, or gender presentation, some participants may have acted differently. However, this same argument could be made about interviewing participants with whom I *did* share identities (see Lune and Berg 2017). Ultimately, my study aimed to observe how participants present a version of themselves they want outsiders to see when promised a confidential space. This space is what I could offer all millennials who participated in the study. Many participants seemed to actually enjoy the interview process. For instance, Leah mentioned that the interview was "therapeutic" and Bridget offered a handshake at the beginning of our interview but a hug at the end.

Boundaries and Limitations

As with any study, this one has its limitations. One limitation is that, as I mentioned previously, this research is not generalizable. Though some participants grew up outside of the area where I conducted interviews, I did focus on those millennials living in a specific area of the country. While this choice offered opportunities—such as the ability to interview many upwardly mobile participants—confining the interviews to one geographic location is a limitation. My results might differ if, for example, I had conducted the interviews in another region with different cultural and economic conditions, such as the Northeast or the South. These regions have different gendered, raced, and classed dynamics—and different histories that shape those dynamics—when compared to the Mountain West. However, generalizability is almost never the goal, nor the accomplishment, of qualitative research methods (Small 2009). Instead, the research questions I described helped structure my methods choice—and to answer my questions, I needed to take a qualitative approach. Further, since I focused on increasing diversity on a number of fronts in my study, inevitably some groups are more represented than others. While a limitation, in treating each participant's interview as its own "case study" and then comparing each case study against the others, generalizability drops out as the ultimate goal in lieu of searching for meaning within—and across—participants' accounts (see Dalessandro and Wilkins 2013; Small 2009). My study also opens up the possibility for others to build upon my initial findings here. For example, future research might further explore stories about interracial relationships between diverse groups of millennials of color, which are stories that I was generally unable to capture.

Further, although my intention with this project was not to verify the "truth" of participants' accounts but rather to explore how millennials derive meaning from their intimacy experiences, the interview method left room for dishonesty. Although it is my impression that most participants were honest, since our meetings were relatively brief it was impossible for me to verify that everything participants told me was true or that the stories they told even happened at all. Again, although examining sense-making processes—rather than verifying participants' claims—was the overall goal of the project, the lack of verifiability should be acknowledged as a limitation. In truth, this same issue befalls other quantitative and qualitative methods—such as survey research or focus group interviews—as well. Human error in reporting life experiences and events is a continuing struggle for social science researchers. However, in-depth interviewing is arguably one of the best methods for capturing how individuals manage and interpret their feelings and emotions, which clues us in to the cultural forces helping shape individuals' accounts. These observations, in turn, help us uncover both what is going on in people's lives and possibilities for action and change (Pugh 2013).

Considering Intersectionality

Intersectionality is also a large part of my project, and it is useful to explain in further detail how I approached it given that intersectionality in research is an ongoing conversation. Intersectionality as an idea is dynamic, and scholars are deciphering in real time the various ways it can—and should—be utilized (P. Collins 2019). One topic under discussion is whether intersectionality should be considered a concept, a framework, a theory, a *critical* theory aimed at social change, a methodology, or all of the above. While this debate is a larger conversation, I can speak to how I've utilized intersectionality in this work. I first used intersectionality as a methodological tool to inform research methods, since I specifically tried to recruit a sample that was diverse on account of the factors I sought to investigate in order to map not just identity, but also power inequalities. Though my approach can undoubtedly be improved upon, what I have shown is that it can be done and that there is much merit in recruiting samples for qualitative studies that are diverse rather than homogenous. By treating each participant as their own "case," and examining how each case was (or was not) in conversation with all the others, I obtained a richness of data that may have been absent had I focused on a narrower demographic group.

Further, though my theoretical approach to the data is primarily an exploration into how personal intimacy stories are influenced by, and construct, emerging adult millennials' realities and identities, I demonstrated throughout that intersectionality can be used to help us understand the process of how millennials use their stories to make sense of themselves and broader categories of difference and the implications of this process. It is my hope that my use of intersectionality helps provide further evidence that millennials' identities and statuses are rooted in structural forces that help organize and perpetuate social inequalities. This approach helps advance one of the original goals of intersectionality—that is, to identify where structural oppression exists in order to address it (Crenshaw 1991; P. Collins 2019). Some of what I found lines up with previous research, but there are also surprises. Thus, I hope I have shown both the merits of applying an intersectional framework and have opened up lines of inquiry that may be taken up and investigated by others.

Acknowledgments

As any academic book author knows, typically many more people are involved in producing a book than just the person whose name is on the cover. Likewise, I couldn't have put this book together without the support of a number of people. First, I must acknowledge the help of the research participants who were willing to open up to me about their personal lives. Though represented here with pseudonyms, these sixty people deserve top billing because without them there would be no book.

Second, several people offered notable guidance through this project in its beginning stages as my dissertation at the University of Colorado Boulder (CU). My early graduate work with Amy Wilkins laid the foundation for what would become this book. My dissertation committee—Emmanuel David, Stefanie Mollborn, C. J. Pascoe, Christina Sue, and advisor/chair Amy Wilkins—all provided feedback, guidance, and support that would shape the direction of the eventual book. Each person on my committee took seriously their commitment to my development as a scholar—even offering mentorship and help after I had my PhD in hand—and I cannot thank them enough for that. Another who served an important role in the early stages of this project is former fellow graduate student and current assistant professor Jennifer Pace, who helped me talk out ideas and sort through my data. Scott Holman and Kristen Drybread in the Writing Center at CU provided feedback on my writing and the organization of my arguments. In addition, Glenda Russell's advice and accountability group at CU helped me stay organized and stay on track during the early days of this project.

In further helping in various capacities as I crafted my manuscript—whether through mentorship, writing feedback, or both—I have to thank Mary Robertson, Catherine Griebel Bowman, Kendra Hutchens, Nicole Lambert, Adelle Monteblanco, Rachel Rinaldo, and Stefanie Mollborn for offering insight, valuable feedback, and their time in helping a first-time book author make sense of her work. I also need to thank the team I've worked with as a postdoc at the University of Utah—including David K. Turok, Kyl Myers, Jessica N. Sanders, Rebecca G. Simmons, and many others who are not named—for offering encouragement and (perhaps most crucially) providing the time I needed to get this book across the finish line. Mirinda Whitaker at the University of Utah also lent a critical view of my writing and arguments from the prospective of someone in an academic field outside my own. Last, but not least, Kim Guinta, Jasper Chang, Alissa Zarro, and the team at Rutgers University Press are responsible for helping bring this book to print and guiding me through the process. Their enthusiasm for the project has been encouraging and exhilarating for me as a first-time author. I also need to thank the anonymous reviewers for lending a critical eye, and for further pushing me to bring this book to its potential.

There are several others who should be acknowledged because their actions and support have directly, or indirectly, helped bring about the production of this book in its final form. First, Leslie Wang, a sociology professor at Saint Mary's College, helped encourage my initial interest in sociology as a discipline and has continued to offer professional support more than a decade after I took his introductory sociology course my first semester as a college student. My spouse, Adam Cardenas, has also encouraged me through the book-writing process and provided feedback on drafts (even though he usually prefers science fiction). In addition to Adam, my father Gary Dalessandro has served as a valuable sounding board for my work and has provided helpful feedback, as he put it, "from an accountant's perspective."

Last but not least, I wanted to thank my Saint Mary's College friends and fellow millennials (Colleen Ferguson, Merah Filko, Taylor Flaherty, and Andrea Plaskett) for the laughs usually unrelated to—but helpful during—the process of writing this book. Here are some of their responses when I asked for alternative title suggestions for this book:

Millennial Dating: Avocado Toast and No Mortgage
How Millennials Are Killing Dating
Millennial Dating: Just Yikes
How Millennials Are Ruining Dating
Millennial Dating: The Illusion of Progress
This Is Why We Can't Have Nice Things

Who says millennials have ruined humor?

Notes

Chapter 1   Introduction

1   Identifying information, including names and other descriptive details, has been changed as needed to protect the confidentiality of the participants. Delilah's age here is that at the time of the interview, which was 2015.

2   According to a number of polls, such as those conducted by the Pew Research Center (2010) and the Brookings Institute (Hoban 2018).

3   Oscar describes himself as both gay and queer regarding his sexual identity. For the participants here, using the term "queer" to describe sexual identity signifies an openness to partners regardless of sex or gender. For example, Oscar mostly dated men, but admitted to being open to dating women. "Queer" is also a political term denoting membership in a community—and indeed, most participants identifying as "queer" also associated with groups of other LGBTQ+ people, which they commonly referred to as "queer" friend groups.

4   As of 2015 and continuing today, millennials outnumber previous generations and are also comparatively more diverse (U.S. Census Bureau 2015).

5   Two Supreme Court decisions led to these changes: in the case of anti-miscegenation laws, *Loving v. Virginia* (1967), and in the case of same-sex marriage, *Obergefell v. Hodges* (2015).

6   While there is always a chance this situation could change and rights could be reversed, as of this writing there are few restrictions on intimacy choices. One exception to this is in the case of marriage, since U.S. citizens may only be legally married to one person at a time.

7   All participants indicated that they have spent the majority of their lives in the United States, with the exception of Isabel (who spent her childhood abroad).

8   "Hooking up," though sometimes ambiguous, usually refers to sexual activity and sex acts that occur outside the context of committed relationships. For a more thorough discussion of hooking up, see Bogle (2008).

9   A simple internet search of millennials "ruining" or "killing" will result in a barrage of popular press articles listing the various social artifacts and traditions in which millennials express decreased interest compared to older generations.

10 While arguably more common knowledge now, millennials were perhaps the first generation to struggle with figuring out the balance of how much personal information to put online in order to protect their privacy and guard against scrutiny from parties such as potential employers, yet still have a digital presence and footprint (which can be advantageous both socially and professionally).

11 Generation Z is the generation immediately following millennials. Though exact dates can vary slightly by the source, Generation Z has birth years extending from approximately the late 1990s to the early to mid-2010s.

12 Jennifer Silva's (2013) analysis of working-class emerging adults' lives also points to the rise in emotionality as an important component; Silva discusses intimacy only briefly, however.

13 Storytelling is thus—as Plummer (1995) points out—a phenomenon that lends itself to symbolic interactionist analysis.

14 My use most closely matches conventional definitions of an analytical (rather than theoretical) framework, since I use intersectionality to help make sense of millennials' stories in the context I have described in this chapter (see Pacheco-Vega 2018).

15 All the interviews were face-to-face with the exception of one that used an online platform. No more digital interviews were conducted due to my own dissatisfaction/technical difficulties with the digitally mediated interview.

16 I speak more about the sampling—including strengths and limitations of my approach—in appendix B.

17 Though "working-class" and "poor" may have been distinct groups historically, economic restructuring has situated working-class people as much more vulnerable to slip into poverty (Cherlin 2014). Most of the young adults I interviewed who belong to these class groups had actually already spent time oscillating between both class statuses by the time of the interview. For this reason, I group them together rather than separately.

18 The participant Jeremy, who identifies as a genderqueer man and also as heterosexual.

19 Arguments in favor of the term "Latinx" point out that the term is gender neutral and, thus, more inclusive by speaking to the experiences of some nonbinary and gender-nonconforming Latinx people. Conversely, others prefer alternatives to the term "Latinx" for various reasons (Trujillo-Pagán 2018). For instance, some argue that while "Latinx" is popular among academics, it is not popular among the majority of "Latinx" people themselves (Hernandez 2017).

Chapter 2   He Said, She Said

1 I did not set out to interview couples, but did so in two cases—Zoey and Connor and Ellie and Reid. This happened by chance—Zoey and Connor were referrals from another participant and did not realize at the time that I had interviewed them both separately. Reid and Ellie were married, and while I initially set out to interview Reid in their home, Ellie also expressed interest and so I interviewed them both separately on the same day. Each of them spent time outside (since it was summertime) while the other was interviewed to preserve confidentiality. One benefit of interviewing the couples is that I could see how each member of the same relationship interpreted their experiences in different gendered ways. At the same time, one potential drawback is that participants might be reluctant to share some information if they believe their partner will eventually seek out the

study results and be able to identify them through their stories. It was for this latter reason that I generally preferred not to interview couples.

2 I discuss some of these patterns—using some different examples—elsewhere as well; see Dalessandro and Wilkins (2017) for an additional discussion of these trends.

3 It is possible that Faith's status as a parent could be part of the reason why she is reluctant to divorce her husband. However, she did not indicate that this was the case, and seemed more focused on trying to convince her husband that they were better off divorced.

4 In this case, a relationship in which one or both partners also have additional sexual (but usually not romantically committed) relationships.

5 For further discussion on this, also see Dalessandro and Wilkins (2017).

6 It would be interesting to explore this further given the press that gender inequality has received since the popularization of discussions around sexual misconduct and the social media–driven "Me Too" movement beginning in 2017, which took place after data collection.

7 Meaning "silly" or "outlandish."

8 A more thorough discussion of race follows in chapter 4.

9 Spencer identifies his sexual identity as both gay and queer.

10 Coincidentally, the language of "treating" became popularized in the early twentieth-century United States as a way to describe heterosexual exchanges between women and men in which men exchanged gifts for women's amorous attentions (Clement 2006). This language also, interestingly, shows up in the quotes of several other participants throughout the book.

Chapter 3   Age Is Nothing but a Number?

1 "Cougar" is a term that refers to a woman, usually in her forties or older, who seeks intimate relationships with younger men, usually in their twenties or thirties (Gibson 2001; Kershaw 2009).

2 Colloquial phrase referring to a deceitful or suspicious situation.

3 And with social class as well, at least in the case of older men.

4 I found no class patterns in LGBTQ+ millennials' stories here, perhaps since all those in the following section were on class-advantaged future trajectories (either as upwardly mobile or coming from an advantaged background already).

5 "Brown" is Leah's term. Another participant—Priya—also uses the term to describe herself, although for Priya "Brown" refers to Indian (South Asian) heritage.

6 Colloquial term for "bourgeoisie."

7 Such as a BDSM or sexual "ageplay" community in which a "daddy" or father figure may be fetishized, and specifically sought out, as a sexual and/or romantic partner.

Chapter 4   The Color of Intimacy

1 For the sake of simplicity, throughout most of this chapter I refer to race and ethnicity, and racial/ethnic difference, as simply "race" or "racial" difference. Though there are distinctions between the terms race and ethnicity, this chapter discusses differences of experience and understanding due to society-wide

racialization of individuals; that is, the placing of people into different "raced" groups based on factors such as skin color, phenotypic characteristics, national origins, and even cultural traits. I've found previously that some young adults themselves often categorize "ethnic" difference as "racial" difference. For more on this, see Dalessandro (2017).

2   "Beaner fever" is a derogatory phrase that's been used to refer to the sexual fetishization of Mexicans, Latin Americans, and other Latinx people. Oscar (who is Latino-Mexican American) provides an example of this in his quote.

3   If this was unapparent before, the 2020 protests resulting from repeated instances of police brutality against Black Americans made abundantly clear the persistence of racial inequality to sections of the U.S. populace who aren't usually confronted with racial inequality in their own lives (namely, White Americans).

4   A reference to the September 11, 2001, terrorist attacks on the United States, which were attributed to Al-Qaeda, an Islamic extremist group.

Chapter 5   No Compromise on Class

1   Danielle uses this term to refer to what is, in her opinion, a small, nondescript town.

2   The name of the town has been changed to protect confidentiality. Here, Lee's friends responded to his social media post by associating the name of the city where he was staying ("Woodland City") with the use of the term "hood," which carries with it specific classed and raced connotations and is derogatory in this example (similar to Lee's term "ghetto").

Chapter 6   Millennial Marriage

1   Including the location where the interview took place.

2   Since I explored this pattern in chapter 2, I do not discuss it in detail here; see that chapter for a thorough discussion of class-disadvantaged men's approaches to commitment.

3   In the years leading up to the 2015 *Obergefell v. Hodges* Supreme Court decision in the United States, the writings of various scholars and social commentators revealed an ideological divide between those who vehemently advocated for the need for marriage equality because of social recognition and civil rights (Gill 2012; Mohr 2005; Rauch 2004) and others who asserted that the fight for marriage equality was actually a setback to social progress because marriage signifies compliance with neoliberal policies that further divert resources away from those who are marginalized in society (D'Emilio [2006] 2014; Duggan 2003).

Chapter 7   Relationship Goals

1   A simple internet search on any of these three charges yields millions of results. For example, one opinion piece from online publication *Grazia UK*, titled "Why Can't Millennials Make Any Damn Decisions?" (Squier 2016), argues that an overabundance of choice has crippled millennials' ability to make decisions. However, not unlike some of the quotes from millennials in this book, arguments such as this tend to take an individualized approach to millennials' problems rather than a nuanced look at how structural factors might be impacting their

ability to make choices. Further, arguments such as those in the *Grazia UK* piece imply that increased choice and freedom is a zero-sum game: if too much choice is bad, doesn't this suggest that less choice is preferable? This seems to set a dangerous precedent. I write about these questions elsewhere (Dalessandro 2018a).

2 The traditions and industries millennials have been accused of "killing" run the gamut from everyday items, such as napkins, to large purchases, such as diamonds (Taylor 2017).

3 For more on millennials' views on social issues compared to other generations, see Pew Research Center (2018).

4 If a "perfect formula" even exists (which it probably does not).

5 Based on the existence of literature from the 1990s that explores links between adult individuals' personal sense of identity and storytelling, such as that by Irvine (1999) and Riessman (1990).

References

Alarie, Milaine. 2019. "'They're the Ones Chasing the Cougar': Relationship Forma-
    tion in the Context of Age-Hypogamous Intimate Relationships." *Gender &
    Society* 33, no. 3: 463–485.

Allen, Renee Nicole, and Deshun Harris. 2018. "#SocialJustice: Combatting Implicit
    Bias in an Age of Millennials, Colorblindness, and Microaggressions." *University
    of Maryland Law Journal of Race, Religion, Gender & Class* 18, no. 1: 1–30.

American Psychological Association. 2020. "Socioeconomic Status." American
    Psychological Association. Accessed July 16, 2020. https://www.apa.org/topics
    /socioeconomic-status/.

Armstrong, Elizabeth, Paula England, and Alison C. K. Fogarty. 2012. "Sexual
    Practices, Learning and Love: Accounting for Women's Orgasm and Sexual
    Enjoyment in College Hookups and Relationships. *American Sociological Review* 77,
    no. 3: 435–462.

Arnett, Jeffery J. 2000. "Emerging Adulthood: A Theory of Development from the
    Late Teens through the Twenties." *American Psychologist* 55, no. 5: 469–480.

———. 2004. *Emerging Adulthood: The Winding Road from Late Teens through the
    Twenties.* New York: Oxford University Press.

Arnett, Jeffrey, and Elizabeth Fishel. 2011. "Generation Me? Maybe Not! Despite the
    Stereotypes, Boomer Parents Can Be Proud of Raising Tolerant and Generous
    Young Adults." *AARP*, October 10. Accessed July 16, 2020. http://www.aarp.org
    /relationships/friends-family/info-10-2011/empathetic-generation.html.

Barroso, Amanda, Kim Parker, and Jesse Bennett. 2020. "As Millennials Near 40,
    They're Approaching Family Life Differently than Previous Generations." Pew
    Research Center, May 27. Accessed August 5, 2020. https://www.pewsocialtrends
    .org/2020/05/27/as-millennials-near-40-theyre-approaching-family-life-differently
    -than-previous-generations/.

Bartholome, Andreanna, Richard Tewksbury, and Alex Bruzzone. 2000. "'I Want a
    Man': Patterns of Attraction in All-Male Personal Ads." *Journal of Men's Studies* 8,
    no. 3: 309–321.

Baumle, Amanda K., and D'Lane R. Compton. 2017. "Love Wins?" *Contexts* 16, no. 1:
    30–35.

Becker, Howard. 2007. *Writing for Social Scientists*. 2nd ed. Chicago: University of Chicago Press.

Bell, Leslie. 2013. *Hard to Get: 20-Something Women and the Paradox of Sexual Freedom*. Berkeley: University of California Press.

Bennhold, Katrin. 2012. "Equality and the End of Marrying Up." *New York Times*, June 12. Accessed July 16, 2020. http://www.nytimes.com/2012/06/13/world /europe/13iht-letter13.html.

Bernstein, Mary, and Verta Taylor. 2013. "Introduction: Marital Discord: Understanding the Contested Place of Marriage in the Lesbian and Gay Movement." In *The Marrying Kind? Debating Same-Sex Marriage within the Gay and Lesbian Movement*, edited by Mary Bernstein and Verta Taylor, 1–35. Minneapolis: University of Minnesota Press.

Bettie, Julie. 2003. *Women without Class: Girls, Race, and Identity*. Berkeley: University of California Press.

Biernacki, Patrick, and Dan Waldorf. 1981. "Snowball Sampling: Problems and Techniques of Chain Referral Sampling." *Sociological Research and Methods* 10, no. 2: 141–163.

Blank, Hanne. 2012. *Straight: The Surprisingly Short History of Heterosexuality*. Boston: Beacon Press.

Bogle, Kathleen A. 2008. *Hooking Up: Sex, Dating, and Relationships on Campus*. New York: New York University Press.

Bonilla-Silva, Eduardo. 2003. *Racism without Racists: Colorblind Racism and the Persistence of Racial Inequality in America*. Lanham, MD: Rowman and Littlefield.

Bourdieu, Pierre. 1993. *The Field of Cultural Production*. New York: Columbia University Press.

Bridges, Tristan, and C. J. Pascoe. 2014. "Hybrid Masculinities: New Directions in the Sociology of Men and Masculinities." *Sociology Compass* 8: 246–258.

Bustillos, Maria. 2019. "The 1% Nightmare Class Politics of Taylor Swift's 'You Need to Calm Down.'" *Popula*, June 25. Accessed July 16, 2020. https://popula.com/2019 /06/25/class-politics-of-you-need-to-calm-down/.

Carbone, June, and Naomi Cahn. 2014. *Marriage Markets: How Inequality Is Remaking the American Family*. New York: Oxford University Press.

Carpenter, Laura, and John DeLamater, eds. 2012. *Sex for Life: From Virginity to Viagra, How Sex Changes throughout Our Lives*. New York: New York University Press.

Cataldi, Emily Forrest, Christopher T. Bennett, and Xianglei Chen. 2018. *First-Generation Students: College Access, Persistence, and Postbachelor's Outcomes*. U.S. Department of Education. https://nces.ed.gov/pubs2018/2018421.pdf.

Cherlin, Andrew J. 2004. "The Deinstitutionalization of American Marriage." *Journal of Marriage and Family* 66, no. 4: 848–861.

———. 2013. "In the Season of Marriage, a Question: Why Bother?" *New York Times*, April 27. Accessed July 16, 2020. http://www.nytimes.com/2013/04/28/opinion /sunday/why-do-people-still-bother-to-marry.html.

———. 2014. *Labor's Love Lost: The Rise and Fall of the Working-Class Family in America*. New York: Russell Sage Foundation.

Ciabattari, Teresa. 2001. "Changes in Men's Conservative Gender Ideologies: Cohort and Period Influences." *Gender & Society* 15, no. 4: 574–591.

Clement, Elizabeth Alice. 2006. *Love for Sale: Courting, Treating, and Prostitution in New York City 1940–1945*. Chapel Hill: University of North Carolina Press.

Collins, Caitlyn M., Liana Christin Landivar, Leah Ruppanner, and William J. Scarborough. 2020. "COVID-19 and the Gender Gap in Work Hours." *Family, Work, & Organization*. https://doi.org/10.1111/gwao.12506.

Collins, Patricia Hill. 1990. *Black Feminist Thought: Knowledge, Consciousness, and Power*. Boston, MA: Unwin Hyman.

———. 2005. *Black Sexual Politics: African Americans, Gender, and the New Racism*. New York: Routledge.

———. 2019. *Intersectionality as Critical Social Theory*. Durham, NC: Duke University Press.

Connell, R. W., and James W. Messerschmidt. 2005. "Hegemonic Masculinity: Rethinking the Concept." *Gender & Society* 19, no. 6: 829–859.

Conrad, Ryan, ed. 2014. *Queer Revolution, Not Mere Inclusion*. Oakland, CA: AK Press.

Contreras, Randol. 2012. *The Stickup Kids: Race, Drugs, Violence, and the American Dream*. Berkeley: University of California Press.

Coontz, Stephanie. 1992. *The Way We Never Were: American Families and the Nostalgia Trip*. New York: Basic Books.

———. 2006. *Marriage, a History: How Love Conquered Marriage*. New York: Penguin.

Cox, Jonathan. 2017. "I Am but I Do Not See: Color-Blind Racial Ideology in College Millennials." PhD diss., University of Maryland.

Crenshaw, Kimberlé. 1991. "Mapping the Margins: Intersectionality, Identity Politics, and Violence against Women of Color." *Stanford Law Review* 43, no. 6: 1241–1299.

Currid-Halkett, Elizabeth. 2017. *The Sum of Small Things: A Theory of the Aspirational Class*. Princeton, NJ: Princeton University Press.

Dalessandro, Cristen. 2017. "Hispanic and Catholic, or Hispanic-Catholic? Racialized Religious Identity for Self-Identified 'Hispanic' Students at a Predominantly White Institution." *NEXT Graduate Journal of Religious Studies* 5, no. 1: 8–23.

———. 2018a. "Internet Intimacy: Authenticity and Longing in the Relationships of Millennial Young Adults." *Sociological Perspectives* 61, no. 4: 626–641.

———. 2018b. "Recruitment Tools for Reaching Millennials: The Digital Difference." *International Journal of Qualitative Methods* 17, no. 1: 1–7.

———. 2019a. "Manifesting Maturity: Gendered Sexual Intimacy and Becoming an Adult." *Sexualities* 22, nos. 1–2: 165–181.

———. 2019b. "'It's a Lifestyle': Social Class, Flexibility, and Young Adults' Stories about Defining Adulthood." *Sociological Spectrum* 39, no. 4: 250–263.

———. 2020. "'My Family and Friends Thought It Was a Horrible Idea': The Classed and Gendered Project of Young Adult Women's Intimacy Choices." *Journal of Youth Studies*. https://doi.org/10.1080/13676261.2020.1713306.

Dalessandro, Cristen, Laurie James-Hawkins, and Christie Sennott. 2019. "Strategic Silence: College Men and Contraceptive Decision Making." *Gender & Society* 33, no. 5: 772–794.

Dalessandro, Cristen, and Amy C. Wilkins. 2017. "Blinded by Love: Women, Men, and Gendered Age in Relationship Stories." *Gender & Society* 31, no. 1: 96–118.

D'Emilio, John. [2006] 2014. "The Marriage Fight Is Setting Us Back." In *Queer Revolution, Not Mere Inclusion*, edited by Ryan Conrad, 51–56. Oakland, CA: AK Press.

Dernberger, Brittany N., and Joanna R. Pepin. 2020. "Gender Flexibility, but Not Equality: Young Adults' Division of Labor Preferences." *Sociological Science*. https://doi.org/10.15195/v7.a2.

DeSante, Christopher D., and Candis Watts Smith. 2019. *Racial Stasis: The Millennial Generation and the Stagnation of Racial Attitudes in American Politics*. Chicago: University of Chicago Press.

DeSantis, Alan D. 2007. *Inside Greek U: Fraternities, Sororities, and the Pursuit of Pleasure, Power, and Prestige*. Lexington: University of Kentucky Press.

Duggan, Lisa. 2003. *The Twilight of Equality?: Neoliberalism, Cultural Politics, and the Attack on Democracy*. Boston: Beacon Press.

Eaton, Asia, and Suzanna Rose. 2011. "Has Dating Become More Egalitarian? A 35 Year Review Using Sex Roles." *Sex Roles* 64, nos. 11–12: 843–862.

Edin, Kathryn, and Maria Kefalas. 2005. *Promises I Can Keep: Why Poor Women Put Motherhood before Marriage*. Berkeley: University of California Press.

Edin, Kathryn, and Timothy L. Nelson. 2013. *Doing the Best I Can: Fatherhood in the Inner City*. Los Angeles: University of California Press.

Edwards, Corie L. 2008. *The Elusive Dream: The Power of Race in Interracial Churches*. New York: Oxford University Press.

England, Paula. 2010. "The Gender Revolution: Uneven and Stalled." *Gender & Society* 24, no. 2: 149–166.

Farrell, Justin. 2020. *Billionaire Wilderness: The Ultra-Wealthy and the Remaking of the American West*. Princeton, NJ: Princeton University Press.

Feliciano, Cynthia, Belinda Robnett, and Golnaz Komaie. 2009. "Gendered Racial Exclusion among White Internet Daters." *Social Science Research* 38, no. 1: 39–54.

Frank, Nathaniel. 2017. *Awakening: How Gays and Lesbians Brought Marriage Equality to America*. Cambridge, MA: Harvard University Press.

Frankenberg, Ruth. 1993. *White Women, Race Matters: The Social Construction of Whiteness*. Minneapolis: University of Minnesota Press.

Freeman, Carla. 2014. *Entrepreneurial Selves: Neoliberal Respectability and the Making of a Caribbean Middle Class*. Durham, NC: Duke University Press.

Freitas, Donna. 2013. *The End of Sex: How Hookup Culture Is Leaving a Generation Unhappy, Sexually Unfulfilled, and Confused about Intimacy*. New York: Basic Books.

Furedi, Frank. 2004. *Therapy Culture: Cultivating Vulnerability in an Uncertain Age*. New York: Routledge.

Gala, Jigisha, and Shagufa Kapadia. 2014. "Romantic Love, Commitment, and Marriage in Emerging Adults in an Indian Context: Views of Emerging Adults and Middle Adults." *Psychology and Development Societies* 26, no. 1: 115–141.

GenForward. 2018. *Millennial Views on Feminism*. GenForward at the University of Chicago, June. Accessed August 19, 2020. http://genforwardsurvey.com/assets/uploads/2018/08/Feminism-Slides_Final.pdf.

Gerson, Kathleen. 2010. *The Unfinished Revolution: Coming of Age in a New Era of Gender, Work, and Family*. New York: Oxford University Press.

Gibson, Valerie. 2001. *Cougar: A Guide for Older Women Dating Younger Men*. Toronto: Key Porter Books.

Giddens, Anthony. 1991. *Modernity and Self-Identity: Self and Society in the Late Modern Age*. Stanford, CA: Stanford University Press.

Gilbert, Dennis. 1998. *The American Class Structure*. New York: Wadsworth.

Gill, Emily R. 2012. *An Argument for Same-Sex Marriage: Religious Freedom, Sexual Freedom, and Public Expressions of Civic Equality*. Washington, DC: Georgetown University Press.

GLAAD. 2017. *Accelerating Acceptance 2017*. GLAAD. Accessed August 29, 2020. http://www.glaad.org/files/aa/2017_GLAAD_Accelerating_Acceptance.pdf.

———. 2019. *Accelerating Acceptance 2019.* GLAAD. Accessed August 29, 2020. https://www.glaad.org/sites/default/files/Accelerating%20Acceptance%20 2019.pdf.

Glenn, Norval, and Elizabeth Marquardt. 2001. *Hooking Up, Hanging Out, and Hoping for Mr. Right: College Women on Mating and Dating Today.* New York: Institute for American Values.

Graf, Nikki L., and Christine L. Schwartz. 2011. "The Uneven Pace of Change in Heterosexual Romantic Relationships: Comment on England." *Gender & Society* 25, no. 1: 101–107.

Guidotti-Hernández, Nicole. 2017. "Affective Communities and Millennial Desires: Latinx, or Why My Computer Won't Recognize Latina/o." *Cultural Dynamics* 29, no. 3: 141–159.

Hamilton, Laura. 2016. *Parenting to a Degree: How Family Matters for College Women's Success.* Chicago: University of Chicago Press.

Hamilton, Laura, and Elizabeth Armstrong. 2009. "Gendered Sexuality in Young Adulthood: Double Binds and Flawed Options." *Gender and Society* 23, no. 5: 589–616.

Harris, Malcolm. 2017. *Kids These Days: Human Capital and the Making of Millennials.* New York: Back Bay Books.

Heath, Melanie. 2012. *One Marriage under God: The Campaign to Promote Marriage in America.* New York: New York University Press.

Hernandez, Daniel. 2017. "Op-ed: The Case against 'Latinx.'" *Los Angeles Times,* December 17. Accessed July 16, 2020. https://www.latimes.com/opinion/op-ed/la -oe-hernandez-the-case-against-latinx-20171217-story.html.

Hiles, David, and Ivo Cermak. 2008. "Narrative Psychology." In *The SAGE Handbook of Qualitative Research in Psychology,* edited by Carla Willig and Wendy Stainton-Rogers, 147–164. Thousand Oaks, CA: SAGE.

Hill, Matthew J. 2015. "Love in the Time of the Depression: The Effect of Economic Conditions on Marriage in the Great Depression." *Journal of Economic History* 75, no. 1: 163–189.

Hitsch, Günter, Ali Hortaçsu, and Dan Ariely. 2010. "What Makes You Click? Mate Preferences in Online Dating." *Qualitative Marketing and Economics* 8, no. 4: 393–427.

Hoban, Brennan. 2018. "Millennials Are on the Frontlines of Political and Cultural Change in America." Brookings Institute, February 2. Accessed December 17, 2020. https://www.brookings.edu/blog/brookings-now/2018/02/02/millennials -are-on-the-frontlines-of-political-and-cultural-change-in-america/.

Hobbes, Michael. 2017. "FML: Why Millennials Are Facing the Scariest Financial Future of Any Generation since the Great Depression." *Huffington Post Highline.* Accessed July 16, 2020. https://highline.huffingtonpost.com/articles/en/poor -millennials-print/.

Hochschild, Arlie. 1989. *The Second Shift: Working Families and the Revolution at Home.* New York: Penguin.

Holstein, James, and Jaber F. Gubrium. 1995. *The Interactive Interview.* Thousand Oaks, CA: SAGE.

Illouz, Eva. 2008. *Saving the Modern Soul: Therapy, Emotions, and the Culture of Self-Help.* Berkeley: University of California Press.

Ingraham, Chrys. 2008. *White Weddings: Romancing Heterosexuality in Popular Culture.* 2nd ed. New York: Routledge.

Irvine, Leslie. 1999. *Codependent Forevermore: The Invention of Self in a Twelve Step Group*. Chicago: University of Chicago Press.

———. 2013. *My Dog Always Eats First: Homeless People and Their Animals*. Boulder, CO: Lynne Rienner.

James-Hawkins, Laurie, Cristen Dalessandro, and Christie Sennott. 2018. "Conflicting Contraceptive Norms for Men: Equal Responsibility vs. Women's Bodily Autonomy." *Culture, Health & Sexuality* 21, no. 3: 263–277.

Jenkins, Tania M. 2020. *Doctor's Orders: The Making of Status Hierarchies in an Elite Profession*. New York: Columbia University Press.

Jensen, Sune Q. 2011. "Othering, Identity Formation, and Agency." *Qualitative Studies* 2, no. 2: 63–78.

Johnson, Monica K., and Stefanie Mollborn. 2009. "Growing Up Faster, Feeling Older: Hardship in Childhood and Adolescence." *Social Psychology Quarterly* 72, no. 1: 39–60.

Jones, Sarah. 2020. "The Pandemic Lavishly Screwed Millennials." *New York Magazine*, May 27. Accessed July 16, 2020. https://nymag.com/intelligencer/2020/05/the-pandemic-lavishly-screwed-millennials.html.

Joyner, Kara, and Grace Kao. 2005. "Interracial Relationships and the Transition to Adulthood." *American Sociological Review* 70, no. 4: 563–581.

Kalish, Emma. 2016. "Millennials Are the Least Wealthy, but Most Optimistic, Generation." Urban Institute, April 2016. Accessed July 16, 2020. https://www.urban.org/sites/default/files/publication/79881/2000753-Millennials-Are-the-Least-Wealthy-but-Most-Optimistic-Generation.pdf.

Kalmijn, Matthijs. 1998. "Intermarriage and Homogamy: Causes, Patterns, Trends." *Annual Review of Sociology* 24: 395–421.

Kaufman, Gayle, and Voon Chin Phua. 2003. "Is Ageism Alive in Date Selection among Men? Age Requests among Gay and Straight Men in Internet Personal Ads." *Journal of Men's Studies* 11, no. 2: 225–235.

Kent, Mary Mederios. 2010. "Most Americans Marry within Their Race." Population Reference Bureau, August 5. Accessed July 16, 2020. http://www.prb.org/Publications/Articles/2010/usintermarriage.aspx.

Kershaw, Sarah. 2009. "Rethinking the Older Woman-Younger Man Relationship." *New York Times*, October 14. Accessed July 16, 2020. http://www.nytimes.com/2009/10/15/fashion/15women.html?_r=0.

Kessler-Harris, Alice. 1990. *A Woman's Wage: Historical Meanings and Social Consequences*. Lexington: University of Kentucky Press.

Khan, Shamus. 2011. *Privilege: The Making of an Adolescent Elite at St. Paul's School*. Princeton, NJ: Princeton University Press.

Koontz, Amanda, and Lauren Norman. 2018. "Happily Ever After? Exploring U.S. Collegiate Women's Understandings of Love as Impermanent and Timeless in the Age of Capitalism." *Sociological Perspectives* 62, no. 2: 167–185.

Labov, William, and Joshua Waletzky. 1997. "Narrative Analysis: Oral Versions of Personal Experience." *Journal of Narrative and Life History* 7, nos. 1–4: 3–38.

Lamont, Ellen. 2014. "Negotiating Courtship: Reconciling Egalitarian Ideals with Traditional Gender Norms." *Gender & Society* 28, no. 2: 189–211.

———. 2017. "'We Can Write the Scripts Ourselves': Queer Challenges to Heteronormative Courtship Practices." *Gender & Society* 31, no. 5: 624–646.

———. 2020. *The Mating Game: How Gender Still Shapes How We Date*. Oakland: University of California Press.

Lee, Gary R. 2015. *The Limits of Marriage: Why Getting Married Won't Solve All Our Problems*. Lanham, MD: Lexington Books.

Lee, Jennifer, and Frank D. Bean. 2004. "America's Changing Color Lines: Immigration, Race/Ethnicity, and Multiracial Identification." *Annual Review of Sociology* 30, no. 2004: 221–242.

Lewis, Kevin. 2013. "The Limits of Racial Prejudice." *Proceedings of the National Academy of Sciences* 110, no. 47: 18814–18819.

Lewis, Rachel. 2019. "Do We Need to Calm Down? A Roundtable on Taylor Swift and Classism in Music Videos." *Bitch Media*, July 3. Accessed July 16, 2020. https://www.bitchmedia.org/article/taylor-swift-you-need-to-calm-down-classism.

Livingston, Gretchen. 2014. "Tying the Knot Again? Chances Are, There's a Bigger Age Gap than the First Time Around." Pew Research Center, December 4. Accessed July 16, 2020. http://www.pewresearch.org/fact-tank/2014/12/04/tying-the-knot-again-chances-are-theres-a-bigger-age-gap-than-the-first-time-around/.

———. 2018. "How Family Life Is Changing in Urban, Suburban, and Rural Communities." Pew Research Center, June 19. Accessed July 16, 2020. https://www.pewresearch.org/fact-tank/2018/06/19/family-life-is-changing-in-different-ways-across-urban-suburban-and-rural-communities-in-the-u-s/.

Lofland, John, David Snow, Leon Anderson, and Lyn Lofland. 2006. *Analyzing Social Settings: A Guide to Qualitative Observation and Analysis*. Belmont, CA: Thompson Wadsworth.

Lune, Howard, and Berg, Bruce L. 2017. *Qualitative Research Methods for the Social Sciences, Global Edition*. 9th ed. Harlow, England: Pearson.

Madfis, Eric. 2014. "Triple Entitlement and Homicidal Anger: An Exploration of the Intersectional Identities of American Mass Murderers." *Men & Masculinities* 17, no. 1: 67–86.

Manning, Wendy D., Susan L. Brown, and Krista K. Payne. 2014. "Two Decades of Stability and Change in Age at First Union Formation." *Journal of Marriage and Family* 76: 247–260.

Martin, Karin. 1996. *Puberty, Sexuality, and the Self: Boys and Girls at Adolescence*. New York: Routledge.

Mason-Schrock, Douglas. 1996. "Transsexuals' Narrative Construction of the 'True Self.'" *Social Psychology Quarterly* 59, no. 3: 176–192.

McAdams, Dan P. 1993. *The Stories We Live By: Personal Myths and the Making of the Self*. New York: Guilford.

McClintock, Elizabeth Aura. 2010. "When Does Race Matter? Race, Sex, and Dating at an Elite University." *Journal of Marriage and Family* 72, no. 1: 45–72.

McIntosh, Peggy. 1990. "White Privilege: Unpacking the Invisible Knapsack." *Independent School* 49, no. 2: 31–35.

McPherson, Miller, Lynn Smith-Lovin, and James M. Cook. 2001. "Birds of a Feather: Homophily in Social Networks." *Annual Review of Sociology* 27: 415–444.

Mears, Ashley. 2011. *Pricing Beauty: The Making of a Fashion Model*. Berkeley: University of California Press.

Mohr, Richard D. 2005. *The Long Arc of Injustice: Lesbian and Gay Marriage, Equality, and Rights*. New York: Columbia University Press.

Mojola, Sanyu. 2014. *Love, Money, and HIV: Becoming a Modern African Woman in the Age of AIDS*. Oakland: University of California Press.

Mollborn, Stefanie. 2017. *Mixed Messages: Norms and Social Control around Teen Sex and Pregnancy*. New York: Oxford University Press.

Montemurro, Beth. 2014. *Deserving Desire: Women's Stories of Sexual Evolution*. New Brunswick, NJ: Rutgers University Press.

Moscowitz, Leigh. 2013. *The Battle over Marriage: Gay Rights Activism through the Media*. Urbana: University of Illinois Press.

Nelson, Larry J., and Stephanie S. Luster. 2015. "'Adulthood' by Whose Definition? The Complexity of Emerging Adults' Conceptions of Adulthood." In *The Oxford Handbook of Emerging Adulthood*, edited by J. J. Arnett, 421–437. New York: Oxford University Press.

Obidoa, Chinekwu A., Bernice A. Dodor, Vivian Tackie-Ofosu, Mabel A. Obidoa, Hilary R. Kalisch, and Larry J. Nelson. 2019. "Perspectives on Markers of Adulthood among Emerging Adults in Ghana and Nigeria." *Emerging Adulthood* 7, no. 4: 270–278.

Orne, Jason. 2017. *Boystown: Sex and Community in Chicago*. Chicago: University of Chicago Press.

Pacheco-Vega, Raul. 2018. "Writing Theoretical Frameworks, Analytical Frameworks, and Conceptual Frameworks." September 28. Accessed December 29, 2020. http://www .raulpacheco.org/2018/09/writing-theoretical-frameworks-analytical-frameworks -and-conceptual-frameworks/.

Parker, Kim, Nikki Graf, and Ruth Igielnik. 2019. "Generation Z Looks a Lot like Millennials on Key Social and Political Issues." Pew Research Center, January 17. Accessed July 16, 2020. https://www.pewsocialtrends.org/2019/01/17/generation-z -looks-a-lot-like-millennials-on-key-social-and-political-issues/.

Pew Research Center. 2010. "Millennials: Confident. Connected. Open to Change." Pew Research Center, February 24. Accessed December 17, 2020. https://www .pewsocialtrends.org/2010/02/24/millennials-confident-connected-open-to -change/.

———. 2018. "The Generation Gap in American Politics." Pew Research Center, March 1. Accessed August 25, 2020. https://www.pewresearch.org/politics/2018/03 /01/the-generation-gap-in-american-politics/.

Plummer, Kenneth. 1995. *Telling Sexual Stories: Power, Change, and Social Worlds*. New York: Routledge.

———. 2005. "Chapter 4: Intimate Citizenship in an Unjust World." In *The Blackwell Companion to Social Inequalities*, edited by Mary Romero and Eric Margolis, 75–99. Hoboken, NJ: John Wiley and Sons.

Polletta, Francesca, Pang Ching Bobby Chin, Beth Gharrity Gardner, and Alice Motes. 2011. "The Sociology of Storytelling." *Annual Review of Sociology* 37 (2011): 109–130.

Pugh, Allison J. 2013. "What Good Are Interviews for Thinking about Culture? Demystifying Interpretive Analysis." *American Journal of Cultural Sociology* 1, no. 1: 42–68.

Pyke, Karen. 1996. "Class-Based Masculinities: The Interdependence of Gender, Class, and Interpersonal Power." *Gender & Society* 10, no. 5: 527–549.

Rao, Aliya Hamid. 2020. *Crunch Time: How Married Couples Confront Unemployment*. Oakland: University of California Press.

Rauch, Jonathan. 2004. *Gay Marriage: Why It Is Good for Gays, Good for Straights, and Good for America*. New York: Henry Holt.

Ray, Rashawn, and Jason A. Rosow. 2010. "Getting Off and Getting Intimate: How Normative Institutional Arrangements Structure Black and White Fraternity Men's Approaches toward Women." *Men and Masculinities* 12, no. 5: 523–546.

Riess, Jana. 2019. *The Next Mormons: How Millennials Are Changing the LDS Church*. New York: Oxford University Press.

Riessman, Catherine K. 1990. *Divorce Talk: Women and Men Make Sense of Personal Relationships*. New Brunswick, NJ: Rutgers University Press.

Rinz, Kevin. 2019. "Did Timing Matter? Life Cycle Differences in the Effects of Exposure to the Great Recession." Center for Economic Studies U.S. Census Bureau (Working Paper).

Risman, Barbara. 2018. *Where the Millennials Will Take Us: A New Generation Wrestles with the Gender Structure*. New York: Oxford University Press.

Robertson, Mary. 2018. *Growing Up Queer: Kids and the Remaking of LGBTQ Identity*. New York: New York University Press.

Robinson, Brandon Andrew. 2015. "'Personal Preference' as the New Racism: Gay Desire and Racial Cleansing in Cyberspace." *Sociology of Race and Ethnicity* 1, no. 2: 317–330.

Robnett, Belinda, and Cynthia Feliciano. 2011. "Patterns of Racial-Ethnic Exclusion by Internet Daters." *Social Forces* 89, no. 3: 807–828.

Rose, Tricia. 2003. *Longing to Tell: Black Women Talk about Sexuality and Intimacy*. New York: Farrar, Giroux, and Straus.

Rosenfeld, Michael. 2009. *The Age of Independence: Interracial Unions, Same-Sex Unions, and the Changing American Family*. Cambridge, MA: Harvard University Press.

Rosentiel, Tom. 2010. "Almost All Millennials Accept Interracial Dating and Marriage." Pew Research Center, February 1. Accessed July 16, 2020. https://www .pewresearch.org/2010/02/01/almost-all-millennials-accept-interracial-dating-and -marriage/.

Rubin, Herbert J., and Irene S. Rubin. 2012. *Qualitative Interviewing: The Art of Hearing Data*. Thousand Oaks, CA: SAGE.

Rubin, Lillian B. 1976. *Worlds of Pain: Life in the Working-Class Family*. New York: Basic Books.

Santos, Cezar, and David Weiss. 2016. "'Why Not Settle Down Already?': A Quantitative Analysis of the Delay in Marriage." *International Economic Review* 57: 425–452.

Sassler, Sharon, and Amanda Miller. 2011. "Waiting to Be Asked: Gender, Power, and Relationship Progression among Cohabiting Couples." *Journal of Family Issues* 32, no. 4: 482–506.

———. 2017. *Cohabitation Nation: Gender, Class, and the Remaking of Relationships*. Berkeley: University of California Press.

Schmalzbauer, Leah. 2014. *The Last Best Place? Gender, Family, and Migration in the New West*. Stanford, CA: Stanford University Press.

Schope, Robert D. 2005. "Who's Afraid of Growing Old? Gay and Lesbian Perceptions of Aging." *Journal of Gerontological Social Work* 45, no. 4: 23–39.

Schwalbe, Michael, and Michelle Wolkomir. 2002. "Interviewing Men." In *Inside Interviewing: New Lenses, New Concerns*, edited by James Holstein and Jaber Gubrium, 55–72. Thousand Oaks, CA: SAGE.

Settersten, Richard, and Barbara Ray. 2010. *Not Quite Adults: Why 20-Somethings Are Choosing a Slower Path to Adulthood, and Why It's Good for Everyone*. New York: Bantam.

Sherman, Rachel. 2017. *Uneasy Street: The Anxieties of Affluence*. Princeton, NJ: Princeton University Press.

Siegler, Ilene C., Beverly H. Brummett, Peter Martin, and Michael J. Helms. 2013. "Consistency and Timing of Marital Transitions and Survival during Midlife:

The Role of Personality and Health Risk Behaviors." *Annals of Behavioral Medicine* 45, no. 3: 338–337.

Silva, Jennifer. 2013. *Coming Up Short: Working-Class Adulthood in an Age of Uncertainty.* New York: Oxford University Press.

Silva, Jennifer, and Sarah Corse. 2018. "Envisioning and Enacting Class Mobility: The Routine Constructions of the Agentic Self." *American Journal of Cultural Sociology* 6, no. 2: 231–265.

Silva, Tony. 2019. "'Daddies,' 'Cougars,' and Their Partners Past Midlife: Gender Attitudes and Relationship and Sexual Well-Being among Older Adults in Age-Heterogenous Partnerships." *Socius.* https://doi.org/10.1177/2378023119869452.

Sizemore, Kayla M., and Spencer B. Olmstead. 2018. "Willingness of Emerging Adults to Engage in Consensual Non-Monogamy: A Mixed-Methods Analysis." *Archives of Sexual Behavior* 47: 1423–1438.

Small, Mario Luis. 2009. "'How Many Cases Do I Need?': On Science and the Logic of Case Selection in Field-Based Research." *Ethnography* 10, no. 1: 5–38.

Somers, Margaret R. 1994. "The Narrative Constitution of Identity: A Relational and Network Approach." *Theory & Society* 23, no. 5: 605–649.

Squier, Chemmie. 2016. "Why Can't Millennials Make Any Damn Decisions?" *Grazia UK*, May 29. Accessed July 16, 2020. https://graziadaily.co.uk/life/opinion/cant-millennials-make-damn-decisions/.

Steinbugler, Amy C. 2012. *Beyond Loving: Intimate Racework in Lesbian, Gay, and Straight Interracial Relationships.* New York: Oxford University Press.

Stepp, Laura Sessions. 2007. *Unhooked: How Women Pursue Sex, Delay Love, and Lose at Both.* New York: Riverhead Books.

Streib, Jessi. 2015a. "Explanations of How Love Crosses Class Lines: Cultural Complements and the Case of Cross-Class Marriages." *Sociological Forum* 20, no. 1: 18–39.

———. 2015b. *The Power of the Past: Understanding Cross-Class Marriages.* New York: Oxford University Press.

Strings, Sabrina. 2019. *Fearing the Black Body: The Racial Origins of Fat Phobia.* New York: New York University Press.

Strully, Kate. 2014. "Racially and Ethnically Diverse Schools and Adolescent Romantic Relationships." *American Journal of Sociology* 120, no. 3: 750–797.

Swartz, Christine R., and Robert D. Mare. 2005. "Trends in Educational Assortative Marriage from 1940 to 2003." *Demography* 42, no. 4: 621–646.

Sweeney, Brian N. 2014. "Masculine Status, Sexual Performance, and the Sexual Stigmatization of Women." *Symbolic Interaction* 37, no. 3: 369–390.

Swidler, Ann. 2001. *Talk of Love: How Culture Matters.* Chicago: University of Chicago Press.

Taylor, Kate. 2017. "'Psychologically Scarred' Millennials Are Killing Countless Industries from Napkins to Applebee's—Here Are the Businesses They Like the Least." *Business Insider*, October 31. Accessed July 17, 2020. https://www.businessinsider.com/millennials-are-killing-list-2017–8.

Trujillo-Pagán, Nicole. 2018. "Crossed Out by LatinX: Gender Neutrality and Genderblind Sexism." *Latino Studies* 16, no. 3: 396–406.

Tsunokai, Glenn T., Augustine J. Kposowa, and Michele A. Adams. 2009. "Racial Preferences in Internet Dating: A Comparison of Four Birth Cohorts." *Western Journal of Black Studies* 33, no. 1: 1–15.

United States Census Bureau. 2015. "Millennials Outnumber Baby Boomers and Are Far More Diverse." United States Census Bureau, June 25. Accessed December 9, 2020. https://www.census.gov/newsroom/press-releases/2015/cb15-113.html.

———. 2017. "The Nation's Older Population Is Still Growing, Census Bureau Reports." United States Census Bureau, June 22. Accessed July 17, 2020. https://www.census.gov/newsroom/press-releases/2017/cb17-100.html.

———. 2018. "Median Age at First Marriage: 1890 to Present." United States Census Bureau. Accessed July 17, 2020. https://www.census.gov/content/dam/Census/library/visualizations/time-series/demo/families-and-households/ms-2.pdf.

Van Dam, Andrew. 2020. "The Unluckiest Generation in U.S. History." *Washington Post*, June 5. Accessed July 17, 2020. https://www.washingtonpost.com/business/2020/05/27/millennial-recession-covid/.

Vasquez, Jessica. 2015. "Disciplined Preferences: Explaining the (Re)Production of Latino Endogamy." *Social Problems* 62, no. 3: 455–475.

Vasquez-Tokos, Jessica. 2017. *Marriage Vows and Racial Choices*. New York: Russell Sage Foundation.

Vidal-Ortiz, Salvador, and Juliana Martínez. 2018. "Latinx Thoughts: Latinidad with an X." *Latino Studies* 16, no. 3: 284–295.

Wade, Lisa. 2009. "Are More Women Marrying Younger Men? Yes, But . . ." *Sociological Images*, October 16. Accessed July 17, 2020. https://thesocietypages.org/socimages/2009/10/16/are-more-women-marrying-younger-men-yes-but/.

———. 2017. *American Hookup: The New Culture of Sex on Campus*. New York: W. W. Norton.

Walker, Alicia M. 2018. *The Secret Life of the Cheating Wife: Power, Pragmatism, and Pleasure in Women's Infidelity*. Lanham, MD: Lexington Books.

Wang, Wendy. 2012. "The Rise of Intermarriage: Rates, Characteristics Vary by Race and Gender." Pew Research Center, February 16. Accessed July 17, 2020. http://www.pewsocialtrends.org/2012/02/16 /the-rise-of-intermarriage/.

———. 2015. "Interracial Marriage: Who Is 'Marrying Out'?" Pew Research Center, June 12. Accessed July 17, 2020. http://www.pewresearch.org/fact-tank/2015/06/12/interracial-marriage-who-is-marrying-out/.

Warren, Carol A. B. 1996. "Older Women, Younger Men: Self and Stigma in Age-Discrepant Relationships." *Clinical Sociology Review* 14, no. 1: 62–86.

Waters, Mary C., Patrick Carr, and Maria Kefalas. 2011. "Introduction." In *Coming of Age in America: The Transition to Adulthood in the Twenty-First Century*, edited by Mary Waters, Patrick Carr, Maria Kefalas, and Jennifer Holladay, 1–27. Berkeley: University of California Press.

Weiss, Robert S. 1994. *Learning from Strangers: The Art and Method of Qualitative Interview Studies*. New York: Simon and Schuster.

Whitehead, Jaye Cee. 2011. *The Nuptial Deal: Same-Sex Marriage and Neo-Liberal Governance*. Chicago: University of Chicago Press.

Wilkins, Amy C. 2004. "'So Full of Myself as a Chick': Goth Women, Sexual Independence, and Gender Egalitarianism." *Gender & Society* 18, no. 3: 328–349.

———. 2012. "Becoming Black Women: Intimate Stories and Intersectional Identities." *Social Psychology Quarterly* 75, no. 2: 173–195.

———. 2014. "Race, Age, and Identity Transformations in the Transition from High School to College for Black and First-Generation White Men." *Sociology of Education* 87, no. 3: 171–187.

Wilkins, Amy C., and Cristen Dalessandro. 2013. "Monogamy Lite: Cheating, College, and Women." *Gender & Society* 27, no. 5: 728–751.

Williams Institute. 2020. "LGBT Data and Demographics." University of California Los Angeles School of Law Williams Institute. Accessed July 17, 2020. https://williamsinstitute.law.ucla.edu/visualization/lgbt-stats/?topic=LGBT#density.

Wong, Jaclyn. 2017. "Competing Desires: How Young Adult Couples Negotiate Moving for Career Opportunities." *Gender & Society* 31, no. 2: 171–196.

Wood, Julia T. 2001. "The Normalization of Violence in Heterosexual Romantic Relationships: Women's Narratives of Love and Violence." *Journal of Social and Personal Relationships* 18, no. 2: 239–261.

Worthen, Elizabeth. 2020. "The Young and the Prejudiced? Millennial Men, 'Dude Bro' Disposition, and LGBTQ Negativity in a US National Sample." *Sexuality Research and Social Policy.* https://doi.org/10.1007/s13178-020-00458-6.

Yau, Nathan. 2007. "Marrying Age: This Is When Americans Get Married." Flowing-Data. Accessed July 17, 2020. https://flowingdata.com/2016/03/03/marrying-age/.

Index

civil rights, 121, 123, 139, 162n3 (chap. 6)

cohabiting, 4, 109–110

Colleen (participant), 31, 110, 131, 129–130, 145

college students: men's experiences as, 51, 60, 68, 95, 99, 113; women's experiences as, 23, 27–28, 32, 74, 95, 100–101, 104–105, 128–129

color blindness, 68–69, 85–86

color-blind racism, defined, 68

compatibility, and social class, viii–ix, 106

Connor (participant), 19–22, 43–45, 113–114, 144

"cougar," 51–52, 161n1 (chap. 3). *See also* age-discrepant relationships

COVID-19, 6, 133, 141

Craigslist, 37, 141

culture, Western global, vii, 8–9, 112, 135; U.S. Mountain regional, 12, 17, 33, 148, 150, 153

"daddy phase," 60–61, 161n7 (chap. 3)

Danielle (participant), 96–97, 145, 162n1 (chap. 5)

date rape, 31, 42, 56. *See also* sexual assault

Dawson (participant), 25–26, 144

Delilah (participant), 1–3, 8, 56–57, 75–76, 94, 127, 145

demographics, of participants, 12–13, 144–145

Dylan (participant), 33, 92–95, 97, 144

economic insecurity, 6–8, 38–39, 107. *See also* finances

Eddie (participant), 30, 33, 122–123, 144

Edin, Kathryn, 6, 22, 36, 38, 58, 111, 117, 119

education, and social class, viii, 2, 13, 17, 89, 91–95, 103, 105–107, 117

Ellie (participant), 145, 160n1

emerging adulthood: characteristics of, 8–9, 97, 147–148, 160n12; defined, 8

emotions: and gender, 21–22, 26, 41–45, 52; manipulation, 25, 27–28, 31, 62; and marriage, 122–123; and millennial intimate life, 9, 20, 135, 138–139; and race, 73–76, 86; and research methods, 152–154; and social class, 34–39, 100–101, 119, 160n12

erotic power, 116–117

exoticization: defined, 71; experiences with, 67–68, 73–78. *See also* objectification

Facebook, 149. *See also* media

Faith (participant), 23, 25, 58, 119–120, 130, 145

family: future plans, 48, 52, 57–58, 64, 94–96, 124–127, 129–130; influence of, 78–84, 89, 99–105, 116, 127–129

femininity: as passive and responsive, 20, 23, 64–65; and self-development, 55–56, 96–97, 103, 115; and social class, 36–39, 55

fertility, 52–54, 64, 114, 116

festivals, 51, 115

finances: goals, 2, 21, 53, 90, 95–97, 109–110, 113–114, 117; security, 57–58, 104–105, 107. *See also* economic insecurity

friendships: and gender, 101, 115, 118–119, 130; and queer identity, 43, 124, 129; and social class, 93–94, 98–99, 162n2 (chap. 5)

Furedi, Frank, 9

Gabriel (participant), 63, 81, 123, 126–129, 144

"gay marriage," 100, 112, 122–123, 162n3 (chap. 6). See also *Obergefell v. Hodges*

gender: and age, 47–66, 103, 96–97, 114–117; binaries, 39, 43, 46, 137; essentialism, 39; expectations, 43, 45, 63, 112–114, 117; participant identifications, 12; queer approaches to, 39–43, 60; and race, 1–2, 73–80, 83–85; and social class, 34–39, 95–98, 100–101, 117; traditional roles of, 22, 37, 53, 65, 95, 112–114, 117

Generation X, 133

Generation Z, 8, 141–142, 160n11

geography: moving, 29–30, 97, 116; participant backgrounds, 119, 149; and participant recruitment, 149–153

grandparents, 3, 78–79, 123, 127

Great Recession, the, 6

Hallie (participant), 27–29, 145

heteronormativity, 112, 131, 137

heterosexuality, 17, 129. *See also* "straight" sexuality

homogamy, educational, 91

homophily, 70

homophobia, 75

About the Author

CRISTEN DALESSANDRO is a sociologist and postdoctoral fellow in the Division of Family Planning at the University of Utah School of Medicine. Most of her past and current research focuses on gender, health, identities, and inequalities in the lives of young adults. Originally from western Pennsylvania, she is currently based in Salt Lake City, Utah.

Printed and bound by CPI Group (UK) Ltd, Croydon, CR0 4YY

09/06/2025